The
LITTLE, BROWN
Compact
Handbook

Jane E. Aaron

New York University

📖 HarperCollins*CollegePublishers*

Acquisitions Editor: Patricia Rossi
Developmental Editor: Marisa L'Heureux
Project Editor: Steven Pisano
Design Supervisor and Cover Design: Dorothy Bungert
Text Design: Robin Hoffmann
Production Administrator: Valerie A. Sawyer
Compositor: Ruttle, Shaw & Wetherill, Inc.
Printer: Haddon Craftsmen, Inc.
Binder: Rand McNally Nicholstone
Cover Printer: The Lehigh Press, Inc.

The Little, Brown Compact Handbook

Copyright © 1993 by HarperCollins College Publishers

The author and publisher are grateful to the many students who have
allowed their work to be reprinted here and to the following:

Excerpt from "Worthy Women Revisited" by Angeline Goreau, *The
New York Times*, December 11, 1986. Copyright © 1986 by The New
York Times Company. Reprinted by permission. ♦ Excerpt from "The
Confounding Enemy of Sleep" by Lawrence A. Mayer, *Fortune*, © 1984
Time Inc. All rights reserved. Reprinted by permission of Fortune,
Time Inc. Magazines. ♦ Excerpt from "Search for Yesterday" by Ruth
Rosen from *Watching Television* by Todd Gitlin. Copyright © 1986 by
Ruth Rosen. Reprinted by permission of Pantheon Books, a division of
Random House, Inc. ♦ Excerpt from "The Decline of Quality" by
Barbara Tuchman, *The New York Times*, November 2, 1980. Copyright
© 1980 by The New York Times Company. Reprinted by permission. ♦
Excerpt from "The Community" by Michael Walzer, *The New Republic*,
March 1, 1982. Reprinted by permission of The New Republic, Inc.

Library of Congress Cataloging-in-Publication Data

Aaron, Jane E.
    The Little, Brown compact handbook / Jane E. Aaron,
        p.   cm.
    Includes index.
    ISBN 0-06-500902-9
        1. English language—Grammar—1950– —Handbooks, manuals, etc.
    2. English language—Rhetoric—Handbooks, manuals, etc.   I. Little,
    Brown and Company.   II. Title.
PE1112.A23   1993
808'.042—dc20   92-2889
                                                                   CIP

    94 95   9 8 7 6 5 4

Preface

This writer's handbook aims for convenience and accessibility. As an offspring of *The Little, Brown Handbook*, it is comprehensive and authoritative. It is also short, handy, easy to use, and suitable for writers of varying experience.

The Little, Brown Compact Handbook concisely covers all the basics of writing: the writing process (including sample drafts), paragraphs, clarity and style, grammar and usage, punctuation, mechanics, and the research paper (including sample papers in both APA and MLA documentation styles). Examples come from many disciplines. Guidance for students using English as a second language is integrated wherever possible with the book's other material on grammar and usage, but for easy reference it is also flagged with a small color block (ESL) and indexed under its own heading.

The format of *The Little, Brown Compact Handbook* invites varied uses. The wire binding allows the book to lie flat and also to fold back on itself; the flexible tabbed dividers allow the book to be opened easily and also to be scanned by thumbing. There are many paths into the book: the guide with questions in the front, the list of symbols in the back, the table of contents immediately after this preface, the tabbed part outlines, the marginal tabs on all pages, and, of course, a detailed index. "Finding What You Need in This Book," a list and illustration of all the book's reference aids, appears inside the back cover. The text, too, has its own internal aids: twenty-five colored boxes contain checklists, summaries, and other key information.

To make these reference aids most useful, *The Little, Brown Compact Handbook* strives to minimize terminology and to help students around unavoidable terms. The guide to the book inside the front cover pairs the book's part and chapter headings with questions like those that students ask, using everyday language and examples in place of terms. Similarly, the detailed part outlines at each tabbed divider prefer examples to terms (or use examples to clarify terms), so that students can quickly find what they need. Headings with the text do the same. Then the text itself handles terminology uniquely: for its principal use, each needed term is carefully defined in the running text (and the page with the definition is boldfaced in the book's index); for secondary uses, terms are defined in out-of-the-way white boxes (see p. 92 for an example). These boxes, always at the bottom of a page, provide much readier assistance than cross-references do for students who want extra help, yet they keep the text unencumbered for other readers.

The organization is also accessible, arranging topics in ways that students can easily grasp without prior experience of handbooks. For instance, students wanting to know when to use *good* or *well* or how to repair a dangling modifier do not have to figure out whether the answer is a matter of sentence effectiveness or sentence grammar: everything about modifiers appears in one sequence of chapters under "Sentence Parts and Patterns."

The Little, Brown Compact Handbook contains no exercises itself, but a separate booklet offers eighty-five activities. There, each exercise set is in connected discourse, so that students work at the level of the paragraph rather than the isolated sentence. And the exercises represent a wide range of academic disciplines.

Acknowledgments

During the development of this book, I have received shrewd and constructive advice from more than two dozen teachers, each of whom has my gratitude:

Valentine C. Angell, Western Michigan University
Sue Belles, California State University, Long Beach
Diane R. Crotty, University of Wisconsin, Oshkosh
Marcia S. Curtis, University of Massachusetts
David L. Elliott, Keystone Junior College
Chrysanthy M. Grieco, Seton Hall University
Mary-Lou Hinman, Plymouth State College
Rebecca Wagner Hite, Southeastern Louisiana University

Paul Hunter, North Lake College
Ruth Y. Jenkins, California State University, Fresno
Marsha Keller, Oklahoma City University
Carolyn Logan, Casper College
George Meese, Eckerd College
H. Brown Miller, City College of San Francisco
Judith Anne Moore, New Mexico State University, Carlsbad
Molly Frances Moore, University of Vermont
Janice Neuleib, Illinois State University
Mary Sue Ply, Southeastern Louisiana University
Michael Rossi, Merrimack College
Judy Shank, Valencia Community College
Joyce Stauffer, Indiana University–Purdue University, Fort
    Wayne
Emily Thiroux, California State University, Bakersfield
John O. White, California State University, Fullerton
Karen W. Willingham, Pensacola Junior College

In addition, Rebecca Bell-Metereau, Southwest Texas State University, and Judy Pierpont, Cornell University, helped generously with the material for ESL students.

At HarperCollins, Patricia Rossi, Marisa L'Heureux, and Ann Stypuloski were, as always, steadfast, creative, and companionable. Maria Paone provided valuable support. And Steven Pisano and Dorothy Bungert marched things along with a fine sensitivity to the book's and its author's needs. My thanks to all.

Contents

VI ❖ Research and Documentation *196*

I

The Writing Process and Paragraphs

Subject, Purpose, and Audience

No matter what you are writing, you will be working within a writing situation: writing on a particular subject, for a particular purpose, to a particular audience of readers.

1a   Finding your subject

A subject for writing has several basic requirements:

❖ It should be suitable for the assignment.
❖ It should be neither too general nor too limited for the length of paper and deadline assigned.
❖ It should be something you care about.

When you receive a writing assignment, ask yourself these questions about it:

❖ What's wanted from you? Many writing assignments contain words such as *describe, analyze, report, interpret, explain, define, argue,* or *evaluate.* These words specify the way you are to approach your subject and what your broad purpose is. (See 1b.)
❖ For whom are you writing? Some assignments will specify your readers, but usually you will have to figure out for yourself whether your audience is your boss, the college community, your instructor, or some other group or individual. (See 1c.)
❖ What kind of research is required? Sometimes an assignment specifies the kinds of sources you are expected to consult, and you can use such information to choose your subject. (If you are unsure whether research is expected, check with your instructor.)
❖ What is the length of the paper? The deadline? Having a week to write three pages or three weeks to write six pages can make a big difference in the subject you select.

Considering these questions will help set some boundaries for your choice of subject. Then, within those boundaries, you can explore your own interests and experiences to discover something you care about. For instance:

❖ What subject do you already know something about or have you been wondering about?

❖ Have you recently participated in a lively discussion about a controversial topic?

❖ What topic in the reading or class discussion for a course has intrigued you or seemed especially relevant to your own experiences?

❖ What have you read or seen at the movies or on television?

❖ What makes you especially happy or especially angry?

❖ Which of your own or others' dislikes and preferences would you like to understand better?

Before you settle on a subject, test it to be sure it's narrow enough to cover adequately within the space and time assigned. Federal aid to college students could be the subject of a book; the kinds of aid available or why the government should increase aid would be a more appropriate subject for a four-page paper due in a week. Here are some guidelines for narrowing broad subjects:

1. Again, pursue your interests, and consider what the assignment tells you about purpose, audience, sources, length, and deadline (see opposite).

2. Break your broad subject into as many specific topics as you can think of. Make a list.

3. For each topic that interests you and fits the assignment, roughly sketch out the main ideas and consider how many paragraphs or pages of specific facts, examples, and other details you would need to pin those ideas down. This thinking should give you at least a vague idea of how much work you'd have to do and how long the resulting paper might be.

4. If an interesting and appropriate topic is still too broad, break it down further and repeat step 3.

1b Defining your purpose

Your PURPOSE in writing is your chief reason for communicating something about your subject to a particular audience of readers. Most writing you do will have one of four main purposes. Occasionally, you will *entertain* readers or *express yourself*—your feelings or ideas—to readers. More often you will *explain* something to readers or *persuade* readers to respect and accept, and sometimes even act on, your well-supported opinion. These purposes often overlap in a single essay, but usually one predominates. And the dominant purpose will influence your particular slant on your subject, the details you choose, and even the words you use.

1c Considering your audience

The readers likely to see your work—your audience—may influence your choice of subject and your definition of purpose. Your audience certainly will influence what you say about your subject and how you say it—for instance, how much background information you give and whether you adopt a serious or a friendly tone. The box opposite contains questions that can help you analyze and address your audience for a particular piece of writing.

2

Invention

Writers use a host of techniques to help invent or discover ideas and information about their subjects. *Whichever of the following techniques you use, do your work in writing, not just in your head.* Your ideas will be retrievable, and the very act of writing will lead you to fresh insights.

2a Keeping a journal

A journal, or diary of ideas, gives you a place to record your reactions to coursework, conversations, movies, and books. It gives you an outlet from the pressures of family, friends, studies, and work. It gives you a private place to find out what you think.

If you write in a journal every day, even for just a few minutes, the routine will loosen up your writing muscles and improve your confidence. And the writing you produce can supply ideas when you are seeking an essay subject or developing an essay. For example, two entries about arguments with your brother may suggest a psychology paper on sibling relations.

Questions about audience

❖ Why are readers going to read my writing? Will they expect information, opinion, entertainment, self-expression, or some combination?

❖ What do I want readers to know or do after reading my work, and how should I make that clear to them?

❖ What characteristic(s) do readers share? For instance:

Age or sex
Occupation: students, professional colleagues, etc.
Social or economic role: adult children, car buyers, potential employers, etc.
Economic or educational background
Ethnic background
Political, religious, or moral beliefs and values
Hobbies or activities

❖ How will the characteristic(s) of readers influence their attitudes toward my topic?

❖ What do readers already know and *not* know about my topic? How much do I have to tell them?

❖ If my topic involves specialized language, how much should I use and define?

❖ What ideas, arguments, or information might surprise readers? excite them? offend them? How should I handle these points?

❖ What misconceptions might readers have of my topic and/or my approach to the topic? How can I dispel these misconceptions?

❖ What is my relationship to my readers? What role and tone should I assume? What role do I want readers to play?

❖ What will readers do with my writing? Should I expect them to read every word from the top, to scan for information, or to look for conclusions? Can I help them with a summary, headings, illustrations, or other special features?

2b   Observing your surroundings

Sometimes you can find a good subject or good ideas by looking around you, not in the half-conscious way most of us move from place to place in our daily lives but deliberately, all senses alert. On a bus, for instance, are there certain types of passengers? What seems to be on the driver's mind? To get the most from observation, you should have a tablet and pen or pencil handy for notes and sketches. Back at your desk, study your notes and sketches for oddities or patterns that you'd like to explore further.

2c   Freewriting and brainstorming

A good way to find or explore a subject is to write without stopping for a certain amount of time (say, ten minutes) or to a certain length (say, one page). The goal of this FREEWRITING is to generate ideas and information from *within* yourself by going around the part of your mind that doesn't want to write or can't think of anything to write. You let words themselves suggest other words. *What* you write is not important; that you *keep* writing is. Don't stop, even if that means repeating the same words until new words come. Don't go back to reread, don't censor ideas, and don't stop to edit: grammar, punctuation, and spelling are irrelevant at this stage.

The physical act of freewriting may give you access to ideas you were unaware of. For example, the following freewriting by a student, Robert Benday, gave him the subject of writing as a disguise.

> Write to write. Seems pretty obvious, also weird. What to gain by writing? never anything before. Writing seems always—always— Getting corrected for trying too hard to please the teacher, getting corrected for not trying hard enuf. Frustration, nail biting, sometimes getting carried away making sentences to tell stories, not even true stories, *esp*. not true stories, *that* feels like creating something. Writing just pulls the story out of me. The story lets me be someone else, gives me a disguise.

(A later phase of Benday's writing appears on p. 8.)

Freewriting is also useful to discover ideas about a specific subject, as the following example shows. The writer, Terry Perez, had an assignment to explore cultural diversity in the United States. She had just read a statement by the writer Ishmael Reed that conflict among cultural groups "is played up and often encouraged by the media."

> Cultural diversity in the media? The media has a one track mind, cultural diversity is bad. Like Reed says the media makes a big deal of conflict between racial and ethnic groups, it's almost constant in the papers, on TV. TV especially—the news vs. all the white bread programs, the sitcoms and ads. That's a whole other view—*no* conflict, *no* tension. No diversity. So we have all people the same except when they're not, then they're at war. Two unreal pictures.

(An outline and drafts of Perez's paper appear on pp. 13, 16–18, 20–21, and 23–27.)

A method similar to freewriting is BRAINSTORMING—focusing intently on a subject for a fixed amount of time (say, fifteen minutes), pushing yourself to list every idea and detail that comes to mind. Like freewriting, brainstorming requires turning off your internal editor so that you keep moving ahead. Here is an example by a student, Johanna Abrams, on what a summer job can teach:

> summer work teaches—
> > how to look busy while doing nothing
> > how to avoid the sun in summer
> > seriously: discipline, budgeting money, value of money
> which job? Burger King cashier? baby sitter? mail-room clerk?
> mail room: how to sort mail into boxes: this is learning??
> how to survive getting fired—humiliation, outrage
> Mrs. King! the mail-room queen as learning experience
> the shock of getting fired: what to tell parents, friends?
> Mrs. K was so rigid—dumb procedures
> initials instead of names on the mail boxes—confusion!
> Mrs. K's anger, resentment: the disadvantages of being smarter than your boss
> The odd thing about working in an office: a world with its own rules for how to act
> what Mr. D said about the pecking order—big chick (Mrs. K) pecks on little chick (me)
> a job can beat you down—make you be mean to other people

(A later phase of Abrams's writing appears on pp. 12–13.)

2d Clustering

Like freewriting and brainstorming, CLUSTERING also draws on free association and rapid, unedited work. But it emphasizes the relations between ideas by combining writing and nonlinear drawing. When clustering, you radiate outward from a center point—your topic. When an idea occurs, you pursue related ideas in a branching structure until they seem exhausted. Then you do the same with other ideas, staying open to connections, continuously branching out or drawing arrows.

The example of clustering on the next page shows how Robert Benday used the technique for ten minutes to expand on the topic of writing as a means of disguise, an idea he arrived at through freewriting (see opposite).

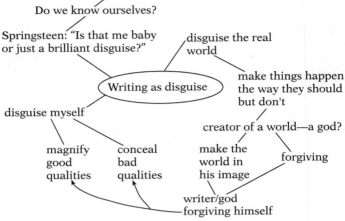

CLUSTERING

Trying <u>not</u> to know myself?

Do we know ourselves?

Springsteen: "Is that me baby or just a brilliant disguise?"

Writing as disguise

disguise the real world

make things happen the way they should but don't

creator of a world—a god?

disguise myself

magnify good qualities

conceal bad qualities

make the world in his image

forgiving

writer/god forgiving himself

2e Reading

Even when reading is not required by an assignment, it can help you locate or develop your topic by introducing you to ideas you didn't know or expanding on what you do know. People often read passively, absorbing content like blotters, not interacting with it. To read for ideas, you need to be more active, probing text and illustrations with your mind. Read with a pen or pencil in your hand and (unless the material is yours to mark up) with a pad of paper by your side. Then you will be able to keep notes on what the reading makes you *think*.

NOTE: Whenever you use the information or ideas of others in your writing, you must acknowledge your sources in order to avoid the serious offense of plagiarism. (See 48e.)

2f Asking questions

Asking yourself a set of questions about your subject—and writing out the answers—can help you look at the topic objectively and see fresh possibilities in it.

1. Journalist's questions

A journalist with a story to report poses a set of questions:

Who was involved?
What happened and what were the results?
When did it happen?
Where did it happen?
Why did it happen?
How did it happen?

These questions can also be useful in probing an essay subject, especially if you are telling a story or examining causes and effects.

2. Questions about patterns

We think about and understand a vast range of subjects through patterns such as narration, classification, and comparison and contrast. Asking questions based on the patterns can help you view your topic from many angles. Sometimes you may want to develop an entire essay using just one pattern.

How did it happen? (Narration)
How does it look, sound, feel, smell, taste? (Description)
What are examples of it or reasons for it? (Illustration or support)
What is it? What does it encompass, and what does it exclude? (Definition)
What are its parts or characteristics? (Division or analysis)
What groups or categories can it be sorted into? (Classification)
How is it like, or different from, other things? (Comparison and contrast)
Why did it happen? What results did or could it have? (Cause-and-effect analysis)
How do you do it, or how does it work? (Process analysis)

For more on these patterns, including paragraph-length examples, see 7c.

Thesis and Organization

Shaping your raw material helps you clear away unneeded ideas, spot possible gaps, and energize your topic. The two main operations in shaping material are focusing on a thesis (3a) and organizing ideas (3b).

3a   Conceiving a thesis sentence

In most essays, you will focus on a single main idea or THESIS, a central proposition or assertion about your subject. You may express this idea in a thesis sentence (or sentences), often at the end of your introduction. A THESIS SENTENCE helps readers in several ways:

❖ It narrows the topic to a single idea that you want readers to gain from your essay.
❖ It asserts something about the topic, conveying your purpose for writing, your opinion of the topic, and your attitude toward it.
❖ It *may* provide a concise preview of how you will arrange your ideas in the essay.

All three thesis sentences below fulfill the first two functions; the last example also fulfills the third.

TOPIC	THESIS SENTENCE
Why the federal government should aid college students	If it hopes to win the technological race, the United States must make higher education possible for any student who qualifies academically.
What public relations is	Although most of us are unaware of the public relations campaigns directed at us, they can significantly affect the way we think and live.
The effects of strip-mining	Strip-mining should be tightly controlled in this region to reduce its pollution of water resources, its permanent destruction of the land, and its devastating effects on people's lives.

Creating a good thesis sentence can take several tries. Ask the following questions about your attempt:

❖ Does it make an *assertion* about your topic?
❖ Does it convey your *purpose*, your *opinion*, and your *attitude?*
❖ Is it *limited* to an assertion of only one idea?
❖ Is the assertion *specific?*
❖ Is the sentence *unified* in that the parts relate to each other?

3b Organizing your ideas

Most essays share a basic pattern of introduction (states the subject), body (develops the subject), and conclusion (pulls the essay's ideas together). Introductions and conclusions are discussed in 7d. Within the body, material may be arranged in an almost infinite number of ways, the choice depending on your subject, purpose, and audience.

1. The general and the specific

To organize material for an essay, you need to distinguish general and specific ideas and see the relations between ideas. GENERAL and SPECIFIC refer to the number of instances or objects included in a group signified by a word. *Plant,* for example, is general because it encompasses all kinds of plants; *rose* is specific because it refers to a certain kind of plant; and *Uncle Dan's prize-winning American Beauty rose* is even more specific. As you arrange your material, pick out the general ideas and then the specific points that support them. Set aside points that seem irrelevant to your key ideas.

2. Outlines

There are many different kinds of outlines, some more flexible than others. All of them can enlarge and toughen your thinking, showing you patterns of general and specific, suggesting proportions, highlighting gaps or overlaps in coverage. An outline can also help you check the underlying structure of a draft during revision (see 5a).

Informal outline

An informal outline includes key general points and may also include the specific evidence for them. In the following example, topic headings correspond to separate paragraphs of the essay.

THESIS SENTENCE

The main street of my neighborhood contains enough variety to make almost any city dweller feel at home.

INFORMAL OUTLINE

The beginning of the street
    high-rise condominium occupied by well-to-do people
    ground floor of building: an art gallery
    across the street: a delicatessen
    above the delicatessen: a tailor's shop, a camera-repair shop, a
        lawyer's office
The middle of the street
    four-story brick apartment buildings on both sides
    at ground level: an Italian bakery and a Spanish bodega
    people sitting on steps
    children playing
The end of the street
    a halfway house for drug addicts
    a boarding house for retired men
    a discount drugstore
    an expensive department store
    a wine shop
    another high-rise condominium

Tree diagram

In a tree diagram, ideas and details branch out in increasing specificity. Unlike more linear outlines, this diagram can be supplemented and extended indefinitely, so it is easy to alter. The following example was developed from Johanna Abrams's brainstorming about a summer job (p. 7).

THESIS SENTENCE

Two months in a mail room taught me a valuable lesson about how people work together.

TREE DIAGRAM

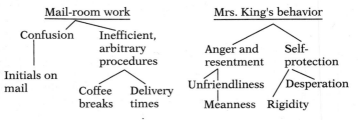

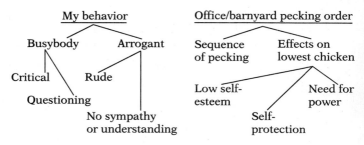

Formal outline

A formal outline not only lays out main ideas and their support but also shows the relative importance of all the essay's elements. Following is Terry Perez's outline. (Her freewriting appears on p. 6, and her drafts appear on pp. 16–18, 20–21, and 23–27.)

THESIS SENTENCE

Judging from the unrealistic images projected by the media, the United States is a nation either of constant ethnic conflict or of untroubled homogeneity.

FORMAL OUTLINE

I. Images of ethnic conflict
  A. News stories
    1. Hispanic-black gang wars
    2. Defaced synagogues
    3. Korean-black disputes
  B. The real story
    1. No war among groups
    2. Groups coexisting
II. Images of untroubled homogeneity
  A. Those pictured in TV shows and ads
    1. Mainly white
    2. Mainly middle class
    3. Mainly attractive
  B. Those missing from TV shows and ads
    1. Ethnic
    2. Poor
    3. Handicapped
    4. Other groups

This example illustrates several principles of outlining that can ensure completeness, balance, and clear relationships.

1. All parts are systematically indented and labeled: Roman nu-

merals (I, II) for primary divisions; indented capital letters (A, B) for secondary divisions; further indented Arabic numerals (1, 2) for supporting examples. (The next level down would be indented further still and labeled with small letters: a, b.)

2. The outline divides the material into several groups. A long list of points at the same level should be broken up into groups.

3. Topics of equal generality appear in parallel headings (with the same indentation and numbering or lettering).

4. All subdivided headings break into at least two parts because a topic cannot logically be divided into only one part.

5. All headings are expressed in parallel grammatical form—in the example, as phrases using a noun or pronoun plus modifiers. This is a topic outline; in a sentence outline all headings are expressed as full sentences.

3. Unity and coherence

Two qualities of effective writing relate to organization: unity and coherence. When you perceive that someone's writing "flows well," you are probably appreciating these qualities.

To check an outline or draft for UNITY, ask these questions:

❖ Is each section relevant to the main idea (thesis) of the essay?
❖ Within main sections, does each example or detail support the principal idea of that section?

To check your outline or draft for COHERENCE, ask these questions:

❖ Do the ideas follow a clear sequence?
❖ Are the parts of the essay logically connected?
❖ Are the connections clear and smooth?

See also 7a and 7b on unity and coherence in paragraphs.

Drafting

Drafting is exploratory. Don't expect to transcribe solid thoughts into polished prose: solidity and polish will come with revision and editing. Instead, while drafting let the very act of writing help you find and form your meaning.

4a Starting to draft

Beginning a draft sometimes takes courage, even for seasoned professionals. Procrastination may actually help if you let ideas for writing simmer at the same time. At some point, though, you'll have to face the blank paper or computer screen. The following techniques can help you begin:

* Read over what you've already written—notes, outlines, and so on—and immediately start your draft with whatever comes to mind.
* Freewrite (see 2c).
* Write scribbles or type nonsense until usable words start coming.
* Pretend you're writing to a friend about your topic.
* Conjure up an image that represents your topic—a physical object, a facial expression, two people arguing over something, a giant machine gouging the earth for a mine, whatever. Describe that image.
* Skip the opening and start in the middle. Or write the conclusion.
* Write a paragraph on what you think your essay will be about when you finish it.
* Using your outline, divide your essay into chunks—say, one for the introduction, another for the first example or reason, and so on. Start writing the chunk that seems most eager to be written, the one you understand best or feel most strongly about.

4b Keeping momentum

Drafting requires momentum: the forward movement opens you to fresh ideas and connections. To keep moving while drafting, try one or more of these techniques.

* Set aside enough time for yourself. (For a brief essay, a first draft is likely to take at least an hour or two.)
* Work in a place where you won't be interrupted.
* Make yourself comfortable.
* If you must stop working, jot a note before leaving the draft about what you expect to do next. Then you can pick up where you left off.

❖ Be as fluid as possible. Spontaneity will allow your attitudes toward your subject to surface naturally in your sentences. It will also make you receptive to ideas and relations you haven't seen before.

❖ Keep going. Skip over sticky spots; leave a blank if you can't find the right word. If an idea pops out of nowhere but doesn't seem to fit in, quickly jot it down on a separate sheet, or write it into the draft and bracket it for later attention.

❖ Resist self-criticism. Don't worry about your style, grammar, spelling, and the like. Don't worry what your readers will think. These are very important matters, but save them for revision.

❖ Use your thesis sentence and outline to remind you of your planned purpose, organization, and content.

❖ But don't feel constrained by your thesis and outline. If your writing leads you in a more interesting direction, follow.

Write or type your first draft only on one side of the paper, leave wide margins, and double- or triple-space all lines. Then you will have room for changes.

4c   Examining a sample first draft

The following is Terry Perez's first draft on the subject of cultural diversity in the media. (Perez's freewriting appears on p. 6 and her formal outline on p. 13.) Like most first drafts, this one is rough, with holes, digressions, misspellings, and grammatical errors. But it gave Perez a good start.

```
                    Title?

    In "America: The Multinational Society,"

Ishmael Reed mentions that the communications

media sensationalizes the "conflict between

people of different backgrounds." Either that,

or it depicts Americans as homogeneous. Judg-

ing from the unrealistic images projected by

television, newspapers, and magazines, the U.S.

is a nation either of constant ethnic conflict

or untroubled homogeneity.
```

It is easy to find examples of the emphasizing of conflict among ethnic groups. The news is full of stories of Hispanic gangs fighting black gangs or Korean shopkeepers pitted against black and Hispanic customers. In fact, New York City, with its dense and ethnically diverse population, regularly supplies stories for other cities' news media when they run out of local stories of hate and mayhem. My brother who lives in San Francisco is always complaining about all the New York stories in the news. What he doesn't realize is that it's not New York's fault, it's the media's for always playing up the bad news. Bad news is what the media specializes in--as everyone is always complaining. When it comes to ethnic relations, this is certainly the case. All sorts of different people mingle together peacefully, but not in the media.

There the only peace belongs to a very narrow band of people. Especially in television fiction and advertising. They have usual characteristics: they are white, married or expecting to be someday, unethnic, white collar, well-to-do, settled, materialistic, good looking, and thin. Many, many groups are excluded from this TV type, such as ethnic groups, poor people, and the handicapped. A

```
certain commercial is typical of TV with the
happy prosperous nuclear family enjoying
breakfast together.
     The problem with this media image, with its
extremes of peace and conflict, is that it is
untrue.  It caters to the ones who feel that the
U.S. should be a "monoculture" and would be.  If
only we could battle down the ones who don't
belong or won't.  A different picture is pos-
sible, but we aren't getting it.
```

Revising and Editing

During revision—literally "re-seeing"—you shift your focus outward from yourself and your subject toward your readers, concentrating on what will help them respond as you want. It's wise to revise in at least two stages, one devoted to fundamental meaning and structure (here called REVISING) and one devoted to word choice, grammar, punctuation, and other features of the surface (here called EDITING). Trying to revise and edit in one sweep can be overwhelming, so each step should be done separately.

5a Revising

One difficulty of revising is gaining enough distance from your work to see it objectively. One of the following techniques may help:

* Take a break after finishing the draft to pursue some other activity. A few hours may be enough; a whole night or day is preferable.
* Ask someone to read and react to your draft.

❖ Outline your draft. A formal outline, especially, can show where organization is illogical or support is skimpy. (See p. 13.)
❖ Listen to your draft: read it out loud, read it into a tape recorder and play the tape, or have someone read the draft to you.

Set aside at least as much time to revise your essay as you took to draft it. Plan on going through the draft several times to answer the questions in the checklist below and to resolve any problems.

Checklist for revision

1. Does the body of the essay carry out the purpose and central idea expressed by the thesis sentence (3a)?

   Is the reason for writing apparent, not only in the thesis sentence but throughout the essay?

   If the body of the essay does not carry out the thesis sentence, is the problem more with the thesis sentence (because it does not reflect a new and better direction in the draft) or with the body (because it wanders)?

2. Do readers need more information at any point to understand the meaning or appreciate the point of view (1c)?

3. Is the essay unified (3b-3)? Does each paragraph and sentence relate clearly to the thesis sentence?

4. Is the essay coherent (3b-3)? Is the sequence of ideas clear? Are the relationships within and among parts logical and clear?

5. Is each paragraph in the body unified (7a), coherent (7b), and well developed (7c)?

6. Does the introduction engage and focus readers' attention (7d-1)? Does the conclusion provide a sense of completion (7d-2)?

5b   Examining a sample revision

The material below is the first half of Terry Perez's revision (first draft pp. 16–18). Some changes are especially notable. (This list is keyed to the revision by number.)

1. Perez added a descriptive title to give readers a sense of her topic.

2. Perez rewrote and expanded the previous abrupt introduction to give more of a sense of Reed's essay and to make a clearer transition to her additional point about the media (the new sentence beginning *Another false media picture*).
3. Perez added examples and other details to support her general statements. This and the following category of changes occupied most of Perez's attention during revision.
4. In response to a reader's comments, Perez added several concessions and exceptions to balance her strong point of view.
5. Perez cut a digression that her reader had found distracting and irrelevant.

~~Title?~~ *America's Media Image*   1

2

Is the United States a "monoculture," a unified homogeneous society? Many Americans would like it to be or they think that it is now. But the writer Ishmael Reed says no. His essay is titled "America: The Multinational Society." In it he speaks out for cultural diversity. He thinks it makes the nation stronger. In passing he

~~In "America: The Multinational Society,"~~

~~Ishmael Reed~~ mentions that the communications

media sensationalizes the "conflict between

another false media picture can be added to Reed's point. The
people of different backgrounds." ~~(Either that,~~
picture of Americans as socially, economically, and ethnically similar.
~~or it depicts Americans as homogeneous.~~ (Judg-

ing from the unrealistic images projected by

television, newspapers, and magazines, the U.S.

is a nation either of constant ethnic conflict

or untroubled homogeneity.

     It is easy to find examples of the empha-

sizing of conflict among ethnic groups. The

news is full of stories of Hispanic gangs

swastikas are painted on Jewish synagogues,
fighting black gangs, ~~or~~ Korean shopkeepers   3

pitted against black and Hispanic customers.
These are real stories, and all-too-real ethnic
~~In fact, New York City, with its dense and~~   4
conflict should not be covered up. However,
~~ethnically diverse population, regularly~~
these stories are blown out of proportion.
~~supplies stories for other cities' news media~~   5

~~when they run out of local stories of hate and~~

~~mayhem. My brother who lives in San Francisco~~

~~is always complaining about all the New York~~

~~stories in the news. What he doesn't realize is~~

~~that it's not New York's fault, it's the media's~~

~~for always playing up the bad news. Bad news is~~

~~what the media specializes in--as~~ *Ø E* ~~e~~veryone ~~is~~
that the news media never present enough good news.
always complaining. When it comes to ethnic

relations, this is certainly the case. All

sorts of different people mingle together

peacefully, but not in the media.

Pakistanis, Russians, Mexicans, Chinese, Mayflower
descendants, great grandchildren of African   3
slaves. All these and more mingle on the
nation's streets, attend school together, work
together. Intergration is very far from   4
complete, severe inequality persists. Real
conflict exists. But for the most part,
cultural groups are not at war.

5c Editing and proofreading

Editing for style, sense, and correctness may come second to
more fundamental revision, but it is far from unimportant. After
revising your draft, try the following approaches to editing:

* Recopy, retype, or print out your revision so that you can read
  it easily and have plenty of room for changes.
* As you read the new draft, try to imagine yourself encountering
  it for the first time, as a reader will.
* Have a friend read your work. Or, if you share your work in
  class, listen to the responses of your classmates or instructor.
* As when revising, read the draft aloud, preferably into a tape
  recorder, listening for awkward rhythms, repetitive sentence
  patterns, and missing or clumsy transitions.
* Be careful to read what you actually see *on the page*, not what
  you may have intended to write but didn't.

Checklist for editing

1. Is the writing clear and effective?

Do the sentences use coordination (8), parallelism (9), and sub-
ordination (10) effectively?
Are the sentences varied and detailed (11)?
Are the words appropriate and exact (12)?
Is the writing concise (14)?

2. Are the sentences grammatically correct?

Are verbs in the correct form (19), tense (20), and mood (21)?
Do subjects and verbs agree (23)?
Are pronouns in the correct case (25)? Do pronouns and ante-
cedents agree (26)? Are the antecedents always clear (27)?
Are adjective and adverb forms correct (28)? Are modifiers
clear and logical (29)?
Are sentences grammatically complete (30)?
Are sentences punctuated correctly to avoid comma splices and
fused sentences (31)?

3. Is the use of commas, semicolons, colons, apostrophes, and
other punctuation correct (33–39)?

4. Are spelling, hyphenation, capital letters, underlining, and
other features correct (41–46)?

In your editing, work first for clarity and a smooth movement among sentences and then for correctness. Use the questions in the checklist opposite to guide your editing, referring to the chapters in parentheses as needed.

After editing your essay, recopy, retype, or print it one last time. Follow the guidelines in Chapter 40 or the wishes of your instructor for an appropriate manuscript form. Be sure to proofread the final essay several times to spot and correct errors. To increase the accuracy of your proofreading, you may need to experiment with ways to keep yourself from relaxing into the rhythm of your prose. Here are a few tricks used by professional proofreaders.

- Read the paper aloud, very slowly, and distinctly pronounce exactly what you see.
- Place a ruler under each line as you read it.
- Read "against copy," comparing your final draft one sentence at a time against the edited draft you copied it from.
- Read the essay backward, end to beginning, examining each sentence as a separate unit. (This technique will help keep the content of your writing from distracting you.)

5d   Examining a sample editing and a final draft

An excerpt from Terry Perez's edited draft and her complete final draft appear below (first draft pp. 16–18; revision pp. 20–21).

EDITED FIRST PARAGRAPH

Is the United States a "monoculture," a

unified, homogeneous society? Many Americans

think that it is or should be.

~~would like it to be or they think that it is~~

~~now.~~ But the writer Ishmael Reed says no. ~~His~~

~~essay is titled~~ *In* "America: The Multinational

Society~~,~~" ~~In it he~~ *Reed* speaks out for cultural

diversity. He thinks it makes the nation

stronger. In passing he mentions that the

communications media sensationalize the

"conflict between people of different back-
grounds." ~~Another false media picture of~~ *To Reed's point can be added*
the media's other false picture of America,
~~America can be added to Reed's point.~~ The

picture of Americans as socially, economically,

and ethnically similar. Judging from the

unrealistic images projected by television,

newspapers, and magazines, the ~~U.S.~~ *United States* is a nation

either of constant ethnic conflict or *of* untroubled

homogeneity.

FINAL DRAFT

America's Media Image

Is the United States a "monoculture," a

unified, homogeneous society? Many Americans

think that it is or should be. But the writer

Ishmael Reed says no. In "America: The Mul-

tinational Society," Reed speaks out for

cultural diversity. He thinks it makes the

nation stronger. In passing he mentions that

the communications media sensationalize the

"conflict between people of different back-

grounds." To Reed's point can be added the

media's other false picture of Americans as

socially, economically, and ethnically similar.

Judging from the unrealistic images projected by

television, newspapers, and magazines, the

United States is a nation either of constant

ethnic conflict or of untroubled homogeneity.

It is easy to find examples of the emphasizing of conflict among ethnic groups. The news is full of stories of Hispanic gangs fighting black gangs, swastikas painted on Jewish synagogues, Korean shopkeepers pitted against black and Hispanic customers. It's not that these aren't real stories, or that all-too-real ethnic conflict should be covered up. It's just that these stories are blown out of proportion.

Everyone complains that the news media never present enough good news. When it comes to ethnic relations, this is certainly the case. Pakistanis, Russians, Mexicans, Chinese, Mayflower descendants, great-grandchildren of African slaves--all these and more mingle on the nation's streets, attend school together, work together. Granted, integration is very far from complete. Severe inequality persists. Real conflict exists. But for the most part, cultural groups are not at war.

In the media, though, especially television fiction and advertising, the only peace belongs to a very narrow band of people. They are usually white, married or expecting to be someday, unethnic, white collar, well-to-do, settled, materialistic, good looking, and thin. These are but a few of the groups excluded from this TV type (some overlap): Polish-Americans, homeless families, homosexuals, factory workers, Lebanese immigrants, teenage mothers, amputees, Japanese-Americans, unmarried couples, loners, stay-at-home fathers, transients, mentally handicapped people, elderly pensioners, homely people, fat people, small people.

Exceptions come and go, of course, such as the working-class and overweight Roseanne and her husband, the older women in Golden Girls, and the Cosbys. However, the norm is easy to recognize. For example, a cereal commercial features a mother who is overseeing her husband's and children's breakfasts. The kitchen is full of the latest appliances and decorations. Everyone is white. Everyone is fit and cute, beautiful, or handsome. Everyone is well dressed and cheerful.

The media's two extremes of peace and conflict create a composite picture of a nation where a "monoculture" is desirable and all but achieved, if only we could battle down the ones who don't belong or won't belong. Imagine a different picture, though. In this one, people coexist who have diverse backgrounds, interests, incomes, living arrangements, and appearances. Sometimes they stay apart; sometimes they blend. Sometimes they clash or prey on each other;

```
sometimes they laugh together.  It all happens

now, and we could be watching.
```

5e Collaborative learning

In many writing courses students work together on writing, from completing exercises to commenting on each other's work. This collaborative learning gives experience in reading written work critically and in reaching others through writing.

If you are a reader of someone else's writing, keep the following principles in mind:

1. You are an interested, supportive reader, not a judge. Your comments will be most helpful when you:
   a. Question the writer or explain your reasons in a way that emphasizes the effect of the work *on you*, a reader: for instance, "I find this paragraph confusing."
   b. Avoid statements that seem to measure the work against a set of external standards: for instance, "This essay is poorly organized."
2. Unless you have other instructions, address only the most significant problems in the work.
3. Use the revision checklist on page 19 as a guide to what is significant in a piece of writing.
4. Be specific. Explain *why* you are confused or *why* you disagree with a conclusion.
5. Remember that you are the reader, not the writer. Resist the temptation to edit sentences, add details, or otherwise assume responsibility for the paper.
6. Be positive as well as honest. Instead of saying "This paragraph bores me," say "You have an interesting detail here that seems buried." And tell the writer what you like about the paper.

When you *receive* the comments of others, whether your classmates or your instructor, you will get more out of the process if you follow these guidelines:

1. Think of your readers as counselors or coaches who will help you see the virtues and flaws in your work and sharpen your awareness of readers' needs.
2. Read or listen to comments closely.
3. Make sure you know what the critic is saying. If you need more information, ask for it.

4. Don't become defensive. Letting comments offend you will only erect a barrier to improvement in your writing.

5. When comments seem appropriate, revise your work in response to them. You will learn more from the act of revision than from just thinking about changes.

6. Though you should be open to suggestions, you are the final authority on your paper. You are free to decline advice when you think it is inappropriate.

7. Keep track of problems that recur in your work so that you can give them special attention in new essays.

6

Writing with a Word Processor

A computerized word processor will not think for you, but it can save time and make writing easier. You need not understand computers or have expert typing skills. A user's manual or tutorial will explain the system and the keystrokes for important commands, such as deleting or saving text. You can avoid losing work accidentally by regularly saving or filing what you've written and by making paper back-up copies.

6a Using a word processor for invention and development

All word processors can aid the initial steps of writing. For instance, you can freewrite or brainstorm (see 2c) and then easily trim or expand the result and even move it directly into a draft. You can free your mind for very creative work by using a technique called INVISIBLE WRITING. Turn the computer screen's brightness control all the way down so that the screen appears blank. The computer will record what you write but keep it from you and thus prevent you from tinkering with your prose. When you're finished freewriting, simply turn up the brightness control to read what you've written and then save or revise it as you see fit.

You can use the computer on a continuing basis to keep a journal (see 2a) or to make notes on your reading. When you are ready to do so, you can transfer journal entries or reading notes (with source information) directly into your draft.

When you come to think about your audience, you can create a standard file of questions by typing the "Questions About Audience" from page 5 into your computer and saving them. For each assignment, duplicate the file and insert appropriate answers between the questions. Save the answers under a new file name, and print a copy for future reference.

A word processor is the ideal tool for shaping and organizing material. Beginning with just a list of ideas, you can isolate the more general points and then use the computer's tab settings to indent the more specific material. Unusable ideas can be deleted; redundant ideas can be merged. Once saved, the outline can be called up and revised as needed to reflect changes in your thinking and writing.

6b   Using a word processor for drafting

Many writers find that a word processor eases the transition from developing ideas to drafting. For instance, you can retrieve notes to the screen and rewrite, delete, or insert as needed.

While drafting, don't stop to correct errors or rewrite—both of which the computer will help you handle easily in a later draft. Use a symbol such as an asterisk (*) to mark gaps or tentative phrasings. Later, you can find these places quickly by instructing the computer to search for the symbol. If it helps, use invisible writing just to keep moving through a draft (see opposite).

6c   Using a word processor for revising and editing

The convenience of extensive revising and editing is the greatest advantage of word processing. With a few keystrokes you can add, delete, and move words, lines, and whole passages.

Here are some guidelines for using a word processor as an effective revision tool.

- Deal with major revisions first: see the revision checklist on page 19. Save editing, formatting the manuscript, and proofreading for later drafts.
- Use commands for deleting and moving blocks of copy as you would cut and paste a handwritten draft.
- Save earlier drafts under their own file names in case you need to consult them for ideas or phrasings. Make a duplicate of any draft you want to revise, and work on the duplicate.
- If you have trouble finding your focus or organizing your paper, print a copy of your entire draft and work on it. Many writers prefer to work on paper copy because it is easier to read and allows a view of the whole. Transferring changes from printed copy to computer is not difficult.

The following guidelines will help you make the most of the machine while editing and proofreading:

- Save your drafts on the computer, print your work, and do your editing on a paper copy. Almost everyone finds it much harder to spot errors on the computer screen than on paper. And paper copy may discourage you from overediting to the point where you say less with less life.
- After editing, return to the draft in the computer. Either work through the draft line by line or use the search command to find particular words or phrases.
- Use the search command as well to find misused words or stylistic problems that tend to crop up in your writing. Such problems might include *there are*, *it is*, and other expletive constructions; *the fact that* and other wordy phrases; and *is*, *are*, and other forms of *be*, which often occur in wordy constructions and passive sentences.
- Make sure that you neither omit needed words nor leave in unneeded words when deleting or inserting text on the computer.
- If your computer is equipped with one, use a spelling checker to locate errors. Be aware, though, that a spelling checker cannot help with many errors, such as *there* for *their*.
- Resist the temptation to view the final draft coming out of the printer as perfect simply because the copy is clean. Always proofread your final draft *carefully*. (See 5c for proofreading tips.)

Paragraphs

Setting off groups of related sentences in paragraphs with beginning indentions helps you and your readers focus on one idea at a time. Effective paragraphs are unified (7a), coherent (7b), and well developed (7c).

7a Maintaining paragraph unity

An effective paragraph develops one central idea—in other words, it is UNIFIED. For example:

> Some people really like chili, apparently, but nobody can agree how the stuff should be made. C. V. Wood, twice winner at Terlingua, uses flank steak, pork chops, chicken, and green chilis. My friend Hughes Rudd of CBS News, who imported five hundred pounds of chili powder into Russia as a condition of accepting employment as Moscow correspondent, favors coarse-ground beef. Isadore Bleckman, the cameraman I must live with on the road, insists upon one-inch cubes of stew beef and puts garlic in his chili, an Illinois affectation. An Indian of my acquaintance, Mr. Fulton Batisse, who eats chili for breakfast when he can, uses buffalo meat and plays an Indian drum while it's cooking. I ask you.
> —CHARLES KURALT, *Dateline America*

Kuralt's paragraph works because it follows through on the central idea stated in the first sentence, the TOPIC SENTENCE. But what if he had written this way instead?

> Some people really like chili, apparently, but nobody can agree how the stuff should be made. C. V. Wood, twice winner at Terlingua, uses flank steak, pork chops, chicken, and green chilis. My friend Hughes Rudd, who imported five hundred pounds of chili powder into Russia as a condition of accepting employment as Moscow correspondent, favors coarse-ground beef. He had some trouble finding the beef in Moscow, though. He sometimes had to scour all the markets and wait in long lines. For any American used to overstocked supermarkets and department stores, Russia can be quite a shock.

In this altered version, the topic of chili preparation is forgotten midway. In Kuralt's original, by contrast, every sentence after the first develops the topic sentence with examples.

A topic sentence need not always come first in the paragraph, and in some paragraphs the central idea may not be stated at all. But always the idea should govern the paragraph's content as if it were standing guard at the opening.

7b Achieving paragraph coherence

When a paragraph is COHERENT, readers can see how it holds together: the sentences seem to flow logically and smoothly into one another. Exactly the opposite happens with this paragraph:

> The ancient Egyptians were masters of preserving dead peo-
> ple's bodies by making mummies of them. Mummies several thou-
> sand years old have been discovered nearly intact. The skin, hair,
> teeth, finger- and toenails, and facial features of the mummies were
> evident. It is possible to diagnose the diseases they suffered in life,
> such as smallpox, arthritis, and nutritional deficiencies. The process
> was remarkably effective. Sometimes apparent were the fatal
> afflictions of the dead people: a middle-aged king died from a blow
> on the head, and polio killed a child king. Mummification consisted
> of removing the internal organs, applying natural preservatives in-
> side and out, and then wrapping the body in layers of bandages.

The paragraph is hard to read. All the sentences seem disconnected from each other, so that the paragraph lurches instead of gliding from point to point.

The paragraph as it was actually written is much clearer. Not only did the writer arrange information differently; he also built links into his sentences so that they would flow smoothly. The high-lighting on the actual paragraph below emphasizes the techniques:

❖ After stating the central idea in a topic sentence, the writer moves to two more specific explanations and illustrates the second with four sentences of examples.

❖ Circled and connected words repeat or restate key terms or concepts.

❖ Boxed words link sentences and clarify relationships.

❖ Underlined and connected phrases are in parallel grammatical form to reflect their parallel content.

Central idea

The ancient Egyptians were masters of preserving dead people's bodies by making mummies of them. Basically, mummification consisted of removing the internal organs, applying natural preservatives inside and out, and then wrapping the body in layers of bandages. And the process was remarkably effective. Indeed, mummies several thousand years old have been discovered nearly intact. Their skin, hair, teeth, finger- and toenails, and facial features are still evident. Their diseases in life, such as smallpox, arthritis, and nutritional deficiencies, are still diagnosable. Even their fatal afflictions are still apparent: a middle-aged king died from a blow on the head; a child king died from polio.

—MITCHELL ROSENBAUM (student),
"Lost Arts of the Egyptians"

1. Paragraph organization

A coherent paragraph organizes information so that readers can easily follow along. These are the most common paragraph schemes:

❖ GENERAL TO SPECIFIC: sentences downshift from more general statements to more specific ones. (See the paragraph above by Rosenbaum.)

❖ CLIMACTIC: sentences increase in drama or interest, ending in a climax. (See the paragraph by Lawrence Mayer on p. 34.)

❖ SPATIAL: scans a person, place, or object from top to bottom, side to side, or some other way that approximates the way people actually look at things. (See the paragraph by Virginia Woolf on pp. 37–38.)

❖ CHRONOLOGICAL: presents events as they occurred in time, earlier to later. (See the paragraph by Kathleen LaFrank on p. 36.)

2. Parallelism

Parallelism helps tie sentences together. In the following paragraph the parallel structures of *She* and a verb (*found, made, plunged, argued, defied*) link all sentences after the first one. Parallelism also appears within many of the sentences. Aphra Behn (1640–89) was the first Englishwoman to write professionally.

> In addition to her busy career as a writer, Aphra Behn also found time to briefly marry and spend a little while in debtor's prison. She found time to take up a career as a spy for the English in their war against the Dutch. She made the long and difficult voyage to Suriname [in South America] and became involved in a slave rebellion there. She plunged into political debate at Will's Coffee House and defended her position from the stage of the Drury Lane Theater. She actively argued for women's rights to be educated and to marry whom they pleased, or not at all. She defied the seventeenth-century dictum that ladies must be "modest" and wrote freely about sex.   —ANGELINE GOREAU, "Aphra Behn"

3. Repetition and restatement

Repeating or restating key words helps make a paragraph coherent and also reminds readers what the topic is. For example:

> Perhaps the simplest fact about sleep is that individual needs for it vary widely. Most adults sleep between seven and nine hours, but occasionally people turn up who need twelve hours or so, while some rare types can get by on three or four. Rarest of all are those legendary types who require almost no sleep at all; respected researchers have recently studied three such people. One of them—a healthy, happy woman in her seventies—sleeps about an hour every two or three days. The other two are men in early middle age, who get by on a few minutes a night. One of them complains about the daily fifteen minutes or so he's forced to "waste" in sleeping.
> —LAWRENCE A. MAYER, "The Confounding Enemy of Sleep"

Note the repetition of *sleep* and the restatement in *adults . . . people . . . rare types . . . legendary types . . . three such people.*

4. Pronouns

Because pronouns refer to nouns, they can help relate sentences to each other. In the paragraph by Angeline Goreau above, *she*, substituting for *Aphra Behn,* works just this way.

PARALLELISM   The use of similar grammatical structures for similar elements of meaning within or among sentences: *The book caused a stir in the media and aroused debate in Congress.* (See also Chapter 9.)

PRONOUN   A word that refers to and functions as a noun, such as *I, you, he, she, it, we, they: The patient could not raise her arm.*

5. Consistency

Consistency (or the lack of it) occurs primarily in the person and number of nouns and pronouns and in the tense of verbs. Any inconsistencies not required by meaning will interfere with a reader's ability to follow the development of ideas. For example:

SHIFTS IN PERSON

An enjoyable form of exercise is modern dance. If *one* wants to stay in shape, *you* will find that dance tones and strengthens most muscles. The leaping and stretching *you* do also improves *a person's* balance and poise. And *I* found that *my* posture improved after only a month of dancing.

SHIFTS IN NUMBER

Politics is not the activity for everyone. It requires quickness and patience at the same time. A *politician* must like speaking to large groups of people and fielding questions without having time to think of the answers. *Politicians* must also be willing to compromise with the people *they* represent. And no matter how good a *politician* is, *they* must give up being popular with all constituents. It isn't possible.

SHIFTS IN TENSE

I *am developing* an interest in filmmaking. I *tried* to take courses that relate to camera work or theater, and I *have read* books about the technical and artistic sides of movies. Though I *would have liked* to get a job on a movie set right away, I *will* probably *continue* my formal education and training in filmmaking after college. There simply *aren't* enough jobs available for all those who *wanted* to be in films but *have* no direct experience.

6. Transitional expressions

Transitional expressions such as *therefore, in contrast*, or *meanwhile* can forge specific connections between sentences, as the italicized expressions do in this paragraph.

PERSON   The form of a pronoun that indicates whether the subject is speaking (first person: *I, we*), spoken to (second person: *you*), or spoken about (third person: *he, she, it, they*). All nouns are in the third person.

NUMBER   The form of a noun, pronoun, or verb that indicates whether it is singular (one) or plural (more than one): *boy, boys*.

TENSE   The form of a verb that indicates the time of its action, such as present (*I run*), past (*I ran*), or future (*I will run*).

Medical science has *thus* succeeded in identifying the hundreds of viruses that can cause the common cold. It has *also* discovered the most effective means of prevention. One person transmits the cold viruses to another most often by hand. *For instance,* an infected person covers his mouth to cough. *Then* he picks up the telephone. *Half an hour later,* his daughter picks up the *same* telephone. *Immediately afterward,* she rubs her eyes. *Within a few days,* she, *too,* has a cold. *And thus* it spreads. To avoid colds, *therefore,* people should wash their hands often and keep their hands away from their faces. —KATHLEEN LAFRANK (student), "Colds: Myth and Science"

Here is a list of transitional expressions, arranged by the functions they perform:

To ADD OR SHOW SEQUENCE

again, also, and, and then, besides, equally important, finally, first, further, furthermore, in addition, in the first place, last, moreover, next, second, still, too

To COMPARE

also, in the same way, likewise, similarly

To CONTRAST

although, and yet, but, but at the same time, despite, even so, even though, for all that, however, in contrast, in spite of, nevertheless, notwithstanding, on the contrary, on the other hand, regardless, still, though, yet

To GIVE EXAMPLES OR INTENSIFY

after all, an illustration of, even, for example, for instance, indeed, in fact, it is true, of course, specifically, that is, to illustrate, truly

To INDICATE PLACE

above, adjacent to, below, elsewhere, farther on, here, near, nearby, on the other side, opposite to, there, to the east, to the left

To INDICATE TIME

after a while, afterward, as long as, as soon as, at last, at length, at that time, before, earlier, formerly, immediately, in the meantime, in the past, lately, later, meanwhile, now, presently, shortly, simultaneously, since, so far, soon, subsequently, then, thereafter, until, until now, when

To REPEAT, SUMMARIZE, OR CONCLUDE

all in all, altogether, as has been said, in brief, in conclusion, in other words, in particular, in short, in simpler terms, in summary, on the whole, that is, therefore, to put it differently, to summarize

To show cause or effect

accordingly, as a result, because, consequently, for this purpose, hence, otherwise, since, then, therefore, thereupon, thus, to this end, with this object

7c Developing paragraphs

An effective, well-developed paragraph always provides the specific information that readers need and expect in order to understand you and to stay interested in what you say. Paragraph length can be a rough gauge of development: anything much shorter than 100 to 150 words may leave readers with a sense of incompleteness.

To develop or shape an idea in a paragraph, one or more of the following patterns may help. (These patterns may also be used to develop entire essays. See p. 9.)

1. Narration

Narration retells a significant sequence of events, usually in the order of their occurrence (that is, chronologically). A narrator is concerned not just with the sequence of events but also with their consequence, their importance to the whole.

> Jill's story is typical for "recruits" to religious cults. She was very lonely in college and appreciated the attention of the nice young men and women who lived in a house near campus. They persuaded her to share their meals and then to move in with them. Between intense bombardments of "love," they deprived her of sleep and sometimes threatened to throw her out. Jill became increasingly confused and dependent, losing touch with any reality besides the one in the group. She dropped out of school and refused to see or communicate with her family. Before long she, too, was preying on lonely college students.
> —HILLARY BEGAS (student), "The Love Bombers"

2. Description

Description details the sensory qualities of a person, scene, thing, or feeling, using concrete and specific words to convey a dominant mood, to illustrate an idea, or to achieve some other purpose.

> The sun struck straight upon the house, making the white walls glare between the dark windows. Their panes, woven thickly with green branches, held circles of impenetrable darkness. Sharp-edged

wedges of light lay upon the window-sill and showed inside the room plates with blue rings, cups with curved handles, the bulge of a great bowl, the criss-cross pattern in the rug, and the formidable corners and lines of cabinets and bookcases. Behind their conglomeration hung a zone of shadow in which might be a further shape to be disencumbered of shadow or still denser depths of darkness.

—VIRGINIA WOOLF, *The Waves*

3. Illustration or support

An idea may be developed with several specific examples, like those used by Charles Kuralt on page 31, or with a single extended example, as here:

> One of my earliest discoveries in the field of intercultural communication was that the position of the bodies of people in conversation varies with the culture. Even so, it used to puzzle me that a special Arab friend seemed unable to walk and talk at the same time. After years in the United States, he could not bring himself to stroll along, facing forward while talking. Our progress would be arrested while he edged ahead, cutting slightly in front of me and turning sideways so we could see each other. Once in this position, he would stop. His behavior was explained when I learned that for the Arabs to view the other person peripherally is regarded as impolite, and to sit or stand back-to-back is considered very rude. You must be involved when interacting with Arabs who are friends.
>
> —EDWARD T. HALL, *The Hidden Dimension*

Sometimes you can develop a paragraph by providing your reasons for stating a general idea. For instance:

> It is time to defend the welfare state—taxes, bureaucrats, rules and regulations—the whole thing. Not only because it actually helps people who need help and subsidizes and enables a range of socially valuable activities—it does all that, and all that has to be done. There is another, and ultimately a more important, reason for defending the welfare state. It expresses a certain civil spirit, a sense of mutuality, a commitment to justice. Without that sense, no society can survive for long as a decent place to live—not for the needy, and not for anyone else.   —MICHAEL WALZER, "The Community"

4. Definition

Defining a complicated, abstract, or controversial term often requires extended explanation. The following definition of the word *quality* comes from an essay asserting that "quality in product and effort has become a vanishing element of current civilization." Notice how the writer pins down her meaning by offering examples and by setting up contrasts with nonquality.

In the hope of possibly reducing the hail of censure which is certain to greet this essay (I am thinking of going to Alaska or possibly Patagonia in the week it is published), let me say that quality, as I understand it, means investment of the best skill and effort possible to produce the finest and most admirable result possible. Its presence or absence in some degree characterizes every man-made object, service, skilled or unskilled labor—laying bricks, painting a picture, ironing shirts, practicing medicine, shoemaking, scholarship, writing a book. You do it well or you do it half-well. Materials are sound and durable or they are sleazy; method is painstaking or whatever is easiest. Quality is achieving or reaching for the highest standard as against being satisfied with the sloppy or fraudulent. It is honesty of purpose as against catering to cheap or sensational sentiment. It does not allow compromise with the second-rate.   —BARBARA TUCHMAN, "The Decline of Quality"

5. Division or analysis

With division or analysis, you separate something into its elements to understand it better—for instance, you might divide a newspaper into its sections, such as national news, regional news, lifestyle, and so on. As in the paragraph below, you may also interpret the meaning and significance of the elements you identify.

The surface realism of the soap opera conjures up an illusion of "liveness." The domestic settings and easygoing rhythms encourage the viewer to believe that the drama, however ridiculous, is simply an extension of daily life. The conversation is so slow that some have called it "radio with pictures." (Advertisers have always assumed that busy housewives would listen, rather than watch.) Conversation is casual and colloquial, as though one were eavesdropping on neighbors. There is plenty of time to "read" the character's face; close-ups establish intimacy. The sets are comfortably familiar: well-lit interiors of living rooms, restaurants, offices, and hospitals. Daytime soaps have little of the glamour of their prime-time relations. The viewer easily imagines that the conversation is taking place in real time.   —RUTH ROSEN, "Search for Yesterday"

6. Classification

When you sort many items into groups, you classify the items to see their relations more clearly. For instance:

In my experience, the parents who hire daytime sitters for their school-age children tend to fall into one of three groups. The first group includes parents who work and want someone to be at home when the children return from school. These parents are looking for an extension of themselves, someone who will give the care they would give if they were at home. The second group includes parents who may be home all day themselves but are too disorganized or too frazzled by their children's demands to handle child care alone. They are looking for an organizer and helpmate. The third and final group includes parents who do not want to be bothered by their children, whether they are home all day or not. Unlike the parents in the first two groups, who care for their children however they can, these parents seek a permanent substitute for themselves.

—NANCY WHITTLE (student), "Modern Parenting"

7. Comparison and contrast

Comparison and contrast may be used separately or together to develop an idea. The following paragraph illustrates one of two common ways of organizing a comparison and contrast: SUBJECT BY SUBJECT, first one subject and then the other.

Consider the differences also in the behavior of rock and classical music audiences. At a rock concert, the audience members yell, whistle, sing along, and stamp their feet. They may even stand during the entire performance. The better the music, the more active they'll be. At a classical concert, in contrast, the better the performance, the more *still* the audience is. Members of the classical audience are so highly disciplined that they refrain from even clearing their throats or coughing. No matter what effect the powerful music has on their intellects and feelings, they sit on their hands.   —TONY NAHM (student), "Rock and Roll Is Here to Stay"

The next paragraph illustrates the other common organization: POINT BY POINT, with the two subjects discussed side by side and matched feature for feature.

The first electronic computer, ENIAC, went into operation not even fifty years ago, yet the differences between it and today's home computer are enormous. ENIAC was enormous itself, consisting of forty panels, each two feet wide and four feet deep. Today's PC or Macintosh, by contrast, fits easily on a small table. ENIAC had to be configured by hand, with its programmers taking up to two days to reset switches and cables. Today, the average home user can change programs in an instant. And for all its size and inconvenience, ENIAC was also slow. In its time, its operating speed of 100,000 pulses per second seemed amazingly fast. However, today's home machine can operate at 4 million pulses per second or faster.

—SHIRLEY KAJIWARA (student), "The Computers We Deserve"

8. Cause-and-effect analysis

When you use analysis to explain why something happened or what did or may happen, then you are determining causes or effects. In the following paragraph the author looks at the causes of an effect—Japanese collectivism.

The *shinkansen* or "bullet train" speeds across the rural areas of Japan giving a quick view of cluster after cluster of farmhouses surrounded by rice paddies. This particular pattern did not develop purely by chance, but as a consequence of the technology peculiar to the growing of rice, the staple of the Japanese diet. The growing of rice requires the construction and maintenance of an irrigation system, something that takes many hands to build. More importantly, the planting and the harvesting of rice can only be done efficiently with the cooperation of twenty or more people. The "bottom line" is that a single family working alone cannot produce enough rice to survive, but a dozen families working together can produce a surplus. Thus the Japanese have had to develop the capacity to work together in harmony, no matter what the forces of disagreement or social disintegration, in order to survive.
— WILLIAM OUCHI, *Theory Z: How American Business Can Meet the Japanese Challenge*

9. Process analysis

When you analyze how to do something or how something works, you explain the steps in a process. For example:

What used to be called "laying on of hands" is now practiced seriously by nurses and doctors. Studies have shown that therapeutic touch, as it is now known, can aid relaxation and ease pain, two effects that may in turn cause physiological healing. A "healer" must first concentrate on helping the patient. Then, hands held a few inches from the patient's body, the healer moves from head to foot. The state of concentration allows the healer to detect energy disturbances in the patient that indicate localized tension, pain, or sickness. With further hand movements, the healer can redirect the energy. Patients report feeling heat from the healer's hands, perhaps indicating an energy transfer between healer and patient.
— LISA KUKLINSKI (student), "Old Ways to Noninvasive Medicine"

7d Writing introductory and concluding paragraphs

1. Introductions

An introduction draws readers from their world into your world. It should focus readers' attention on the topic and arouse their curiosity about what you have to say.

- It should be concise.
- It should specify your subject and imply your attitude.
- It should be sincere.
- It should be interesting without misrepresenting the content of the essay that follows.

Depending on your purpose and your main idea (thesis), you can use one of the following techniques for opening an essay:

- State the subject.
- Use a quotation.
- Relate an incident.
- Create an image.
- Ask a question.
- State an opinion.
- Make a historical comparison or contrast.
- Describe a problem or dilemma.

The most common kind of introduction opens with a statement of the essay's general subject, clarifies or limits the subject in one or more sentences, and then, in the thesis sentence, asserts the point of the essay. (See 3a for more on thesis sentences.)

> We Americans are a clean people. We bathe or shower regularly and spend billions of dollars each year on soaps and deodorants to wash away or disguise our dirt and odor. Yet cleanliness is a relatively recent habit with us. From the time of the Puritans until the turn of the twentieth century, bathing in the United States was rare and sometimes even illegal.
> —AMANDA HARRIS (student), "The Cleaning of America"

When writing and revising your introduction, avoid the following approaches that are likely to bore readers or make them question your sincerity or control.

- Don't reach back too far with vague generalities or truths, such as those beginning "Throughout human history . . ." or "In today's world. . . ." You may have needed a warm-up paragraph to start drafting, but your readers can do without it.
- Don't start with "The purpose of this essay is . . . ," "In this essay I will . . . ," or any similar flat announcement of your intention or topic.
- Don't refer to the title of the essay in the first sentence—for example, "This is my favorite activity" or "This is a big problem."
- Don't start with "According to Webster . . ." or a similar phrase leading to a dictionary definition. A definition can be an effective springboard to an essay, but this kind of lead-in has become dull with overuse.
- Don't apologize for your opinion or for inadequate knowledge with "I'm not sure if I'm right, but I think . . . ," "I don't know much about this, but . . . ," or similar lines.

2. Conclusions

Your conclusion finishes off your essay and tells readers where you think you have brought them. Usually set off in its own paragraph, the conclusion may consist of a single sentence or a group of sentences. It may take one or more of the approaches below.

- ❖ Create an image.
- ❖ Strike a note of hope or despair.
- ❖ Use a quotation.
- ❖ Give a symbolic or powerful fact or other detail.
- ❖ Recommend a course of action.
- ❖ Summarize the paper.
- ❖ Echo the introduction.
- ❖ Restate the thesis in a fresh way.

The following paragraph concludes the essay on bathing habits whose introduction was on the facing page. The writer both summarizes her essay and echoes her introduction.

> Thus changed attitudes and advances in plumbing finally freed us to bathe whenever we want. Perhaps partly to make up for our ancestors' bad habits, we have transformed that freedom into a national obsession.
> —AMANDA HARRIS (student), "The Cleaning of America"

Conclusions have several pitfalls you'll want to avoid:

- ❖ Don't simply restate your introduction—statement of subject, thesis sentence, and all. Presumably the paragraphs in the body of your essay have contributed something to the opening statements, and it's that something you want to capture in your conclusion.
- ❖ Don't start off in a new direction, with a subject different from or broader than the one your essay has been about.
- ❖ Don't conclude more than you reasonably can from the evidence you have presented. If your essay is about your frustrating experience trying to clear a parking ticket, you cannot reasonably conclude that *all* local police forces are too tied up in red tape to be of service to the people.
- ❖ Don't apologize for your essay or otherwise cast doubt on it. Don't say, "Even though I'm no expert," or "This may not be convincing, but I believe it's true," or anything similar. Rather, to win your readers' confidence, display confidence.

II

Clarity and Style

8

Coordination

With COORDINATION you can show that two or more elements in a sentence are equally important in meaning.

❖ Two main clauses may be linked with a comma and a coordinating conjunction, such as *and* or *but*.

Independence Hall in Philadelphia is now restored, <u>but</u> *fifty years ago it was in bad shape.*

❖ Two main clauses may be linked with a semicolon alone or a semicolon and a conjunctive adverb, such as *however*.

The building was standing; <u>however,</u> *it suffered from decay and vandalism.*

❖ Within clauses, words and phrases may be linked with a coordinating conjunction, such as *and* or *or*.

The people <u>and</u> *officials of the nation were indifferent to Independence Hall* <u>or</u> *took it for granted.*

8a   Using coordination to relate equal ideas

Coordination shows the equality between elements, as illustrated above. At the same time that it clarifies meaning, it can also help smooth choppy sentences.

MAIN CLAUSE   A word group that contains a subject and a verb and does not begin with a subordinating word: *The books were expensive.*

COORDINATING CONJUNCTIONS   *And, but, or, nor,* and sometimes *for, so, yet.*

CONJUNCTIVE ADVERBS   Modifiers that describe the relation of the ideas in two clauses, such as *hence, however, indeed,* and *thus.* (See p. 136 for a fuller list.)

CHOPPY
SENTENCES

We should not rely so heavily on oil. Coal and uranium are also overused. We have a substantial energy resource in the moving waters of our rivers. Smaller streams add to the total volume of water. The resource renews itself. Coal and oil are irreplaceable. Uranium is also irreplaceable. The cost of water does not increase much over time. The costs of coal, oil, and uranium rise dramatically.

IDEAS
COORDINATED

We should not rely so heavily on coal, oil, and uranium, for we have a substantial energy resource in the moving waters of our rivers and streams. Coal, oil, and uranium are irreplaceable and thus subject to dramatic cost increases; water, however, is self-renewing and more stable in cost.

The information in both passages is essentially the same, but the second is shorter and considerably easier to understand because it builds connections among coordinate elements.

8b Using coordination effectively

Use coordination only to express the *equality* of ideas or details. A string of coordinated elements—especially main clauses—implies that all points are equally important.

EXCESSIVE
COORDINATION

We were near the end of the trip, and the storm kept getting worse, and the snow and ice covered the windshield, and I could hardly see the road ahead, and I knew I should stop, but I kept on driving, and once I barely missed a truck.

Passages with such excessive coordination need editing to emphasize the main points (*the storm kept getting worse* and *I kept on driving*) and to de-emphasize the less important information.

REVISED

As we neared the end of the trip, *the storm kept getting worse*, covering the windshield with snow and ice until I could barely see the road ahead. Even though I knew I should stop, *I kept on driving*, once barely missing a truck. [The revision uses main clauses only for the main ideas, in italics.]

Even within a single sentence, coordination should express a logical equality between ideas.

FAULTY   John Stuart Mill was a nineteenth-century utilitarian, and he believed that actions should be judged by their usefulness or by the happiness they cause. [The two clauses are not separate and equal: the second expands on the first by explaining what a utilitarian such as Mill believed.]

REVISED   John Stuart Mill, *a nineteenth-century utilitarian,* believed that actions should be judged by their usefulness or by the happiness they cause.

Parallelism

PARALLELISM is a similarity of grammatical form between two or more coordinated elements.

| The air is dirtied by and | ‖ | factories cars | ‖ | belching spewing | ‖ | smoke exhaust. |

With parallelism, form reflects meaning: the parts of compound constructions have the same function and importance, so they also have the same grammatical form.

9a Using parallelism with *and, but,* or another coordinating conjunction

The coordinating conjunctions *and, but, or, nor,* and *yet* always signal a need for parallelism.

The industrial base is *shifting* <u>and</u> *shrinking.* [Parallel words.]

Politicians rarely *acknowledge the problem* <u>or</u> *propose alternatives.* [Parallel phrases.]

Industrial workers are understandably disturbed *that they are losing their jobs* <u>and</u> *that no one seems to care.* [Parallel clauses.]

> COORDINATING CONJUNCTIONS   *And, but, or, nor,* and sometimes *for, so, yet.*

FAULTY	Three reasons why steel companies keep losing money are that their plants are inefficient, high labor costs, <u>and</u> foreign competition is increasing. [Two elements are clauses; one is a phrase.]
REVISED	Three reasons why steel companies keep losing money are *inefficient plants*, *high labor costs*, and *increasing foreign competition*.

All the words required by idiom or grammar must be stated in compound constructions (see also 13a).

FAULTY	Given training, workers can acquire the skills <u>and</u> interest in other jobs. [Idiom dictates different prepositions with *skills* and *interest*.]
REVISED	Given training, workers can acquire the skills *for* and interest in other jobs.

9b Using parallelism with *both . . . and, either . . . or,* or another correlative conjunction

Correlative conjunctions stress equality and balance between elements. Parallelism confirms the equality.

It is <u>not</u> *a tax bill* <u>but</u> *a tax relief bill,* providing relief <u>not</u> *for the needy* <u>but</u> *for the greedy.*   —FRANKLIN DELANO ROOSEVELT

At the end of the novel, Huck Finn <u>both</u> *rejects society's values by turning down money and a home* <u>and</u> *affirms his own values by setting out for "the territory."*

With correlative conjunctions, the element after the second connector must match the element after the first connector.

NONPARALLEL	Huck Finn learns <u>not only</u> that human beings have an enormous capacity for folly <u>but also</u> enormous dignity. [The first element includes *that human beings have;* the second element does not.]
REVISED	Huck Finn learns *that human beings have not only* an enormous capacity for folly but also enormous dignity. [Repositioning *not only* makes the two elements parallel.]

CORRELATIVE CONJUNCTIONS   Pairs of connectors, such as *both . . . and, either . . . or, neither . . . nor, not . . . but, not only . . . but also, whether . . . or.*

9c Using parallelism with lists and outlines

The elements of a list or outline are coordinate and should be parallel in structure. Parallelism is essential in a formal topic outline (see 3b-2).

FAULTY	IMPROVED
Changes in Renaissance England	Changes in Renaissance England
1. An extension of trade routes	1. Extension of trade routes
2. Merchant class became more powerful	2. Increasing power of the merchant class
3. The death of feudalism	3. Death of feudalism
4. Upsurging of the arts	4. Upsurge of the arts
5. The sciences were encouraged	5. Encouragement of the sciences
6. Religious quarrels began	6. Rise of religious quarrels

10

Subordination

With SUBORDINATION you use words or word groups to indicate that some elements in a sentence are less important than others to your meaning. Usually, the main idea appears in the main clause, and supporting details appear in subordinate structures such as phrases or subordinate clauses.

Various subordinate structures can de-emphasize information:

❖ Subordinate clauses beginning with *although, because, if, who (whom), that, which,* or another subordinating word.

Although production costs have declined, they are still high.
Costs, *which include labor and facilities,* are difficult to control.

❖ Phrases.

Despite some decline, production costs are still high.
Costs, *including labor and facilities,* are difficult to control.

❖ Single words.

Declining costs have not matched prices.
Labor costs are difficult to control.

10a Emphasizing main ideas

A string of main clauses can make everything in a passage seem equally important. Subordination with words, phrases, or subordinate clauses, as illustrated above, will highlight what's important.

STRING OF MAIN CLAUSES	In recent years computer prices have dropped, and production costs have dropped more slowly, and computer manufacturers have had to struggle, for their profits have been shrinking.
REVISED	*Because* production costs have dropped more slowly *than computer prices* in recent years, computer manufacturers have had to struggle *with shrinking profits*.

Generally, subordinate clauses give the most emphasis to secondary information, phrases give less, and single words give the least.

10b Using subordination effectively

Subordination should be used only for the less important information in a sentence.

FAULTY	Ms. Angelo was in her first year of teaching, although she was a better instructor than others with many years of experience. [The sentence suggests that Angelo's inexperience is the main idea, whereas the writer almost certainly intended to stress her skill *despite* her inexperience.]
REVISED	Although Ms. Angelo was in her first year of teaching, *she was a better instructor than others with many years of experience*.

MAIN CLAUSE   A word group that contains a subject and a verb and does not begin with a subordinating word: *Words can do damage*.

SUBORDINATE CLAUSE   A word group that contains a subject and a verb, begins with a subordinating word such as *because* or *who*, and is not a question: *Words can do damage <u>when they hurt feelings</u>*. (See pp. 77 and 133 for fuller lists of subordinating words.)

PHRASE   A word group that lacks a subject or verb or both: *Words can do damage <u>by hurting feelings</u>*.

Subordination loses its power to organize and emphasize information when too much loosely related detail crowds into one long sentence.

OVERLOADED   The boats that were moored at the dock when the hurricane, which was one of the worst in three decades, struck were ripped from their moorings, because the owners had not been adequately prepared, since the weather service had predicted the storm would blow out to sea, which they do at this time of year.

REVISED   Struck by one of the worst hurricanes in three decades, *the boats at the dock were ripped from their moorings. The owners were unprepared* because the weather service had said that hurricanes at this time of year blow out to sea. [The details are sorted into two sentences, each with its own main clause.]

Variety and Details

Writing that's interesting as well as clear has at least two features: the sentences vary in length and structure, and they are well textured with details.

11a Varying sentence length

In most contemporary writing, sentences tend to vary from about ten words on the short side to about forty words on the long. The average is between fifteen and twenty-five words, depending on the writer's purpose, audience, and style.

Your sentences should not be all at one extreme or the other; if they are, your readers may have difficulty focusing on main ideas and seeing the relations among them.

❖ If most of your sentences contain thirty-five words or more, you probably need to break some up into shorter, simpler sentences.
❖ If most of your sentences contain fewer than ten or fifteen words, you probably need to add details to them (11c) or combine them through coordination (8a) and subordination (10a).

11b Varying sentence structure

A passage will be monotonous if all its sentences follow the same pattern, like soldiers marching in a parade. Try these techniques for varying structure.

1. Subordination

A string of main clauses in simple or compound sentences can be especially plodding.

MONOTONOUS   The moon is now drifting away from the earth. It moves away at the rate of about one inch a year. Our days on earth are getting longer, and they grow a thousandth of a second longer every century. A month will someday be forty-seven of our present days long, and we might eventually lose the moon altogether. Such great planetary movement rightly concerns astronomers, but it need not worry us. It will take 50 million years.

Enliven such writing—and make the main ideas stand out—by expressing the less important information in subordinate clauses and phrases. In the revision below, italics indicate subordinate structures that used to be main clauses.

REVISED   The moon is now drifting away from the earth *at the rate of about one inch a year. At the rate of a thousandth of a second or so every century,* our days on earth are getting longer. A month will someday be forty-seven of our present days long, *if we don't eventually lose the moon altogether.* Such great planetary movement rightly concerns astronomers, but it need not worry us. It will take 50 million years.

MAIN CLAUSE   A word group that contains a subject and a verb and does not begin with a subordinating word: *Tourism is an industry. It brings in over $2 billion a year.*

SUBORDINATE CLAUSE   A word group that contains a subject and verb, begins with a subordinating word such as *because* or *who,* and is not a question: *Tourism is an industry <u>that brings in over $2 billion a year.</u>* (See pp. 77 and 133 for fuller lists of subordinating words.)

PHRASE   A word group that lacks a subject or verb or both: *Tourism is an industry <u>valued at over $2 billion a year.</u>*

2. Varied sentence beginnings

Another cause of monotony is an unbroken sequence of sentences beginning with their subjects.

MONOTONOUS   The lawyer cross-examined the witness for two days. The witness had expected to be dismissed within an hour and was visibly irritated. He did not cooperate. He was reprimanded by the judge.

Simply beginning some of these sentences with a modifier or conjunction dramatically improves readability.

REVISED   *For two days*, the lawyer cross-examined the witness. *Expecting to be dismissed within an hour*, the witness was visibly irritated. He did not cooperate. *Indeed*, he was reprimanded by the judge.

The italicized expressions represent the most common choices for varying sentence beginnings.

❖ Adverb modifiers, such as *For two days* (modifies the verb *cross-examined*).
❖ Adjective modifiers, such as *Expecting to be dismissed within an hour* (modifies *witness*).
❖ Transitional expressions, such as *Indeed*. (See pp. 36–37 for a list of such expressions.)

3. Varied word order

Occasionally, you can vary a sentence and emphasize it at the same time by inverting the usual order of parts:

A dozen witnesses testified for the prosecution, and the defense attorney barely questioned eleven of them. *The twelfth, however, he grilled.* [Compare normal word order: *He grilled the twelfth, however.*]

Inverted sentences used without need are artificial. Use them only when emphasis demands.

11c   Adding details

Adding relevant details such as facts and examples to sentences creates the texture and life that keep readers awake and help them grasp your meaning. For instance:

FLAT   Constructed after World War II, Levittown, NY, con-
            sisted of thousands of houses in two basic styles. Over
            the decades, residents have altered the houses so dra-
            matically that the original styles are often unrecogniz-
            able.

DETAILED   Constructed *on potato fields* after World War II, Levit-
            town, NY, consisted of *more than 17,000* houses in *Cape
            Cod and ranch* styles. Over the decades, residents have
            *added expansive front porches, punched dormer windows
            through roofs, converted garages to sun porches, and
            otherwise* altered the houses so dramatically that the
            original styles are often unrecognizable.

Appropriate and Exact Words

The clarity and effectiveness of your writing will depend greatly
on the use of words that are appropriate for your writing situation
(12a) and that express your meaning exactly (12b).

12a Choosing the appropriate word

Appropriate words suit your writing situation—your subject,
purpose, and audience. In most college and career writing you
should rely on standard English, the English normally expected and
used by educated readers and writers.

The vocabulary of standard English is huge, allowing expression
of an infinite range of ideas and feelings; but it does exclude words
that only some groups of people use, understand, or find inoffensive.
Some of these more limited vocabularies should be avoided altogether; others should be used cautiously and in relevant situations,
as when aiming for a special effect with an audience you know will
appreciate it. Whenever you doubt a word's status, consult a dictionary.

1. Slang

SLANG is the language used by a group, such as musicians or
computer programmers, to reflect common experiences and to make

technical references efficient. The following example is from an essay on the slang of "skaters" (skateboarders):

> Curtis slashed ultra-punk crunchers on his longboard, while the Rube-man flailed his usual Gumbyness on tweaked frontsides and lofty fakie ollies.　　—MILES ORKIN, "Mucho Slingage by the Pool"

Among those who understand it, slang may be vivid and forceful. It often occurs in dialogue, and an occasional slang expression can enliven an informal essay. But most slang is too flippant and imprecise for effective communication, and it is generally inappropriate for college or business writing. Notice the gain in seriousness and precision achieved in the following revision.

SLANG	Many students start out *pretty together* but then *get weird.*
REVISED	Many students start out *with clear goals* but then *lose their direction.*

2. Colloquial language

COLLOQUIAL LANGUAGE is the everyday spoken language, including expressions such as *get together, go crazy,* and *do the dirty work.*

When you write informally, colloquial language may be appropriate to achieve the casual, relaxed effect of conversation. An occasional colloquial word dropped into otherwise more formal writing can also help you achieve a desired emphasis. But most colloquial language is not precise enough for college or career writing. In such writing you should generally avoid any words and expressions labeled "informal" or "colloquial" in your dictionary.

COLLOQUIAL	According to a Native American myth, the Great Creator *had a dog hanging around with him* when he created the earth.
REVISED	According to a Native American myth, the Great Creator *was accompanied by a dog* when he created the earth.

3. Nonstandard language

Many intelligent people who speak dialects of English use expressions considered unacceptable in standard English. Usually labeled "nonstandard" in dictionaries, these expressions include *nowheres;* such pronoun forms as *hisn, hern, hisself,* and *theirselves; them* as an adjective, as in *them dishes, them courses;* the expressions *this here* and *that there,* as in *that there elevator;* verb forms such as *knowed, throwed, hadn't ought,* and *could of;* and double negatives such as *didn't never* and *haven't no*. Avoid or revise all nonstandard expressions in speaking and writing situations calling for standard English.

4. Technical words

All disciplines and professions rely on specialized language that allows the members to communicate precisely and efficiently with each other. Chemists, for instance, have their *phosphatides*, and literary critics have their *motifs* and *subtexts*. Without explanation technical words are meaningless to the nonspecialist. When you are writing for a general audience, avoid unnecessary technical terms. If your subject requires words the reader may not understand, be careful to define them.

5. Indirect and pretentious writing

Small, plain, and direct words are almost always preferable to big, showy, or evasive words. Take special care to avoid euphemisms, double talk, and pretentious writing.

A EUPHEMISM is a presumably inoffensive word that a writer or speaker substitutes for a word deemed potentially offensive or too blunt, such as *passed away* for *died* or *misspeak* for *lie*. Use euphemisms only when you know that blunt, truthful words would needlessly hurt or offend members of your audience.

A kind of euphemism that deliberately evades the truth is DOUBLE TALK (also called DOUBLESPEAK or WEASEL WORDS): language intended to confuse or to be misunderstood. Today double talk is unfortunately common in politics and advertising—the *revenue enhancement* that is really a tax, the *peace-keeping function* that is really war making, the *biodegradable* bags that last decades. Double talk has no place in honest writing.

Euphemism and sometimes double talk seem to keep company with PRETENTIOUS WRITING, fancy language that is more elaborate than its subject requires. Choose your words for their exactness and economy. The big, ornate word may be tempting, but pass it up. Your readers will be grateful.

PRETENTIOUS	Many institutions of higher education recognize the need for youth at the threshold of maturity to confront the choice of life's endeavor and thus require students to select a field of concentration.
REVISED	Many colleges and universities force students to make decisions about their careers by requiring them to select a major.

6. Sexist and other biased language

Even when we do not mean it to, our language can reflect and perpetuate hurtful prejudices toward groups of people, especially racial, ethnic, religious, age, and sexual groups. Insulting language reflects more poorly on the user than on the person or persons designated. Unbiased language does not submit to stereotypes. It refers to people as they would wish to be referred to.

Among the most subtle and persistent biased language is sexist

---

Eliminating sexist language

❖ Avoid demeaning and patronizing language.

SEXIST Pushy broads are entering almost every occupation.
REVISED *Women* are entering almost every occupation.

SEXIST President Reagan came to Nancy's defense.
REVISED President Reagan came to *Mrs. Reagan's* defense.

❖ Avoid occupational or social stereotypes.

SEXIST The caring doctor commends his nurse when she does a good job.
REVISED Caring *doctors* commend *their nurses* on jobs well done.

SEXIST The grocery shopper should save her coupons.
REVISED *Grocery shoppers* should save *their* coupons.

❖ Avoid using *man* or words containing *man* to refer to all human beings.

SEXIST Man has not reached the limits of social justice.
REVISED *Humankind* (or *Humanity*) has not reached the limits of social justice.

SEXIST The furniture consists of manmade materials.
REVISED The furniture consists of *synthetic* materials.

❖ Avoid using the generic *he* to refer to both genders. (See also 26c.)

SEXIST The person who studies history knows his roots.
REVISED The person who studies history knows *his or her* roots.
REVISED *People* who study history know *their* roots.

language that distinguishes needlessly between men and women in such matters as occupation, ability, behavior, temperament, and maturity. It can wound or irritate readers, and it indicates the writer's thoughtlessness or unfairness. The box on the facing page suggests some ways of eliminating sexist language.

12b Choosing the exact word

To write clearly and effectively, you will want to find the words that fit your meaning exactly and convey your attitude precisely.

1. The right word for your meaning

All words have one or more basic meanings (called DENOTATIONS)—the meanings listed in the dictionary, without reference to emotional associations. If readers are to understand you, you must use words according to their established meanings.

* Become acquainted with a dictionary. Consult it whenever you are unsure of a word's meaning.
* Distinguish between similar-sounding words that have widely different denotations.

INEXACT   Older people often suffer *infirmaries* [places for the sick].

EXACT   Older people often suffer *infirmities* [disabilities].

Some words, called HOMONYMS, sound exactly alike but differ in meaning: for example, *principal/principle* or *rain/reign/rein*. (See 41a for a list of commonly confused homonyms.)

* Distinguish between words with related but distinct denotations.

INEXACT   Television commercials *continuously* [unceasingly] interrupt programming.

EXACT   Television commercials *continually* [regularly] interrupt programming.

In addition to their emotion-free meanings, many words also carry associations with specific feelings. These CONNOTATIONS can shape readers' responses and are thus a powerful tool for writers. The following word pairs have related denotations but very different connotations: *desire/lust, firm/stubborn, enthusiasm/mania, pride/vanity, lasting/endless, daring/reckless.*

Several resources can help you track down words with the exact connotations you want:

- ❖ A dictionary is essential. Many dictionaries list and distinguish among synonyms.
- ❖ A dictionary of synonyms lists and defines synonyms in groups.
- ❖ A thesaurus lists synonyms but does not distinguish among them. Because it lacks definitions, a thesaurus can only suggest possibilities; you will still need a dictionary to discover the words' connotations.

2. Concrete and specific words

Clear, exact writing balances abstract and general words, which outline ideas and objects, with concrete and specific words, which sharpen and solidify.

- ❖ ABSTRACT WORDS name qualities and ideas: *beauty, inflation, management, culture, liberal.* CONCRETE WORDS name things we can know by our five senses of sight, hearing, touch, taste, and smell: *sleek, humming, brick, bitter, musty.*
- ❖ GENERAL WORDS name classes or groups of things, such as *buildings, weather,* or *birds,* and include all the varieties of the class. SPECIFIC WORDS limit a general class, such as *buildings,* by naming one of its varieties, such as *skyscraper, Victorian courthouse,* or *hut.*

Abstract and general words are useful in the broad statements that set the course for your writing.

The wild horse in America has a *romantic* history.

Relations between the sexes today are only a *little* more *relaxed* than they were in the past.

But such statements need development with concrete and specific detail. Look at how such detail turns a vague sentence into an exact one:

VAGUE   The size of his hands made his smallness real. [How big were his hands? How small was he?]

EXACT   Not until I saw his white, doll-like hands did I realize that he stood a full head shorter than most other men.

3. Idioms

IDIOMS are expressions in any language that do not fit the rules for meaning or grammar—for instance, *put up with, plug away at, make off with.*

Because they are not governed by rules, idioms usually cause particular difficulty for people learning to speak and write a new language. But even native speakers of English misuse some combinations of verb and preposition or adjective and preposition, such as those listed below.

accords *with*

according *to*

accuse *of* a crime

adapt *from* a source

adapt *to* a situation

agree *on* a plan

agree *to* a proposal

agree *with* a person

angry *with*

capable *of*

charge *for* a purchase

charge *with* a crime

compare *to* something in a different class

compare *with* something in the same class

concur *in* an opinion

concur *with* a person

contend *for* a principle

contend *with* a person

differ *about* or *over* a question

differ *from* in appearance

differ *with* a person

identical *with* or *to*

impatient *at* her conduct

impatient *of* restraint

impatient *for* a raise

impatient *with* a person

independent *of*

infer *from*

inferior *to*

occupied *by* a person

occupied *in* study

occupied *with* a thing

part *from* a person

part *with* a possession

prior *to*

rewarded *by* the judge

rewarded *for* something done

rewarded *with* a gift

superior *to*

wait *at* a place

wait *for* a train, a person

wait *on* a customer

For more on prepositions with verbs, see 24c.

4. Figurative language

FIGURATIVE LANGUAGE (or a FIGURE OF SPEECH) departs from the literal meanings of words, usually by comparing very different ideas or objects.

LITERAL   As I try to write, I can think of nothing to say.

FIGURATIVE As I try to write, *my mind is a blank slab of black slate.*

Imaginatively and carefully used, figurative language can capture meaning more precisely and feelingly than literal language.

The two most common figures of speech are the simile and the metaphor. Both compare two things of different classes, often one abstract and the other concrete. A SIMILE makes the comparison explicit and usually begins with *like* or *as*.

> Whenever we grow, we tend to feel it, *as* a young seed must feel the weight and inertia of the earth when it seeks to break out of its shell on its way to becoming a plant.   —ALICE WALKER

A METAPHOR claims that the two things are identical, omitting such words as *like* and *as*.

> A school is a hopper into which children are heaved while they are young and tender; therein they are pressed into certain standard shapes and covered from head to heels with official rubber stamps.
> —H. L. MENCKEN

To be successful, figurative language must be fresh and unstrained, calling attention not to itself but to the writer's meaning. Be especially wary of mixed metaphors, which combine two or more incompatible figures.

MIXED   Various thorny problems that we try to sweep under the rug continue to bob up all the same.

IMPROVED   Various thorny problems that we try to weed out continue to thrive all the same.

5. Trite expressions

TRITE EXPRESSIONS, or CLICHÉS, are phrases so old and so often repeated that they become stale. They include:

acid test	moving experience
add insult to injury	needle in a haystack
better late than never	point with pride
beyond the shadow of a doubt	pride and joy
cool, calm, and collected	ripe old age
crushing blow	rude awakening
dyed in the wool	sadder but wiser
easier said than done	shoulder the burden
face the music	shoulder to cry on
few and far between	sneaking suspicion
gentle as a lamb	sober as a judge
green with envy	stand in awe
hard as a rock	strong as an ox
heavy as lead	thin as a rail
hit the nail on the head	tired but happy
hour of need	tried and true
ladder of success	wise as an owl

To prevent clichés from sliding into your writing, be wary of any expression you have heard or used before. Substitute fresh words of your own, or restate the idea in plain language.

Completeness

The most serious kind of incomplete sentence is the grammatical fragment (see Chapter 30). But sentences are also incomplete when they omit one or more words needed for clarity.

13a Writing complete compounds

You may omit words from a compound construction when the omission will not confuse readers.

> Environmentalists have hopes for alternative fuels and (for) public transportation.
>
> Some cars will run on electricity; some (will run) on methane.

Such omissions are possible only when the words omitted are common to all the parts of a compound construction. When the parts differ in grammar or idiom, all words must be included in all parts.

> One new car *gets* eighty miles per gallon; some old cars *get* as little as five miles per gallon. [One verb is singular, the other plural.]
>
> Environmentalists believe *in* and work *for* fuel conservation. [Idiom requires different prepositions with *believe* and *work.*]

13b Adding needed words

In haste or carelessness, do not omit small words that are needed for clarity.

COMPOUND CONSTRUCTION   Two or more elements (words, phrases, clauses) that are equal in importance and that function as a unit: *dogs and cats* (words); *Rain fell; streams overflowed* (clauses).

| INCOMPLETE | Regular payroll deductions are a type painless savings. You hardly notice missing amounts, and after period of years the contributions can add a large total. |
| REVISED | Regular payroll deductions are a type *of* painless savings. You hardly notice *the* missing amounts, and after *a* period of years the contributions can add *up to* a large total. |

Attentive proofreading is the only insurance against this kind of omission. *Proofread all your papers carefully.* See page 23 for tips.

Writers whose first language is not English often omit the articles *a, an,* and *the* because their native language uses such words differently or not at all. For guidelines on when to use articles, see 28f.

Conciseness

Writing concisely means making every word count toward your meaning. Conciseness is not the same as mere brevity: detail and originality should not be cut with needless words. Rather, the length of an expression should be appropriate to the thought.

14a   Cutting or shortening empty words and phrases

Empty words and phrases walk in place, gaining little or nothing in meaning. Many can be cut entirely. For example:

all things considered	in a manner of speaking
as far as I'm concerned	in my opinion
for all intents and purposes	last but not least
for the most part	more or less

Others can also be cut, usually along with some of the words around them:

area	element	kind	situation
aspect	factor	manner	thing
case	field	nature	type

Ways to achieve conciseness

WORDY

The highly pressured nature of critical-care nursing is due to the fact that the patients have life-threatening illnesses. Critical-care nurses must have possession of steady nerves to care for patients who are critically ill and very sick. The nurses must also have possession of interpersonal skills. They must also have medical skills. It is considered by most health-care professionals that these nurses are essential if there is to be improvement of patients who are now in critical care from that status to the status of intermediate care.

- Cut or shorten empty words and phrases (14a).
- Use strong verbs (14e).
- Cut unneeded repetition (14b).
- Combine sentences (14c).
- Rewrite passive sentences as active (14f).
- Eliminate expletive constructions (14g).
- Reduce clauses to phrases (14d).
- Reduce phrases to single words (14d).

CONCISE

Critical-care nursing is highly pressured because the patients have life-threatening illnesses. Critical-care nurses must possess steady nerves and interpersonal and medical skills. Most health-care professionals consider these nurses essential if patients in critical care are to improve to intermediate care.

Still others can be reduced from several words to a single word:

FOR	SUBSTITUTE
at all times	always
at the present time	now
for the purpose of	for
due to the fact that	because
because of the fact that	because
by virtue of the fact that	because
in the final analysis	finally

Cutting or reducing such words and phrases will make your writing move faster and work harder.

WORDY   As far as I am concerned, because of the fact that a situation of discrimination continues to exist in the field of medicine, women have not at the present time achieved equality with men.

CONCISE   Because of continuing discrimination in medicine, women have not yet achieved equality with men.

14b Cutting unneeded repetition

Unnecessary repetition weakens sentences.

WORDY   Many unskilled workers *without training in a particular job* are unemployed *and do not have any work.*

CONCISE   Many unskilled workers are unemployed.

Be especially alert to phrases that say the same thing twice. In the examples below, the unneeded words are italicized.

circle *around*   *important* (*basic*) essentials
consensus *of opinion*   puzzling *in nature*
cooperate *together*   repeat *again*
final completion   return *again*
frank and honest exchange   square (round) *in shape*
the future *to come*   *surrounding* circumstances

14c Combining sentences

Often the information in two or more sentences can be combined into one tight sentence.

WORDY   The French and British collaborated on building the Channel Tunnel. The tunnel links France and Britain. The French drilled from Sangatte. The British drilled from Dover.

CONCISE   The French and British collaborated on building the Channel Tunnel between their countries, the French drilling from Sangatte and the British from Dover.

14d Reducing clauses and phrases

Modifiers—subordinate clauses, phrases, and single words—can be expanded or contracted depending on the emphasis you want to achieve. (Generally, the longer a construction, the more emphasis it has.) When editing your sentences, consider whether any modifiers can be reduced without loss of emphasis or clarity.

WORDY   The tunnel, *which was drilled for twenty-three miles*, runs *through a bed of solid chalk that lies under the English Channel*.

CONCISE The *twenty-three-mile* tunnel runs *through solid chalk under the English Channel*.

14e Using strong verbs

Weak verbs such as *is, has,* and *make* stall sentences. Strong verbs such as *slice, bicker,* and *stroll* energize sentences, moving them along. Weak verbs usually carry extra baggage, too, such as unneeded prepositional phrases and long, abstract nouns or adjectives.

WORDY   The drillers *made slow advancement*, and costs *were over* $5 million a day. The slow progress *was worrisome for* backers, who *had had expectations of* high profits.

CONCISE The drillers *advanced slowly*, and costs *topped* $5 million a day. The slow progress *worried* backers, who *had expected* high profits.

MODIFIER   A word or word group that limits or qualifies another word: *slippery* road.

PHRASE   A word group that lacks a subject or a verb or both. Many phrases serve as modifiers: road *with a slippery surface*.

SUBORDINATE CLAUSE   A word group that contains a subject and a verb, begins with a subordinating word such as *because* or *who*, and is not a question. Most subordinate clauses serve as modifiers: *Two accidents occurred on the road, which was unusually slippery*. (See pp. 77 and 133 for fuller lists of subordinating words.)

14f Using the active voice

The active voice uses fewer words than the passive voice and is much more direct, because it names the performer of the verb's action up front. Change passive sentences to active by changing the verb and positioning the actor as the subject. (If you need help with this change, see pp. 96–97.)

> **WORDY**   As many as *fifteen feet* of chalk an hour *could be chewed through* by the drill.
>
> **CONCISE**   The *drill could chew through* as many as fifteen feet of chalk an hour.

14g Eliminating expletive constructions

Expletive constructions are sometimes useful to emphasize a change in direction, but usually they just add needless words.

> **WORDY**   *There are more than half a million shareholders who* have invested in the tunnel. *It is they and the banks that* expect to profit when the tunnel opens to trains.
>
> **CONCISE**   *More than half a million shareholders* have invested in the tunnel. *They and the banks* expect to profit when the tunnel opens to trains.

14h Rewriting jargon

JARGON is vague, inflated language that is overcomplicated, even incomprehensible. When it comes from government or business, we call it *bureaucratese.*

ACTIVE VOICE   The verb form when the subject names the *performer* of the verb's action: *The drillers <u>used</u> huge rotary blades.*

PASSIVE VOICE   The verb form when the subject names the *receiver* of the verb's action: *Huge rotary blades <u>were used</u> by the drillers.*

EXPLETIVE CONSTRUCTION   A sentence that begins with *there* or *it* and postpones the sentence subject: *There is a tunnel under the channel.* Compare *A tunnel is under the channel.*

You may find yourself writing jargon when you are unsure of your subject or when your thoughts are tangled. It's fine, even necessary, to stumble and grope while drafting. But you should straighten out your ideas and eliminate jargon during revision and editing.

JARGON   The necessity for individuals to become separate entities in their own right may impel children to engage in open rebelliousness against parental authority or against sibling influence, with resultant confusion of those being rebelled against.

TRANSLATION   Children's natural desire to become themselves may make them rebel against bewildered parents or siblings.

III

Sentence Parts and Patterns

Basic Grammar

Grammar describes how language works, and understanding it can help you create clear and accurate sentences. This section explains the kinds of words in sentences (Chapter 15) and how to build basic sentences (16), expand them (17), and classify them (18).

Parts of Speech

All English words fall into eight groups, called PARTS OF SPEECH: nouns, pronouns, verbs, adjectives, adverbs, prepositions, conjunctions, and interjections.

NOTE: In different sentences a word may serve as different parts of speech. For example:

> The government sent *aid* to the city. [*Aid* is a noun.]
> Governments *aid* citizens. [*Aid* is a verb.]

The *function* of a word in a sentence always determines its part of speech in that sentence.

15a Recognizing nouns

Nouns name. They may name a person (*Lily Tomlin, Arsenio Hall, astronaut*), a thing (*chair, book, Mt. Rainier*), a quality (*pain, mystery, simplicity*), a place (*city, Washington, ocean, Red Sea*), or an idea (*reality, peace, success*).

The forms of nouns depend partly on where they fit in certain groups. As the examples indicate, the same noun may appear in more than one group.

❖ COUNT NOUNS name things considered countable in English. Most add -*s* or -*es* to distinguish between singular (one) and plural (more than one): *citizen, citizens; city, cities*. Some count nouns form irregular plurals: *woman, women; child, children*.

❖ MASS NOUNS name things that aren't considered countable in

English (*earth, sugar*), or they name qualities (*chaos, fortitude*). Mass nouns do not form plurals.

❖ COLLECTIVE NOUNS are singular in form but name groups: *army, family, herd, U.S. Congress.*

❖ COMMON NOUNS name general classes of things and do not begin with capital letters: *earthquake, citizen, earth, fortitude, army.*

❖ PROPER NOUNS name specific people, places, and things and begin with capital letters: *Arsenio Hall, Mt. Rainier, Washington, U.S. Congress.*

In addition, most nouns form the POSSESSIVE by adding *-'s* to show ownership (*Nadia's books, citizen's rights*), source (*Auden's poems*), and some other relationships.

15b Recognizing pronouns

Most PRONOUNS substitute for nouns and function in sentences as nouns do: *Susanne Ling enlisted in the Air Force when <u>she</u> graduated.*

Pronouns fall into several subclasses depending on their form or function.

❖ PERSONAL PRONOUNS refer to a specific individual or to individuals: *I, you, he, she, it, we,* and *they.*

❖ INDEFINITE PRONOUNS, such as *everybody* and *some,* do not substitute for any specific nouns, though they function as nouns (<u>*Everybody*</u> *speaks*).

❖ DEMONSTRATIVE PRONOUNS, including *this, that,* and *such,* identify or point to nouns (<u>*This*</u> *is the problem*).

❖ RELATIVE PRONOUNS—*who, whoever, which, that*—relate groups of words to nouns or other pronouns (*The book <u>that</u> won is a novel*).

❖ INTENSIVE PRONOUNS—a personal pronoun plus *-self* or *-selves* (*himself, ourselves*)—emphasize a noun or other pronoun (*He <u>himself</u> asked that question*).

❖ REFLEXIVE PRONOUNS have the same form as intensive pronouns but indicate that the sentence subject also receives the action of the verb (*They injured <u>themselves</u>*).

❖ INTERROGATIVE PRONOUNS, such as *who, which,* and *what,* introduce questions (<u>*Who*</u> *will contribute?*).

The personal pronouns *I, he, she, we,* and *they* and the relative pronouns *who* and *whoever* change form depending on their function in the sentence. (See Chapter 25.)

15c Recognizing verbs

Verbs express an action (*bring, change, grow, consider*), an occurrence (*become, happen, occur*), or a state of being (*be, seem, remain*).

Verbs have five distinctive forms. If the form can change as described here, the word is a verb.

❖ The PLAIN FORM is the dictionary form of the verb. When the subject is a plural noun or the pronoun *I, we, you,* or *they,* the plain form indicates action that occurs in the present, occurs habitually, or is generally true.

A few artists *live* in town today.
They *hold* classes downtown.

❖ The -*s* FORM ends in -*s* or -*es*. When the subject is a singular noun, a pronoun such as *everyone,* or the personal pronoun *he, she,* or *it,* the -*s* form indicates action that occurs in the present, occurs habitually, or is generally true.

The artist *lives* in town today.
She *holds* classes downtown.

❖ The PAST-TENSE FORM indicates that the action of the verb occurred in the past. It usually adds -*d* or -*ed* to the plain form, although most irregular verbs create it in different ways (see 19a).

Many artists *lived* in town before this year.
They *held* classes downtown. [Irregular verb.]

❖ The PAST PARTICIPLE is usually the same as the past-tense form, except in most irregular verbs. It combines with forms of *have* or *be* (*has climbed, was created*), or by itself it modifies nouns and pronouns (*the sliced apples*).

Artists have *lived* in town for decades.
They have *held* classes downtown. [Irregular verb.]

❖ The PRESENT PARTICIPLE adds -*ing* to the verb's plain form. It combines with forms of *be* (*is buying*), modifies nouns and pronouns (*the boiling water*), or functions as a noun (*Running exhausts me*).

A few artists are *living* in town today.
They are *holding* classes downtown.

The verb *be* has eight forms rather than the five forms of most other verbs.

PLAIN FORM	be		
PRESENT PARTICIPLE	being		
PAST PARTICIPLE	been		
	I	*HE, SHE, IT*	*WE, YOU, THEY*
PRESENT TENSE	am	is	are
PAST TENSE	was	was	were

Some verb forms combine with HELPING VERBS to indicate time and other kinds of meaning.

> *Having been trained* to draw, some artists *can train* others.
> The techniques *have changed* little.

These are the helping verbs:

| can | may | must | shall | will |
| could | might | ought | should | would |

Forms of *be*: be, am, is, are, was, were, been, being
Forms of *have*: have, has, had, having
Forms of *do*: do, does, did

15d Recognizing adjectives and adverbs

ADJECTIVES describe or modify nouns and pronouns. They specify which one, what quality, or how many.

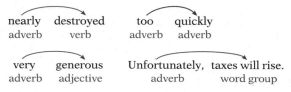

old   city   generous   one   two   pears
adjective   noun   adjective   pronoun   adjective   noun

ADVERBS describe or modify verbs, adjectives, other adverbs, and whole groups of words. They specify when, where, how, and to what extent.

nearly   destroyed   too   quickly
adverb   verb   adverb   adverb

very   generous   Unfortunately, taxes will rise.
adverb   adjective   adverb   word group

An *-ly* ending often signals an adverb, but not always: *friendly* is an adjective; *never, not,* and *always* are adverbs. The only way to tell whether a word is an adjective or an adverb is to determine what it modifies.

Adjectives and adverbs appear in three forms: the POSITIVE (*green, angrily*), COMPARATIVE (*greener, more angrily*), and SUPERLATIVE (*greenest, most angrily*).

15e Recognizing connecting words: prepositions and conjunctions

Connecting words are mostly small words that link parts of sentences. They never change form.

1. Prepositions

PREPOSITIONS form nouns or pronouns (plus any modifiers) into word groups called PREPOSITIONAL PHRASES: <u>*about*</u> *love,* <u>*down*</u> *the steep stairs.* These phrases usually serve as modifiers in sentences, as in *The plants trailed <u>down the steep stairs</u>.* (See p. 81 for more on prepositional phrases.)

Common prepositions

about	before	except for	of	throughout
above	behind	excepting	off	till
according to	below	for	on	to
across	beneath	from	onto	toward
after	beside	in	out	under
against	between	in addition to	out of	underneath
along	beyond	inside	outside	unlike
along with	by	in spite of	over	until
among	concerning	instead of	past	up
around	despite	into	regarding	upon
as	down	like	round	with
at	during	near	since	within
because of	except	next to	through	without

NOTE: Specific prepositions and verbs are sometimes linked in two-word verbs, such as *take in* and *take off.* These verbs are discussed in 24c.

2. Subordinating conjunctions

SUBORDINATING CONJUNCTIONS form sentences into word groups called SUBORDINATE CLAUSES, such as <u>*when*</u> *the meeting ended.*

These clauses serve as parts of sentences: *Everyone was relieved when the meeting ended.* (See p. 83 for more information on subordinate clauses.)

Common subordinating conjunctions

after	even if	since	until
although	even though	so that	when
as	if	than	whenever
as if	if only	that	where
as long as	in order that	though	whereas
as though	now that	till	wherever
because	once	unless	while
before	rather than		

3. Coordinating and correlative conjunctions

Coordinating and correlative conjunctions connect words or word groups of the same kind, such as nouns, adjectives, or sentences.

COORDINATING CONJUNCTIONS consist of a single word.

Coordinating conjunctions

and	nor	for	yet
but	or	so	

Biofeedback *or* simple relaxation can relieve headaches.
Relaxation works well, *and* it is inexpensive.

CORRELATIVE CONJUNCTIONS are combinations of coordinating conjunctions and other words.

Common correlative conjunctions

both . . . and	neither . . . nor
not only . . . but also	whether . . . or
not . . . but	as . . . as
either . . . or	

Both biofeedback *and* relaxation can relieve headaches.

The headache sufferer learns *not only* to recognize the causes of headaches *but also* to control those causes.

15f Recognizing interjections

INTERJECTIONS express feeling or command attention. They are rarely used in academic or business writing.

Oh, the meeting went fine.
They won seven thousand dollars! *Wow*!

16

The Sentence

The SENTENCE is the basic unit of expression. It is grammatically complete and independent: it does not serve as an adjective, adverb, or other single part of speech.

16a Recognizing subjects and predicates

Most sentences make statements. First the SUBJECT names something; then the PREDICATE makes an assertion about the subject or describes an action by the subject.

SUBJECT	PREDICATE
Art	*can be* controversial.
It	*has caused* disputes in Congress and in artists' studios.
Its *meaning and value* to society	*are* often the focus of dispute.

The SIMPLE SUBJECT is usually one or more nouns or pronouns (italicized in the sentences above). The COMPLETE SUBJECT is the simple subject plus any modifiers. The SIMPLE PREDICATE is the verb (italicized in the sentences above). The COMPLETE PREDICATE adds any words needed to complete the meaning of the verb, plus any modifiers.

16b Recognizing predicate patterns

All English sentences are based on five patterns, each differing in the complete predicate (the verb and any words following it).

Pattern 1: The earth trembled.

In the simplest pattern the predicate consists only of an INTRANSITIVE VERB, a verb that does not require a following word to complete its meaning.

SUBJECT	PREDICATE
	Intransitive verb
The earth	trembled.
The hospital	may reopen.

Pattern 2: The earthquake destroyed the city.

In pattern 2 the verb is followed by a DIRECT OBJECT, a noun or pronoun that identifies who or what receives the action of the verb. A verb that requires a direct object to complete its meaning is called TRANSITIVE.

SUBJECT	PREDICATE	
	Transitive verb	*Direct object*
The earthquake	destroyed	the city.
Education	opens	doors.

Pattern 3: The result was chaos.

In pattern 3 the verb is followed by a SUBJECT COMPLEMENT, a word that renames or describes the subject. A verb in this pattern is called a LINKING VERB because it links its subject to the description following. Subject complements are usually nouns or adjectives.

SUBJECT	PREDICATE	
	Linking verb	*Subject complement*
The result	was	chaos.
The man	became	an accountant.
The apartments	seem	expensive.

Pattern 4: The government sent the city aid.

In pattern 4 the verb is followed by a direct object and an IN-DIRECT OBJECT, a word identifying to or for whom the action of the verb is performed. The direct object and indirect object refer to different things, people, or places.

SUBJECT	PREDICATE		
	Transitive verb	*Indirect object*	*Direct object*
The government	sent	the city	aid.
One company	offered	its employees	bonuses.

Pattern 5: The citizens considered the earthquake a disaster.

In pattern 5 the verb is followed by a direct object and an OBJECT COMPLEMENT, a word that renames or describes the direct object. Object complements may be nouns or adjectives.

SUBJECT	PREDICATE		
	Transitive verb	*Direct object*	*Object complement*
The citizens	considered	the earthquake	a disaster.
The class	elected	Joan O'Day	president.
Success	makes	some people	nervous.

17

Phrases and Subordinate Clauses

Most sentences contain word groups that serve as adjectives, adverbs, or nouns. These word groups cannot stand alone as sentences.

❖ A PHRASE lacks either a subject or a predicate or both: *fearing an accident; in a panic.*
❖ A SUBORDINATE CLAUSE contains a subject and a predicate (like a sentence) but begins with a subordinating word: *when prices rise; whoever laughs.*

17a Recognizing phrases

1. Prepositional phrases

A PREPOSITIONAL PHRASE consists of a preposition plus a noun, a pronoun, or a word group serving as a noun, called the OBJECT OF THE PREPOSITION. A list of prepositions appears on page 76.

PREPOSITION	OBJECT
of	spaghetti
on	the surface
with	great satisfaction
upon	entering the room
from	where you are standing

Prepositional phrases usually function as adjectives or adverbs.

Life *on a raft* was an opportunity *for adventure.*
   adjective phrase   adjective phrase

Huck Finn rode the raft *by choice.*
                 adverb phrase

2. Verbal phrases

Certain forms of verbs, called VERBALS, can serve as modifiers or nouns. Often these verbals appear with their own modifiers and objects in VERBAL PHRASES.

NOTE: Verbals cannot serve as verbs in sentences. *The sun <u>rises</u> over the dump* is a sentence; *The sun <u>rising</u> over the dump* is a sentence fragment. (See 30a.)

Participial phrases

Phrases made from present participles (ending in -*ing*) or past participles (usually ending in -*d* or -*ed*) serve as adjectives.

Strolling shoppers fill the malls.
 adjective

They make selections *determined by personal taste.*
                 adjective phrase

NOTE: With irregular verbs, the past participle may have a different ending—for instance, *<u>hidden</u> funds.*

Gerund phrases

A GERUND is the *-ing* form of a verb when it serves as a noun. Gerunds and gerund phrases can do whatever nouns can do.

sentence
subject
Shopping satisfies personal needs.
noun

object of preposition
Malls are good at *creating such needs.*
noun phrase

Infinitive phrases

An INFINITIVE is the plain form of a verb plus *to: to hide.* Infinitives and infinitive phrases serve as adjectives, adverbs, or nouns.

sentence subject ┌─────── subject complement────────┐
To design a mall is *to create an artificial environment.*
noun phrase   noun phrase

Malls are designed *to make shoppers feel safe.*
adverb phrase

The environment supports the impulse *to shop.*
adjective

3. Absolute phrases

An ABSOLUTE PHRASE consists of a noun or pronoun and a participle, plus any modifiers. It modifies the entire rest of the sentence it appears in.

┌───── absolute phrase ──────┐
Their own place established, many ethnic groups are making way
for new arrivals.

4. Appositive phrases

An APPOSITIVE is usually a noun that renames another noun. An appositive phrase includes modifiers as well.

appositive phrase
Bizen ware, *a dark stoneware,* is produced in Japan.

Appositives and appositive phrases sometimes begin with *that is, such as, for example,* or *in other words.*

Bizen ware is used in the Japanese tea ceremony, *that is, the Zen*
─────────────────appositive phrase ───────────────┐
Buddhist observance that links meditation and art.

17b Recognizing subordinate clauses

A CLAUSE is any group of words that contains both a subject and a predicate. There are two kinds of clauses, and the distinction between them is important.

- ❖ A MAIN CLAUSE can stand alone as a sentence: *The sky darkened.*
- ❖ A SUBORDINATE CLAUSE is just like a main clause *except* that it begins with a subordinating word: <u>*when*</u> *the sky darkened,* <u>*whoever*</u> *calls.* The subordinating word reduces the clause to a single part of speech: an adjective, adverb, or noun.

NOTE: A subordinate clause punctuated as a sentence is a sentence fragment. (See 30a.)

Adjective clauses

An ADJECTIVE CLAUSE modifies a noun or pronoun. It usually begins with the relative pronoun *who, whom, which,* or *that.* The relative pronoun is the subject or object of the clause it begins. The clause ordinarily falls immediately after the word it modifies.

adjective clause
Parents *who are illiterate* may have bad memories of school.

adjective clause
One school, *which is open year-round,* helps parents learn to read.

Adverb clauses

An ADVERB CLAUSE modifies a verb, adjective, other adverb, or whole word group. It always begins with a subordinating conjunction, such as *although, because, if,* or *when* (see p. 77 for a list).

adverb clause
The school began teaching parents *when adult illiteracy gained national attention.*

adverb clause ————————— main clause
Because it was directed at people who could not read, advertising had to be inventive.

Noun clauses

A NOUN CLAUSE replaces a noun in a sentence and serves as a subject, object, or complement. It begins with *that, what, whatever, who, whom, whoever, whomever, when, where, whether, why,* or *how.*

sentence subject

Whether the program would succeed depended on door-to-door advertising.
noun clause

direct object

Teachers explained in person *how the program would work.*
noun clause

Sentence Types

The four basic sentence structures vary in the number of main and coordinate clauses.

18a Recognizing simple sentences

A SIMPLE SENTENCE consists of a single main clause and no subordinate clause.

main clause
Last summer was unusually hot.

main clause
The summer made many farmers leave the area for good or reduced them to bare existence.

18b Recognizing compound sentences

A COMPOUND SENTENCE consists of two or more main clauses and no subordinate clause.

main clause   main clause
Last July was hot, but August was even hotter.

main clause   main clause
The hot sun scorched the earth, and the lack of rain killed many crops.

18c Recognizing complex sentences

A COMPLEX SENTENCE consists of one main clause and one or more subordinate clauses.

┌─main clause─┐ ┌──────── subordinate clause ────────┐
Rain finally came, although many had left the area by then.

┌──────────── main clause ────────────┐┌─ subordinate clause
Those who remained were able to start anew because the govern-
   └── subordinate clause

ment came to their aid.

18d Recognizing compound-complex sentences

A COMPOUND-COMPLEX SENTENCE has the characteristics of both the compound sentence (two or more main clauses) and the complex sentence (at least one subordinate clause).

┌──────── subordinate clause ────────┐ ┌───── main clause ─────
Even though government aid finally came, many people had already

└────────────────────────┘ ┌───── main clause ─────┐
been reduced to poverty, and others had been forced to move.

Verbs

VERBS express actions, conditions, and states of being. The basic uses and forms of verbs are described on pages 74–75. This section explains and solves the most common problems with verbs' forms (Chapter 19), tenses (20), mood (21), and voice (22). It shows how to make verbs match their subjects (23). And it treats some special challenges of English verbs for nonnative speakers (24).

Verb Forms

Verb forms may give you trouble when the verb is irregular or when you omit certain endings or helping verbs.

19a Use the correct forms of *sing/sang/sung* and other irregular verbs.

Most verbs are REGULAR: they form their past tense and past participle by adding *-d* or *-ed* to the plain form.

PLAIN FORM	PAST TENSE	PAST PARTICIPLE
live	lived	lived
act	acted	acted

PLAIN FORM   The dictionary form of the verb: *I walk. You forget*.

PAST-TENSE FORM   The verb form indicating action that occurred in the past: *I walked. You forgot*.

PAST PARTICIPLE   The verb form used with *have, has,* or *had*: *I have walked*. It may also serve as a modifier: *This is a forgotten book*.

About two hundred English verbs are IRREGULAR: they form their past tense and past participle in some irregular way. Check a dictionary under the verb's plain form if you have any doubt about its other forms. If the verb is irregular, the dictionary will list the plain form, the past tense, and the past participle in that order (*go, went, gone*). If the dictionary gives only two forms (as in *think, thought*), then the past tense and the past participle are the same.

The following list includes the most common irregular verbs. (When two forms are possible, as in *dove* and *dived*, both are included.)

PLAIN FORM	PAST TENSE	PAST PARTICIPLE
arise	arose	arisen
become	became	become
begin	began	begun
bid	bid	bid
bite	bit	bitten, bit
blow	blew	blown
break	broke	broken
bring	brought	brought
burst	burst	burst
buy	bought	bought
catch	caught	caught
choose	chose	chosen
come	came	come
cut	cut	cut
dive	dived, dove	dived
do	did	done
draw	drew	drawn
dream	dreamed, dreamt	dreamed, dreamt
drink	drank	drunk
drive	drove	driven
eat	ate	eaten
fall	fell	fallen
find	found	found
flee	fled	fled
fly	flew	flown
forget	forgot	forgotten, forgot
freeze	froze	frozen
get	got	got, gotten
give	gave	given
go	went	gone
grow	grew	grown
hang (suspend)	hung	hung
hang (execute)	hanged	hanged
hear	heard	heard
hide	hid	hidden
hold	held	held

PLAIN FORM	PAST TENSE	PAST PARTICIPLE
keep	kept	kept
know	knew	known
lay	laid	laid
lead	led	led
leave	left	left
let	let	let
lie	lay	lain
lose	lost	lost
pay	paid	paid
prove	proved	proved, proven
ride	rode	ridden
ring	rang	rung
rise	rose	risen
run	ran	run
say	said	said
see	saw	seen
set	set	set
shake	shook	shaken
sing	sang	sung
sink	sank, sunk	sunk
sit	sat	sat
slide	slid	slid
speak	spoke	spoken
spring	sprang, sprung	sprung
stand	stood	stood
steal	stole	stolen
swim	swam	swum
take	took	taken
tear	tore	torn
throw	threw	thrown
wear	wore	worn
write	wrote	written

19b Distinguish between *sit* and *set* and between *lie* and *lay*.

The forms of *sit* and *set* and of *lie* and *lay* are easy to confuse.

PLAIN FORM	PAST TENSE	PAST PARTICIPLE
sit	sat	sat
set	set	set
lie	lay	lain
lay	laid	laid

Sit and *lie* mean "be seated" and "recline," respectively. They do not require any following words (objects) to complete their meaning.

> Obediently, the children *sit*.
> There the sunbathers *lie*.

Set and *lay* both mean "put" or "place." They usually do require following words (objects) to complete their meaning.

> José *lays* the plans on the table.
> Mr. Flood *sets* the jug down roughly.

19c Use the *-s* and *-ed* forms of the verb when they are required.

Some English dialects use the verb's plain form when the subject is *he, she, it,* or a singular noun and the verb's action occurs in the present. But standard English requires the *-s* form of the verb.

> The roof *leaks* (not *leak*).   Tina *has* (not *have*) a car.
> He *doesn't* (not *don't*) care.   She *is* (not *be*) happy.

Some dialects also omit the *-ed* or *-d* ending from a verb when the ending is not clearly pronounced. Standard English requires the ending whenever (1) the verb's action occurred in the past, (2) the verb form functions as a modifier, or (3) the verb form combines with a form of *be* or *have*.

> We *bagged* (not *bag*) groceries.   I *used* (not *use*) to dance.
> He was *supposed* (not *suppose*)   Sue has *asked* (not *ask*) us.
>   to call.

20

Verb Tenses

TENSE shows the time of a verb's action. The following table illustrates the tense forms for a regular verb. (Irregular verbs have different past-tense and past-participle forms. See 19a.)

PRESENT: action that is occurring now, occurs habitually, or is generally true

SIMPLE PRESENT: plain form or -s form

I *walk.*
You/we/they *walk.*
He/she/it *walks.*

PRESENT PROGRESSIVE: *am, is,* or *are* plus -*ing* form

I *am walking.*
You/we/they *are walking.*
He/she/it *is walking.*

PAST: action that occurred before now

SIMPLE PAST: past-tense form (-*d* or -*ed*)

I/he/she/it *walked.*
You/we/they *walked.*

PAST PROGRESSIVE: *was* or *were* plus -*ing* form

I/he/she/it *was walking.*
You/we/they *were walking.*

FUTURE: action that will occur in the future

SIMPLE FUTURE: plain form plus *will*

I/you/he/she/it/we/they *will walk.*

FUTURE PROGRESSIVE: *will be* plus -*ing* form

I/you/he/she/it/we/they *will be walking.*

PRESENT PERFECT: action that began in the past and is linked to the present

PRESENT PERFECT: *have* or *has* plus past participle (-*d* or -*ed*)

I/you/we/they *have walked.*

He/she/it *has walked.*

PRESENT PERFECT PROGRESSIVE: *have been* or *has been* plus -*ing* form

I/you/we/they *have been walking.*
He/she/it *has been walking.*

PAST PERFECT: action that was completed before another past action

PAST PERFECT: *had* plus past participle (*d* or -*ed*)

I/you/he/she/it/we/they *had walked.*

PAST PERFECT PROGRESSIVE: *had been* plus -*ing* form

I/you/he/she/it/we/they *had been walking.*

FUTURE PERFECT: action that will be completed before another future action

FUTURE PERFECT: *will have* plus past participle (-*d* or -*ed*)

I/you/he/she/it/we/they *will have walked.*

FUTURE PERFECT PROGRESSIVE: *will have been* plus -*ing* form

I/you/he/she/it/we/they *will have been walking.*

20a Observe the special uses of the present tense (*sing*).

The present tense has several uses.

TO INDICATE ACTION OCCURRING NOW
She *understands* what you mean.

TO INDICATE HABITUAL OR RECURRING ACTION
The store *opens* at ten o'clock.

TO STATE A GENERAL TRUTH
The earth *is* round.

TO DISCUSS THE CONTENT OF LITERATURE, FILM, AND SO ON
Huckleberry Finn *has* adventures we all envy.

TO INDICATE FUTURE TIME
The theater *closes* in a month.

20b Observe the uses of the perfect tenses (*have/had/will have sung*).

The perfect tenses generally indicate an action completed before another specific time or action. The present perfect tense also indicates action begun in the past and continued into the present.

PRESENT PERFECT
The dancer *has performed* here only once.

PAST PERFECT
The dancer *had trained* in Asia before his performance.

FUTURE PERFECT
He *will have performed* here again by next month.

20c Keep tenses consistent.

Within a sentence, the tenses of verbs and verb forms need not be identical as long as they reflect actual changes in time: *Ramon will graduate from college twenty years after his father arrived in America.* But needless shifts in tense will confuse or distract readers.

INCONSISTENT	Immediately after Booth *shot* Lincoln, Major Rathbone *threw* himself upon the assassin. But Booth *pulls* a knife and *plunges* it into the major's arm.
REVISED	Immediately after Booth *shot* Lincoln, Major Rathbone *threw* himself upon the assassin. But Booth *pulled* a knife and *plunged* it into the major's arm.
INCONSISTENT	The main character in the novel *suffers* psychologically because he *has* a clubfoot, but he eventually *triumphed* over his handicap.
REVISED	The main character in the novel *suffers* psychologically because he *has* a clubfoot, but he eventually *triumphs* over his handicap.

20d Use the appropriate sequence of verb tenses. ESL

The SEQUENCE OF TENSES is the relation between the verb tense in a main clause and the verb tense in a subordinate clause. The tenses are often different, as in *He will leave before I arrive*.

English tense sequence can be tricky for native speakers and especially challenging for nonnative speakers. The main difficulties are discussed below.

1. Past or past perfect tense in main clause

When the verb in the main clause is in the past or past perfect tense, the verb in the subordinate clause must also be past or past perfect.

The researchers *discovered* (past) that people *varied* (past) widely in their knowledge of public events.

The variation *occurred* (past) because respondents *had been born* (past perfect) in different decades.

None of them *had been born* (past perfect) when Warren G. Harding *was* (past) President.

MAIN CLAUSE   A word group that contains a subject and a verb and does not begin with a subordinating word: *Books are valuable*.

SUBORDINATE CLAUSE   A word group that contains a subject and a verb, begins with a subordinating word such as *because* or *who*, and is not a question: *Books are valuable when they enlighten*.

EXCEPTION: When the subordinate clause expresses a general truth, such as *The earth is round*, use the present tense even if the verb in the main clause is past or past perfect.

Few *understood* [past] that popular Presidents *are* [present] not necessarily good Presidents.

2. Conditional sentences

A CONDITIONAL SENTENCE states a factual relation between cause and effect, makes a prediction, or speculates about what might happen. Such a sentence usually consists of a subordinate clause beginning *if*, *when*, or *unless* along with a main clause stating the result. The three kinds of conditional sentences use distinctive verbs.

Factual relation

❖ For statements that something always or usually happens whenever something else happens, use the present tense in both clauses.

When a voter *casts* [present] a ballot, he or she *has* [present] complete privacy.

❖ If the linked events occurred in the past, use the past tense in both clauses.

When voters *registered* [past] in some states, they *had* [past] to pay a poll tax.

Prediction

❖ For a prediction, generally use the present tense in the subordinate clause and the future tense in the main clause.

Unless citizens *regain* [present] faith in politics, they *will* not *vote* [future].

❖ Sometimes the verb in the main clause consists of *may, can, should*, or *might* plus the verb's plain form: *If citizens regain faith, they may vote.*

Speculation

Speculations are mainly of two kinds, each with its own verb pattern.

❖ Events that are possible though unlikely. For such events in the present (by far the most common pattern), use the past tense in the subordinate clause and *would, could*, or *might* plus the verb's plain form in the main clause.

past   would + verb
If voters *had* more confidence, they *would vote* more often.

Use *were* instead of *was* when the subject is *I, he, she, it,* or a
singular noun. (See 21a for more on this distinctive verb form.)

past   would + verb
If the voter *were* more confident, he or she *would vote* more often.

❖ Events that are impossible, that are contrary to fact. In the
present, use the same forms as above (including the distinctive
were when applicable).

past   might + verb
If Lincoln *were* alive, he *might inspire* confidence.

For the past, use the past perfect tense in the subordinate clause
and *would, could,* or *might* plus the present perfect tense in the
main clause.

past perfect   might + present perfect
If Lincoln *had lived* past the Civil War, he *might have helped* stabilize
the country.

3.   Indirect quotations

An INDIRECT QUOTATION reports what someone said or wrote but
not in the exact words and not in quotation marks: *Lincoln said <u>that
events had controlled him</u>* (quotation "Events have controlled me").
Indirect quotations generally appear in subordinate clauses (underlined above), with certain conventions governing verb tense in most
cases.

❖ When the verb in the main clause is in the present tense, the
verb in the indirect quotation (subordinate clause) is in the same
tense as the original quotation.

present   present
Haworth *says* that Lincoln *is* our noblest national hero. [Quotation:
"Lincoln *is* our noblest national hero."]

present   past
He *says* that Lincoln *was* a complicated person. [Quotation:
"Lincoln *was* a complicated person."]

❖ When the verb in the main clause is in the past tense, the verb
in the indirect quotation usually changes tense from the original
quotation. Present tense changes to past tense.

past   past
An assistant to Lincoln *said* that he *was* always generous. [Quota-
tion: "He *is* always generous."]

Past tense and present perfect tense change to past perfect tense. (Past perfect tense does not change.)

past   past perfect
Lincoln *said* that events *had controlled* him. [Quotation: "Events *have controlled* me."]

NOTE: As the previous example shows, an indirect quotation differs in at least two additional ways from the original quotation: (1) the indirect quotation is usually preceded by *that,* and (2) the indirect quotation changes pronouns, especially from forms of *I* or *we* to forms of *he, she,* or *they.*

Verb Mood

MOOD in grammar is a verb form that indicates the writer's or speaker's attitude toward what he or she is saying. The INDICATIVE MOOD states a fact or opinion or asks a question: *The theater needs help.* The IMPERATIVE MOOD expresses a command or gives a direction. It omits the subject of the sentence, *you: Help the theater.*

The SUBJUNCTIVE MOOD is trickier and requires distinctive verb forms described below.

21a Use the subjunctive verb forms appropriately, as in *I wish I were.*

The subjunctive mood expresses a suggestion, requirement, or desire, or it states a condition that is contrary to fact (that is, imaginary or hypothetical).

❖ Suggestion or requirement with the verb *ask, insist, urge, require, recommend,* or *suggest*: use the verb's plain form with all subjects.

Rules require that donations *be* mailed.

❖ Desire or present condition contrary to fact: use the verb's past-tense form; for *be*, use the past-tense form *were*.

If the theater *were* in better shape and *had* more money, its future would be guaranteed.

❖ Past condition contrary to fact: use the verb's past-perfect form (*had* + past participle).

The theater would be better funded if it *had been* better managed.

NOTE: In a sentence expressing a condition contrary to fact, the helping verb *would* or *could* does not appear in the clause beginning *if*.

NOT   Many people would have helped if they *would have* known.

BUT   Many people would have helped if they *had* known.

See also page 93 for more on verb tenses in conditional sentences like this one.

21b Keep mood consistent.

Shifts in mood within a sentence or among related sentences can be confusing. Such shifts occur most frequently in directions.

INCONSISTENT   *Cook* the mixture slowly, and *you should stir* it until the sugar is dissolved. [Mood shifts from imperative to indicative.]

REVISED   *Cook* the mixture slowly, and *stir* it until the sugar is dissolved. [Consistently imperative.]

22

Verb Voice

The VOICE of a verb tells whether the subject of the sentence performs the action or is acted upon.

Active and passive voice

ACTIVE VOICE: The subject acts.

| Subject = actor | Transitive verb in active voice | Direct object |
| The city | controls | rents. |

PASSIVE VOICE: The subject is acted upon.

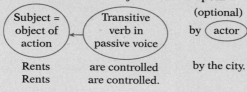

| Subject = object of action | Transitive verb in passive voice | (optional) by actor |
| Rents Rents | are controlled are controlled. | by the city. |

22a **Generally, prefer the active voice. Use the passive voice when the actor is unknown or unimportant.**

The active voice is usually stronger, clearer, and more forthright than the passive voice.

WEAK PASSIVE   The exam was thought by us to be unfair because we were tested on material that was not covered in the course.

STRONG ACTIVE   We thought the exam unfair because it tested us on material the course did not cover.

The passive voice is useful in two situations: when the actor is unknown and when the actor is unimportant or less important than the object of the action.

Ray Appleton *was murdered* after he returned home. [The murderer may be unknown, and in any event Ray Appleton's death is the point of the sentence.]

In the first experiment acid *was added* to the solution. [The person who added the acid, perhaps the writer, is less important than the fact that acid was added. Passive sentences are common in scientific writing.]

22b Keep voice consistent.

A shift in voice may sometimes help focus the reader's attention on a single subject, as in *The <u>candidate campaigned</u> vigorously and <u>was nominated</u> on the first ballot.* However, most shifts in voice also involve shifts in subject. They are unnecessary and confusing.

> INCONSISTENT   In the morning the *children rode* their bicycles; in the afternoon *their skateboards were given* a good workout.

> REVISED   In the morning the *childen rode* their bicycles; in the afternoon *they gave* their skateboards a good workout.

23

Agreement of Subject and Verb

A subject and its verb should agree in number and person.

More *Japanese-Americans live* in Hawaii and California than elsewhere.
          subject   verb

Daniel Inouye was the first Japanese-American in Congress.
  subject   verb

Most problems of subject-verb agreement arise when endings are omitted from subjects or verbs or when the relation between sentence parts is uncertain.

	NUMBER	
PERSON	SINGULAR	PLURAL
FIRST	I eat.	We eat.
SECOND	You eat.	You eat.
THIRD	He/she/it eats.	They eat.
	The bird eats.	Birds eat.

23a Subject and verb should agree even when other words come between them.

A catalog of courses and requirements often *baffles* (not *baffle*) students.

The requirements stated in the catalog *are* (not *is*) unclear.

NOTE: Phrases beginning with *as well as, together with, along with,* and *in addition to* do not change the number of the subject.

The president, as well as the deans, *has* (not *have*) agreed to revise the catalog.

23b Subjects joined by *and* usually take plural verbs.

Frost and Roethke *were* contemporaries.

EXCEPTIONS: When the parts of the subject form a single idea or refer to a single person or thing, they take a singular verb.

Avocado and bean sprouts *is* a California sandwich.

When a compound subject is preceded by the adjective *each* or *every*, the verb is usually singular.

Each man, woman, and child *has* a right to be heard.

23c When parts of a subject are joined by *or* or *nor*, the verb agrees with the nearer part.

Either the painter or the carpenter *knows* the cost.

The cabinets or the bookcases *are* too costly.

When one part of the subject is singular and the other plural, avoid awkwardness by placing the plural part closer to the verb so that the verb is plural.

AWKWARD   Neither the owners nor the contractor *agrees*.

IMPROVED   Neither the contractor nor the owners *agree*.

23d Generally, use singular verbs with *everyone* and other indefinite pronouns.

Most indefinite pronouns are singular in meaning (they refer to a single unspecified person or thing), and they take singular verbs.

Something *smells*.   Neither *is* right.

A few indefinite pronouns such as *all, any, none,* and *some* may take a singular or plural verb depending on meaning.

All of the money *is* reserved for emergencies. [*All* refers to the singular noun *money*, so the verb is singular.]

All of the funds *are* reserved for emergencies. [*All* refers to the plural noun *funds*, so the verb is plural.]

23e Collective nouns such as *team* take singular or plural verbs depending on meaning.

Use a singular verb with a collective noun when the group acts as a unit.

The group *agrees* that action is necessary.

Any band *sounds* good in that concert hall.

But when the group's members act separately, use a plural verb.

The old group *have* gone their separate ways.

The band *do* not agree on where to play.

INDEFINITE PRONOUN A pronoun that does not refer to a specific person or thing:

all	each	neither	one
any	either	nobody	some
anybody	everybody	none	somebody
anyone	everyone	no one	someone
anything	everything	nothing	something

COLLECTIVE NOUN A noun with singular form that names a group of individuals or things—for instance, *army, audience, committee, crowd, family, group, team.*

23f *Who, which,* and *that* take verbs that agree with their antecedents.

When used as subjects, *who, which,* and *that* refer to another word in the sentence, called the ANTECEDENT. The verb agrees with the antecedent.

Mayor Garber ought to listen to the people who *work* for her.

Bardini is the only aide who *has* her ear.

Agreement problems often occur with relative pronouns when the sentence includes *one of the* or *the only one of the*.

Bardini is one of the aides who *work* unpaid. [Of the aides who work unpaid, Bardini is one.]

Bardini is the only one of the aides who *knows* the community. [Of the aides, only one, Bardini, knows the community.]

23g *News* and other singular nouns ending in *-s* take singular verbs.

Singular nouns ending in *-s* include *athletics, economics, mathematics, news, physics, politics,* and *statistics*.

After so long a wait, the news *has* to be good.

Statistics *is* required of psychology majors.

Measurements and figures ending in *-s* may also be singular when the quantity they refer to is a unit.

Three years *is* a long time to wait.

Three-fourths of the library *consists* of reference books.

NOTE: These words take plural verbs when they describe individual items rather than whole bodies of activity or knowledge.

The statistics *prove* him wrong.

23h The verb agrees with the subject even when the normal word order is inverted.

Inverted subject-verb order occurs mainly in questions and in constructions beginning with *there* or *it* and a form of *be*.

Is voting a right or a privilege?

Are a right and a privilege the same thing?

There *are* differences between them.

23i *Is, are,* and other linking verbs agree with their subjects, not subject complements.

Make a linking verb agree with its subject, usually the first element in the sentence, not with the noun or pronoun serving as a subject complement.

Henry's sole support *is* his mother and father.

Henry's mother and father *are* his sole support.

24

Other Complications with Verbs   ESL

If your native language is not English, you may have difficulty with combinations of verbs and other words: helping verbs (24a), gerunds and infinitives (24b), and prepositions and adverbs (24c).

LINKING VERB   A verb that connects or equates the subject and subject complement: for example, *seem, become,* and forms of *be*.

SUBJECT COMPLEMENT   A word that describes or renames the subject: *They became <u>chemists</u>*.

24a Combine helping verbs and main verbs appropriately for your meaning.   ESL

A VERB PHRASE consists of a MAIN VERB (which expresses the primary meaning) preceded by a HELPING VERB (which indicates time, possibility, and other shades of meaning).

VERB PHRASE

Helping verb	*Main verb*
The experiments *are*	*completed.*
They *have been*	*controlled.*
The results *could*	*arrive* soon.
Should we	*post* the results?

Helping verbs combine with main verbs in specific ways.

1. Forms of *be*

Eight forms of *be* serve as helping verbs: *be, am, is, are, was, were, been, being.*

Form of *be* + present participle

Create the progressive tenses with *be, am, is, are, was, were,* or *been* followed by the main verb's present participle.

She *is working* on a new book.

Be and *been* require additional helping verbs to form progressive tenses.

can	might	should			have		
could	must	will	} *be* working		has	} *been* working	
may	shall	would			had		

When forming the progressive tenses, be sure to use the *-ing* form of the main verb.

PRESENT PARTICIPLE   The *-ing* form of the verb: *flying, writing.*

PROGRESSIVE TENSES   Verb tenses expressing action in progress—for instance, *I am flying* (present progressive), *I was flying* (past progressive), *I will be flying* (future progressive). See page 90 for a list of verb tenses.

FAULTY   Her ideas are *grow* more complex. She is *developed* a new approach to ethics.

REVISED   Her ideas are *growing* more complex. She is *developing* a new approach to ethics.

NOTE: Verbs that express mental states or activities rather than physical actions do not usually appear in the progressive tenses. These verbs include *adore, appear, believe, belong, have, hear, know, like, love, need, see, taste, think, understand,* and *want.*

FAULTY   She *is wanting* to understand contemporary ethics.

REVISED   She *wants* to understand contemporary ethics.

Form of *be* + past participle

Create the passive voice with *be, am, is, are, was, were, being,* or *been* followed by the main verb's past participle.

Her latest book *was completed* in four months.

Be, being, and *been* require additional helping verbs to form the passive voice.

$$\left.\begin{array}{l}\text{have}\\\text{has}\\\text{had}\end{array}\right\}\ been \text{ completed} \qquad \left.\begin{array}{ll}\text{am} & \text{was}\\\text{is} & \text{were}\\\text{are}\end{array}\right\}\ being \text{ completed}$$

will *be* completed

Be sure to use the main verb's past participle for the passive voice.

FAULTY   Her next book will be *publish* soon.

REVISED   Her next book will be *published* soon.

NOTE: Use only transitive verbs to form the passive voice.

FAULTY   A philosophy conference *will be occurred* in the same week. [*Occur* is not a transitive verb.]

REVISED   A philosophy conference *will occur* in the same week.

See 22a for advice on when to use and when to avoid the passive voice.

PASSIVE VOICE   The verb form when the subject names the receiver of the verb's action: *An essay was written by every student.*

TRANSITIVE VERB   A verb that requires an object to complete its meaning: *Every student completed an essay* (*essay* is the object of *completed*).

2. Forms of *have*

Four forms of *have* serve as helping verbs: *have, has, had, having*. One of these forms plus the main verb's past participle creates one of the perfect tenses.

Some students *have complained* about the laboratory.
Others *had complained* before.

Will and other helping verbs sometimes accompany forms of *have* in the perfect tenses.

Several more students *will have complained* by the end of the week.

3. Forms of *do*

Always with the plain form of the main verb, three forms of *do* serve as helping verbs: *do, does, did. Do* has three uses:

❖ To pose a question: *Whom <u>did</u> the officers <u>arrest</u>?*
❖ To emphasize the main verb: *They <u>did arrest</u> someone.*
❖ To negate the main verb, along with *not* or *never*: *The suspect <u>did not escape</u>.*

Be sure to use the main verb's plain form with any form of *do*.

FAULTY   They did *captured* someone.
REVISED   They did *capture* someone.

4. Modals

The MODALS are ten helping verbs that never change form.

can	may	must	shall	will
could	might	ought	should	would

The modals indicate necessity, obligation, permission, possibility, and other meanings. They are always used with the plain form of the main verb.

They *can speak* English. They *could translate*. *Will* you *ask* them?

PAST PARTICIPLE   The *-d* or *-ed* form of a regular verb: *hedged, walked*. Most irregular verbs have distinctive past participles: *eaten, swum*.

PERFECT TENSES   Verb tenses expressing an action completed before another specific time or action—for instance, *We have eaten* (present perfect), *We had eaten* (past perfect), *We will have eaten* (future perfect). See page 90 for a list of verb tenses.

24b Use a gerund or an infinitive after a verb as appropriate.   ESL

Gerunds and infinitives may follow certain verbs but not others. And sometimes the use of a gerund or infinitive with the same verb changes the meaning of the verb.

1. Either gerund or infinitive

A gerund or an infinitive may follow these verbs with no significant difference in meaning:

begin	hate	love
continue	like	start

The pump began *working*. The pump began *to work*.

2. Meaning change with gerund or infinitive

With four verbs, a gerund has quite a different meaning from an infinitive.

forget	remember	stop	try

The engineer stopped *eating*. [He no longer ate.]
The engineer stopped *to eat*. [He stopped in order to eat.]

3. Gerund, not infinitive

Do not use an infinitive after these verbs:

adore	detest	imagine	recall
admit	discuss	miss	resist
appreciate	enjoy	practice	risk
avoid	escape	put off	suggest
deny	finish	quit	tolerate

GERUND   The *-ing* form of the verb used as a noun: *Smoking is unhealthful*.

INFINITIVE   The plain form of the verb usually preceded by *to*: *to smoke*. An infinitive may serve as an adjective, adverb, or noun.

FAULTY   He finished *to eat* lunch.
REVISED   He finished *eating* lunch.

4. Infinitive, not gerund

Do not use a gerund after these verbs:

agree	decide	mean	refuse
ask	expect	offer	say
assent	have	plan	wait
beg	hope	pretend	want
claim	manage	promise	wish

FAULTY   He decided *checking* the pump.
REVISED   He decided *to check* the pump.

5. Noun or pronoun + infinitive

Some verbs may be followed by an infinitive alone or by a noun or pronoun and an infinitive. The presence of a noun or pronoun changes the meaning.

ask	need	would like
expect	want	

He expected *to watch*.
He expected *his workers to watch*.

Some verbs *must* be followed by a noun or pronoun before an infinitive:

advise	command	order	require
admonish	convince	persuade	tell
allow	encourage	remind	warn
cause	instruct		

He instructed *his workers to watch*.

Do not use *to* before the infinitive when it follows one of these verbs and a noun or pronoun:

feel	make ("force")
have	see
hear	watch
let	

He let his workers *learn* by observation.

24c Use the appropriate particles with two-word verbs. ESL

Some verbs consist of two words: the verb itself and a PARTICLE, a preposition or adverb that affects the meaning of the verb. For example:

Look up the answer. [Research the answer.]
Look over the answer. [Check the answer.]

The meanings of these two-word verbs are often quite different from the meanings of the individual words that make them up, and many are defined in dictionaries. (There are some three-word verbs, too, such as *put up with* and *run out of.*)

Some two-word verbs may be separated in a sentence; others may not.

1. Inseparable two-word verbs

Verbs and particles that may not be separated by any other words include the following:

catch on	go out	look into	speak up
come across	go over	play around	stay away
get along	grow up	run into	stay up
give in	keep on	run out of	take care of

FAULTY   Childen *grow* quickly *up.*
REVISED   Children *grow up* quickly.

2. Separable two-word verbs

Most two-word verbs that take direct objects may be separated by the object.

PREPOSITION   A word such as *about, for,* or *to* that takes a noun or pronoun as its object: *at the house, in the woods.* See page 76 for a list of prepositions.

ADVERB   A word that modifies a verb (*went down*), adjective (*very pretty*), another adverb (*too sweetly*), or a whole word group (*Eventually, the fire died*). Adverbs tell when, where, how, and to what extent.

Parents *help out* their children.
Parents *help* their children *out*.

If the direct object is a pronoun, the pronoun *must* separate the verb from the particle.

FAULTY   Parents *help out* them.

REVISED   Parents *help* them *out*.

The separable two-word verbs include the following:

bring up	give back	make up	take out
call off	hand in	pick up	take over
call up	hand out	point out	try on
drop off	help out	put away	try out
fill out	leave out	put back	turn down
fill up	look over	put off	turn on
give away	look up	see off	wrap up

Pronouns

PRONOUNS—words such as *she* and *who* that refer to nouns— merit special care because all their meaning comes from the other words they refer to. This section discusses pronoun forms (Chapter 25), matching pronouns and the words they refer to (26), and making sure pronouns refer to the right nouns (27).

25

Pronoun Case

CASE is the form of a noun or pronoun that shows the reader how it functions in a sentence.

- ❖ The SUBJECTIVE CASE indicates that the word is a subject or subject complement.
- ❖ The OBJECTIVE CASE indicates that the word is an object of a verb or preposition.
- ❖ The POSSESSIVE CASE indicates that the word owns or is the source of a noun in the sentence.

Nouns change form only to show possession: *teacher's* (see 37a). Certain pronouns change much more frequently, as shown at the top of the facing page.

SUBJECT   Who or what a sentence is about: *Biologists study animals*.

SUBJECT COMPLEMENT   A word that renames the subject: *Biologists are scientists*.

OBJECT OF VERB   The receiver of the verb's action (DIRECT OBJECT): *Biologists study animals*. Or the person or thing the action is performed for (INDIRECT OBJECT): *Some give animals homes*.

OBJECT OF PREPOSITION   The word(s) linked by *with*, *for*, or another preposition to the rest of the sentence: *Many biologists work in laboratories*.

SUBJECTIVE	OBJECTIVE	POSSESSIVE
I	me	my, mine
you	you	your, yours
he	him	his
she	her	her, hers
it	it	its
we	us	our, ours
you	you	your, yours
they	them	their, theirs
who	whom	whose
whoever	whomever	—

25a Distinguish between compound subjects and compound objects: *she and I* vs. *her and me.*

Compound subjects or objects—those consisting of two or more nouns or pronouns—have the same case forms as they would if one noun or pronoun stood alone.

compound subject
She and Clinton discussed the proposal.

compound object
The proposal disappointed *her and him.*

If you are in doubt about the correct form, try the test below.

1. Identify a compound construction (one connected by *and, but, or, nor*).

(*He, Him*) and (*I, me*) won the prize.
The prize went to (*he, him*) and (*I, me*).

2. Write a separate sentence for each part of the compound.

(*He, Him*) won the prize. (*I, Me*) won the prize.
The prize went to (*he, him*). The prize went to (*I, me*).

3. Choose the pronouns that sound correct.

He won the prize. *I* won the prize. [Subjective.]
The prize went to *him*. The prize went to *me*. [Objective.]

4. Put the separate sentences back together.

He and *I* won the prize.
The prize went to *him* and *me*.

25b Use the subjective case for subject complements: *It was she*.

Since a subject complement renames the subject, it, too, is in the subjective case.

subject
complement

The ones who care most are *he and she*.

Sentences like these may sound stilted because expressions such as *It was her* are common in speech. Generally, use the more natural order: *He and she are the ones who care most.*

25c The use of *who* vs. *whom* depends on the pronoun's function in its clause.

1. Questions

At the beginning of a question use *who* for a subject and *whom* for an object.

subject ⌐↓   object ←⌐
Who wrote the policy? *Whom* does it affect?

To find the correct case of *who* in a question, try the test below.

1. Pose the question.
   (*Who, Whom*) makes that decision?
   (*Who, Whom*) does one ask?

2. Answer the question, using a personal pronoun. Choose the pronoun that sounds correct, and note its case.
   (*She, Her*) makes that decision. *She* makes that decision. [Subjective.]
   One asks (*she, her*). One asks *her*. [Objective.]

3. Use the same case (*who* or *whom*) in the question.
   Who makes that decision? [Subjective.]
   Whom does one ask? [Objective.]

2. Subordinate clauses

In subordinate clauses use *who* and *whoever* for all subjects, *whom* and *whomever* for all objects.

subject
Give old clothes to *whoever* needs them.

object
I don't know *whom* the mayor appointed.

To determine which form to use, try the test below.

1. Locate the subordinate clause.

   Few people know (*who, whom*) they should ask.
   They are unsure (*who, whom*) makes the decision.

2. Rewrite the subordinate clause as a separate sentence, substituting a personal pronoun for *who, whom*. Choose the pronoun that sounds correct, and note its case.

   They should ask (*she, her*). They should ask *her*. [Objective.]
   (*She, her*) makes the decision. *She* makes the decision. [Subjective.]

3. Use the same case (*who* or *whom*) in the subordinate clause.

   Few people know *whom* they should ask. [Objective.]
   They are unsure *who* makes the decision. [Subjective.]

NOTE: Don't let expressions such as *I think* and *she says* confuse you when they come between the subject *who* and its verb.

subject
He is the one *who* I think is best qualified.

To choose between *who* and *whom* in such constructions, delete the interrupting phrase: *He is the one who is best qualified.*

25d Use the appropriate case in other constructions.

1. *We* or *us* with a noun

The choice of *we* or *us* before a noun depends on the use of the noun.

object of
preposition
Freezing weather is welcomed by *us* skaters.

subject
We skaters welcome freezing weather.

SUBORDINATE CLAUSE   A word group that contains a subject and a verb and also begins with a subordinating word, such as *who, whom,* or *because.*

2. Pronoun in an appositive

In an appositive the case of a pronoun depends on the function of the word the appositive describes or identifies.

object of verb
The class elected two representatives, DeShawn and *me*.

subject
Two representatives, DeShawn and *I*, were elected.

3. Pronoun after *than* or *as*

When a pronoun follows *than* or *as* in a comparison, the case of the pronoun indicates what words may have been omitted. A subjective pronoun must be the subject of the omitted verb:

subject
Annie liked Nancy more than *he* (liked Nancy).

An objective pronoun must be the object of the omitted verb:

object
Annie liked Nancy more than (Annie liked) *him*.

4. Subject and object of infinitive

Both the object *and* the subject of an infinitive are in the objective case.

subject of
infinitive
The school asked *him* to speak.

object of
infinitive
Students chose to invite *him*.

5. Case before a gerund

Ordinarily, use the possessive form of a pronoun or noun immediately before a gerund.

The coach disapproved of *their* lifting weights.

The *coach's* disapproving was a surprise.

APPOSITIVE   A noun or noun substitute that renames another noun immediately before it.

INFINITIVE   The plain form of the verb plus *to*: *to run*.

GERUND   The *-ing* form of a verb used as a noun: *Running is fun*.

Agreement of Pronoun and Antecedent

The ANTECEDENT of a pronoun is the noun or other pronoun it refers to.

Home owners fret over *their* tax bills.
antecedent   pronoun

Its constant increases make the *tax bill* a dreaded document.
pronoun   antecedent

For clarity, a pronoun should agree with its antecedent in person, number, and gender.

26a Antecedents joined by *and* usually take plural pronouns.

Mr. Bartos and I cannot settle *our* dispute.

The dean and my adviser have offered *their* help.

EXCEPTIONS: When the compound antecedent refers to a single idea, person, or thing, then the pronoun is singular.

My friend and adviser offered *her* help.

		NUMBER
PERSON	SINGULAR	PLURAL
FIRST	*I*	*we*
SECOND	*you*	*you*
THIRD	*he, she, it,*	*they*
	indefinite pronouns,	plural nouns
	singular nouns	
GENDER		
MASCULINE	*he,* nouns naming males	
FEMININE	*she,* nouns naming females	
NEUTER	*it,* all other nouns	

When the compound antecedent follows *each* or *every*, the pronoun is singular.

Every girl and woman took *her* seat.

26b When parts of an antecedent are joined by *or* or *nor*, the pronoun agrees with the nearer part.

Tenants or owners must present *their* grievances.

Either the tenant or the owner will have *her* way.

When one subject is plural and the other singular, the sentence will be awkward unless you put the plural one second.

AWKWARD   Neither the tenants nor the owner has yet made *her* case.

REVISED   Neither the owner nor the tenants have yet made *their* case.

26c Generally, use a singular pronoun with *everyone* and other indefinite pronouns.

Most indefinite pronouns are singular in meaning. When they serve as antecedents to other pronouns, the other pronouns are singular.

Everyone on the team had *her* own locker.

Each of the boys likes *his* teacher.

In speech we commonly use a plural pronoun when the indefinite pronoun means "many" or "all" rather than "one." In writing, however, you should revise sentences to avoid the misuse.

INDEFINITE PRONOUN   A pronoun that does not refer to a specific person or thing:

all	each	neither	one
any	either	nobody	some
anybody	everybody	none	somebody
anyone	everyone	no one	someone
anything	everything	nothing	something

FAULTY   Everyone feared for *their* lives.

REVISED   *All the riders* feared for *their* lives.

The generic *he*

The meaning of an indefinite pronoun often includes both masculine and feminine genders, not one or the other. The same is true of other indefinite words such as *child, adult, individual,* and *person.* In such cases tradition has called for *he* (*him, his*) to refer to the antecedent. But this so-called GENERIC *HE* (or generalized *he*) appears to exclude females. To avoid it, try one of the techniques below:

GENERIC *HE*   Nobody in the class had the credits *he* needed.

❖ Substitute *he or she.*

REVISED   Nobody in the class had the credits *he or she* needed.

To avoid awkwardness, don't use *he or she* more than once in several sentences.

❖ Recast the sentence using a plural antecedent and pronoun.

REVISED   *All the students* in the class lacked the credits *they* needed.

❖ Rewrite the sentence to avoid the pronoun.

REVISED   Nobody in the class had the *needed credits.*

26d Collective nouns such as *team* take singular or plural pronouns depending on meaning.

Use a singular pronoun with a collective noun when referring to the group as a unit.

The committee voted to disband *itself.*

When referring to the individual members of the group, use a plural pronoun.

The old group have gone *their* separate ways.

COLLECTIVE NOUN   A noun with singular form that names a group of individuals or things—for instance, *army, audience, committee, crowd, family, group, team.*

27

Reference of Pronoun to Antecedent

A pronoun should refer clearly to its ANTECEDENT, the noun it substitutes for. Otherwise, readers will have difficulty grasping the pronoun's meaning.

27a Make a pronoun refer clearly to one antecedent.

When either of two nouns can be a pronoun's antecedent, the reference will not be clear.

> CONFUSING   The workers removed all the furniture from the room and cleaned *it*.

Revise such a sentence in one of two ways:

❖ Replace the pronoun with the appropriate noun.

> CLEAR   The workers removed all the furniture from the room and cleaned *the room* (or *the furniture*).

❖ Avoid repetition by rewriting the sentence with the pronoun but with only one possible antecedent.

> CLEAR   After removing all the furniture from *it*, the workers cleaned the room.

> CLEAR   The workers cleaned all the furniture after removing *it* from the room.

27b Place a pronoun close enough to its antecedent to ensure clarity.

A clause beginning *who, which,* or *that* should generally fall immediately after the word it refers to.

> CONFUSING   Jody found a dress in the attic *that* her aunt had worn.

> CLEAR   In the attic Jody found a dress *that* her aunt had worn.

27c Make a pronoun refer to a specific antecedent, not an implied one.

A pronoun should refer to a specific noun or other pronoun. When the antecedent is not specifically stated but is implied by the context, the reference can only be inferred by the reader.

1. Vague *this, that, which,* or *it*

This, that, which, or *it* should refer to a specific noun, not to a whole word group expressing an idea or situation.

CONFUSING   The faculty agreed on a change in the requirements, but *it* took time.

CLEAR   The faculty agreed on a change in the requirements, but *agreeing* took time.

CLEAR   The faculty agreed on a change in the requirements, but *the change* took time.

CONFUSING   The British knew little of the American countryside and had no experience with the colonists' guerrilla tactics. *This* gave the colonists an advantage.

CLEAR   The British knew little of the American countryside and had no experience with the colonists' guerrilla tactics. This *ignorance and inexperience* gave the colonists an advantage.

2. Implied nouns

A noun may be implied in some other word or phrase: *happiness* is implied in *happy, news* in *newspaper.* But a pronoun cannot refer clearly to such an implied noun; it must refer to a specific, stated antecedent.

CONFUSING   In the speaker's advice *she* was not concrete enough.

CLEAR   The *speaker's advice* was not concrete enough.

CONFUSING   She spoke once before, but *it* was sparsely attended.

CLEAR   She spoke once before, but *the speech* was sparsely attended.

3. Indefinite *it, they,* or *you*

It, they, and *you* should have definite antecedents—nouns for *it* and *they,* an actual reader being addressed for *you.* Rewrite the sentence if the antecedent is missing.

CONFUSING   In Chapter 4 of this book *it* describes the early flights of the Wright brothers.

CLEAR   *Chapter 4* of this book describes the early flights of the Wright brothers.

CONFUSING   In the average television drama *they* present a false picture of life.

CLEAR   The average television *drama* presents a false picture of life.

In all but very formal writing, *you* is acceptable when the meaning is clearly "you, the reader." But the context must be appropriate for such a meaning.

INAPPROPRIATE   In the fourteenth century *you* had to struggle simply to survive.

REVISED   In the fourteenth century *one* (or *a person*) had to struggle simply to survive.

27d Keep pronouns consistent.

Within a sentence or a group of related sentences, pronouns should be consistent. Partly, consistency comes from making pronouns and their antecedents agree (see Chapter 26). In addition, the pronouns within a passage should match each other.

INCONSISTENT   *One* finds when studying that *your* concentration improves with practice, so that *I* now get better results from the same amount of time.

REVISED   *I* find when studying that *my* concentration improves with practice, so that I now get better results from the same amount of time.

Modifiers

MODIFIERS describe or limit other words in a sentence. They are adjectives, adverbs, or word groups serving as adjectives or adverbs. This section identifies and solves problems in the forms of modifiers (Chapter 28) and in their relation to the rest of the sentence (29).

Adjectives and Adverbs

ADJECTIVES modify nouns (*happy child*) and pronouns (*special someone*). ADVERBS modify verbs (*almost see*), adjectives (*very happy*), other adverbs (*not very*), and whole word groups (*Otherwise, the room was empty*). The only way to tell if a modifier should be an adjective or an adverb is to determine its function in the sentence.

28a Use adjectives only to modify nouns and pronouns.

Using adjectives instead of adverbs to modify verbs, adverbs, or other adjectives is nonstandard.

NONSTANDARD   They took each other *serious*.

STANDARD   They took each other *seriously*.

NONSTANDARD   Playing *good* is the goal of practice.

STANDARD   Playing *well* is the goal of practice.

28b Use an adjective after a linking verb to modify the subject. Use an adverb to modify a verb.

Some verbs may or may not be linking verbs, depending on their meaning in the sentence. When the word after the verb modifies the

subject, the verb is linking and the word should be an adjective.
When the word modifies the verb, however, it should be an adverb.

The evidence proved *conclusive*.
　　　　linking adjective
　　　　verb

The evidence proved *conclusively* that he was guilty.
　　　　verb　　　adverb

　　Two word pairs are especially troublesome in this context: *bad/
badly* and *good/well*.

The weather grew *bad*. She felt *bad*.

Flowers grow *badly* in such soil.

Well may serve as an adverb with a host of meanings or as an adjective meaning only "fit" or "healthy." *Good* serves only as an adjective.

Decker trained *well*.

She felt *well*.

Her prospects were *good*.

28c Use the comparative and superlative forms of adjectives and adverbs appropriately.

　　Adjectives and adverbs can show degrees of quality or amount
with the endings *-er* and *-est* or with the words *more* and *most* or *less*
and *least*. Most modifiers have three forms:

	ADJECTIVES	**ADVERBS**
POSITIVE: the basic form listed in the dictionary	red, good, awful	soon, badly, quickly

> LINKING VERB   A verb that links, or connects, a subject and a word
> that describes the subject: *They are golfers*. Linking verbs are forms
> of *be*, the verbs associated with our five senses (*look, sound, smell,
> feel, taste*), and a few others (*appear, seem, become, grow, turn, prove,
> remain*).

	ADJECTIVES	**ADVERBS**
COMPARATIVE: a greater or lesser degree of the quality named	redder, better, more/less awful	sooner, worse, more/less quickly
SUPERLATIVE: the greatest or least degree of the quality named	reddest, best, most/least awful	soonest, worst, most/least quickly

If sound alone does not tell you whether to use *-er/-est* or *more/ most*, consult a dictionary. If the endings can be used, the dictionary will list them. Otherwise, use *more* or *most*.

1. Irregular adjectives and adverbs

The irregular modifiers change the spelling of their positive form to show comparative and superlative degrees.

POSITIVE	**COMPARATIVE**	**SUPERLATIVE**
Adjectives		
good	better	best
bad	worse	worst
little	littler, less	littlest, least
many ⎫		
some ⎬	more	most
much ⎭		
Adverbs		
well	better	best
badly	worse	worst

2. Double comparisons

A double comparative or double superlative combines the *-er* or *-est* ending with the word *more* or *most*. It is redundant.

Chang was the *wisest* (not *most wisest*) person in town.
He was *smarter* (not *more smarter*) than anyone else.

3. Logical comparisons

Absolute modifiers

Some adjectives and adverbs cannot logically be compared— for instance, *perfect, unique, dead, impossible, infinite*. These absolute words can be preceded by adverbs like *nearly* or *almost* that mean "approaching," but they cannot logically be modified by *more* or *most* (as in *most perfect*).

NOT   He was the *most unique* teacher we had.

BUT   He was a *unique* teacher.

Completeness

To be logical, a comparison must also be complete.

❖ The comparison must state a relation fully enough to ensure clarity.

UNCLEAR   Car makers worry about their industry more than environmentalists.

CLEAR   Car makers worry about their industry more than environmentalists *do*.

CLEAR   Car makers worry about their industry more than *they worry about* environmentalists.

❖ The items being compared should in fact be comparable.

ILLOGICAL   The cost of an electric car is greater than a gasoline-powered car. [Illogically compares a cost and a car.]

REVISED   The cost of an electric car is greater than *the cost of* (or *that of*) a gasoline-powered car.

Any versus *any other*

Comparing a person or thing with all others in the same group creates two units: (1) the individual person or thing and (2) all *other* persons or things in the group. The two units need to be distinguished.

ILLOGICAL   Los Angeles is larger than *any* city in California. [Since Los Angeles is itself a city in California, the sentence seems to say that Los Angeles is larger than itself.]

LOGICAL   Los Angeles is larger than *any other* city in California.

Comparing a person or thing with the members of a *different* group assumes separate units to begin with. The two units do not need to be distinguished with *other*.

ILLOGICAL   Los Angeles is larger than *any other* city in Canada. [The cities in Canada constitute a group to which Los Angeles does not belong.]

LOGICAL   Los Angeles is larger than *any* city in Canada.

28d Avoid double negatives.

A DOUBLE NEGATIVE is a nonstandard construction in which two negative words such as *no, none, neither, barely, hardly,* or *scarcely* cancel each other out. For instance, *Jenny did <u>not</u> feel <u>nothing</u>* asserts that Jenny felt other than nothing, or something. For the opposite meaning, one of the negatives must be eliminated or changed to a positive: *She felt <u>nothing</u>* or *She did <u>not</u> feel anything.*

> FAULTY   We could *not hardly* hear the speaker. *None* of her ideas *never* made it to the back of the room.
>
> REVISED   We could *hardly* hear the speaker. *None* of her ideas made it to the back of the room.
>
> REVISED   We could *not* hear the speaker. Her ideas *never* made it to the back of the room.

28e Distinguish between present and past participles as adjectives. ESL

Both present participles and past participles may serve as adjectives: *a <u>burning</u> bush, a <u>burned</u> bush.* As in the examples, the two participles usually differ in the time they indicate.

But some present and past participles—those derived from verbs expressing feeling—can have altogether different meanings. The present participle refers to something that causes the feeling: *That was a <u>frightening</u> storm.* The past participle refers to something that experiences the feeling: *They quieted the <u>frightened</u> horses.*

The following participles are among those likely to be confused:

annoying/annoyed
astonishing/astonished
boring/bored
confusing/confused
depressing/depressed
exciting/excited
exhausting/exhausted

fascinating/fascinated
frightening/frightened
pleasing/pleased
satisfying/satisfied
surprising/surprised
tiring/tired
worrying/worried

28f Use *a, an,* and *the* where they are required. ESL

The words *a, an,* and *the*—called ARTICLES—are sometimes considered adjectives and sometimes considered DETERMINERS, words that mark nouns because they always precede nouns. Articles usually trouble native English speakers only in the choice of *a* versus *an*: *a* for words beginning with consonant sounds (*a bridge*, *a uniform*), *an* for words beginning with vowel sounds, including silent *h*'s (*an apple*, *an urge*, *an hour*).

For nonnative speakers, *a, an,* and *the* can be difficult, because many other languages use such words quite differently. In English, their uses depend on the kinds of nouns they precede and the context they appear in.

1.   Singular count nouns

A COUNT NOUN is a singular noun that names something countable and can form a plural: *glass/glasses, child/children.*

❖ *A* or *an* precedes a singular count noun when the reader does not already know its identity, usually because you have not mentioned it before.

A scientist in our chemistry department developed *a* process to strengthen metals. [*Scientist* and *process* are being introduced for the first time.]

❖ *The* precedes a singular count noun that has a specific identity for the reader, usually because (1) you have mentioned it before or (2) you identify it immediately before or after you state it.

A scientist in our chemistry department developed a process to strengthen metals. *The* scientist patented *the* process. [*Scientist* and *process* were identified in the preceding sentence.]

The most productive laboratory is *the* research center in the chemistry department. [*Most productive* identifies *laboratory,* and *in the chemistry department* identifies *research center.*]

2.   Plural nouns

A or *an* never precedes a plural noun. *The* does not precede a plural noun that names a general category. *The* does precede a plural noun that names specific representatives of a category.

Men and *women* are different. [*Men* and *women* name general categories.]

The women formed a team. [*Women* refers to specific people.]

3.   Mass nouns

A MASS NOUN is a singular noun that names something not usually considered countable in English. For example:

| advice | cereal | confidence | furniture |

health	lumber	pollution	supervision
honesty	mail	research	truth
information	meat	satisfaction	water
love	oil	silver	work

A or *an* never precedes a mass noun. *The* does precede a mass noun that names specific representatives of a general category.

> *Vegetation* suffers from drought. [*Vegetation* names a general category.]

> *The* vegetation in the park withered or died. [*Vegetation* refers to specific plants.]

> NOTE: Many nouns are sometimes count nouns and sometimes mass nouns.

> The library has *a room* for readers. [*Room* is a count noun meaning "walled area."]

> The library has *room* for reading. [*Room* is a mass noun meaning "space."]

4. Proper nouns

A PROPER NOUN names a particular person, place, or thing and begins with a capital letter: *February, Joe Allen. A* or *an* never precedes a proper noun. *The* rarely does.

> *Garcia* lives in *Boulder*, where he attends *the University of Colorado*.

Misplaced and Dangling Modifiers

The arrangement of words in a sentence is an important clue to their relationships. Modifiers will be unclear if readers can't connect them to the words they modify.

29a Reposition misplaced modifiers.

A MISPLACED MODIFIER falls in the wrong place in a sentence. It may be awkward, confusing, or even unintentionally funny.

1. Clear placement

Readers tend to link a modifier to the nearest word it could modify. Any other placement can link the modifier to the wrong word.

CONFUSING   She served steak to the men *on paper plates*.

CLEAR   She served the men steak *on paper plates*.

CONFUSING   According to the police, many dogs are killed by automobiles and trucks *roaming unleashed*.

CLEAR   According to the police, many dogs *roaming unleashed* are killed by automobiles and trucks.

2. *Only* and other limiting modifiers

LIMITING MODIFIERS include *almost, even, exactly, hardly, just, merely, nearly, only, scarcely,* and *simply*. They should fall immediately before the word or word group they modify.

UNCLEAR   They *only* saw each other during meals.

CLEAR   They saw *only* each other during meals.

CLEAR   They saw each other *only* during meals.

3. Infinitives and other grammatical units

Some grammatical units should generally not be split by long modifiers. For example, a long modifier between subject and verb can be awkward and confusing.

AWKWARD   The *wreckers*, soon after they began demolishing the old house, *discovered* a large box of coins.

REVISED   Soon after they began demolishing the old house, the *wreckers discovered* a large box of coins.

A SPLIT INFINITIVE—a modifier placed between *to* and the verb— can be especially awkward and annoys many readers.

INFINITIVE   A verb form consisting of *to* plus the verb's plain (or dictionary) form: *to produce, to enjoy*.

AWKWARD   The weather service expected temperatures *to* not *rise*.

REVISED   The weather service expected temperatures not *to rise*.

A split infinitive may sometimes be natural and preferable, though it may still bother some readers.

Several U.S. industries expect *to* more than *triple* their use of robots.

Here the split infinitive is more economical than the alternatives, such as *Several U.S. industries expect to increase their use of robots by more than three times.*

4. Order of adjectives   ESL

English follows distinctive rules for arranging two or three adjectives before a noun. (A string of more than three adjectives before a noun is rare.) Adjectives always precede the noun except when they are subject complements, and they follow this order:

1. Article or other word marking the noun: *a, an, the, this, Mary's*
2. Word of opinion: *beautiful, disgusting, important, fine*
3. Word about measurement: *small, huge, short, towering*
4. Word about shape: *round, flat, square, triangular*
5. Word about age: *old, young, new, ancient*
6. Word about color: *green, white, black, magenta*
7. Word about origin (nationality, religion, etc.): *European, Iranian, Jewish, Parisian*
8. Word about material: *wooden, gold, nylon, stone*

29b Connect dangling modifiers to their sentences.

A DANGLING MODIFIER does not sensibly modify anything in its sentence.

DANGLING   *Passing the building*, the vandalism became visible. [The modifying phrase seems to describe *vandalism*, but vandalism does not pass buildings. Who was passing the building? Who saw the vandalism?]

SUBJECT COMPLEMENT   A word following the verb that describes or renames the subject: *The essay is brief.*

Dangling modifiers usually introduce sentences, contain a verb form, and imply but do not name a subject: in the example above, the implied subject is the someone or something passing the building. Readers assume that this implied subject is the same as the subject of the sentence (*vandalism* in the example). When it is not, the modifier "dangles" unconnected to the rest of the sentence.

Revise dangling modifiers by recasting the sentences they appear in. The choice of method depends on what you want to emphasize in the sentence.

❖ Rewrite the dangling modifier as a complete clause with its own stated subject and verb. Readers can accept that the new subject and the sentence subject are different.

DANGLING   *Passing the building,* the vandalism became visible.

REVISED   *As we passed* the building, the vandalism became visible.

❖ Change the subject of the sentence to a word the modifier properly describes.

DANGLING   *Trying to understand the causes,* vandalism has been extensively studied.

REVISED   Trying to understand the causes, *researchers have* extensively *studied* vandalism.

Sentence Faults

A word group punctuated as a sentence will confuse or annoy readers if it lacks needed parts, has too many parts, or has parts that don't fit together.

Sentence Fragments

A SENTENCE FRAGMENT is part of a sentence that is set off as if it were a whole sentence by an initial capital letter and a final period or other end punctuation. Although writers occasionally use fragments deliberately and effectively (see 30c), readers perceive most fragments as serious errors.

Complete sentence versus sentence fragment

A COMPLETE SENTENCE or MAIN CLAUSE
1. contains a subject and a verb (*The wind blows*);
2. *and* is not a subordinate clause (beginning with a word such as *because* or *who*).

A SENTENCE FRAGMENT
1. lacks a verb (*The wind blowing*);
2. *or* lacks a subject (*And blows*);
3. *or* is a subordinate clause not attached to a complete sentence (*Because the wind blows*).

NOTE ESL Some languages other than English allow the omission of the subject or verb. Except in commands (*Close the door*), English always requires you to state the subject and verb.

30a Test your sentences for completeness.

A word group punctuated as a sentence should pass *all three* of the following tests. If it does not, it is a fragment and needs to be revised.

Test 1: Find the verb.

Look for a verb in the group of words.

FRAGMENT   The baboon with a stick in his mouth. [Compare a complete sentence: *The baboon* <u>held</u> *a stick in his mouth.*]

Any verb form you find must be a FINITE VERB, one that changes form as indicated below. A verbal does not change; it cannot serve as a sentence verb without the aid of a helping verb.

	FINITE VERBS IN COMPLETE SENTENCES	VERBALS IN SENTENCE FRAGMENTS
SINGULAR	The baboon *looks*.	The baboon *looking*.
PLURAL	The baboons *look*.	The baboons *looking*.
PRESENT	The baboon *looks*.	
PAST	The baboon *looked*.	The baboon *looking*.
FUTURE	The baboon *will look*.	

Test 2: Find the subject.

The subject of the sentence will usually come before the verb. If there is no subject, the word group is probably a fragment.

FRAGMENT   And eyed the guard nervously. [Compare a complete sentence: *And* <u>he</u> *eyed the guard nervously.*]

VERB   The part of a sentence that asserts something about the subject: *Ducks* <u>swim</u>. Also called PREDICATE.

VERBAL   A verb form that can serve as a noun, a modifier, or a part of a sentence verb, but not alone as the only verb of a sentence: *drawing, to draw, drawn.*

HELPING VERB   A verb such as *is, were, have, might,* and *could* that combines with various verb forms to indicate time and other kinds of meaning: for instance, <u>were</u> *drawing,* <u>might</u> *draw.*

SUBJECT   The part of a sentence that names who or what performs the action or makes the assertion of the verb: <u>Ducks</u> *swim.*

Test 3: Make sure the clause is not subordinate.

A subordinate clause usually begins with a subordinating word.

SUBORDINATING CONJUNCTIONS			RELATIVE PRONOUNS	
after	once	until	that	who/whom
although	since	when	which	whoever/whomever
as	than	where		
because	that	whereas		
if	unless	while		

Subordinate clauses serve as parts of sentences (nouns or modifiers), not as whole sentences.

FRAGMENT   When the next cage rattled. [Compare a complete sentence: *The next cage rattled.*]

NOTE: Questions beginning *who, whom,* or *which* are not sentence fragments: *Who rattled the cage?*

30b Rewrite sentence fragments as complete sentences.

Correct sentence fragments in one of two ways depending on the importance of the information in the fragment.

❖ Rewrite the fragment as a complete sentence. The information in the fragment will then have the same importance as that in other complete sentences.

FRAGMENT   The baboon stared at his challenger. *Poised for combat.*

REVISED   The baboon stared at his challenger. *He was* poised for combat.

❖ Combine the fragment with the appropriate main clause. The information in the fragment will then be subordinated to that in the main clause.

FRAGMENT   The challenger was a newcomer. *Who was unusually fierce.*

REVISED   The challenger was a newcomer who was unusually fierce.

SUBORDINATE CLAUSE   A word group that contains a subject and a verb, begins with a subordinating word such as *because* or *who*, and is not a question: *Ducks can swim <u>when they are young</u>.* A subordinate clause may serve as a modifier or as a noun.

30c Be aware of the acceptable uses of incomplete sentences.

A few word groups lacking the usual subject-predicate combination are incomplete sentences, but they are not fragments because they conform to the expectations of most readers. They include exclamations (*Oh no!*); questions and answers (*Where next? To Kansas.*); and commands (*Move along. Shut the window.*).

Experienced writers sometimes use sentence fragments when they want to achieve a special effect. Such fragments appear more in informal than in formal writing. Unless you are experienced and thoroughly secure in your own writing, you should avoid all fragments and concentrate on writing clear, well-formed sentences.

Comma Splices and Fused Sentences

Two problems commonly occur in punctuating consecutive main clauses. One is the COMMA SPLICE, in which the clauses are joined (or spliced) *only* with a comma.

> COMMA SPLICE   The ship was huge, its mast stood eighty feet high.

The other is the FUSED SENTENCE, in which no punctuation or conjunction appears between the clauses.

> FUSED SENTENCE   The ship was huge its mast stood eighty feet high.

31a Separate main clauses not joined by *and, but,* or another coordinating conjunction.

Readers need a signal that one main clause is ending and another is beginning. No punctuation at all or even a comma alone (without *and, but, or, nor, for, so,* or *yet*) fails to provide that signal.

MAIN CLAUSE   A word group that contains a subject and a verb and does not begin with a subordinating word: *A dictionary is essential.*

Revision of comma splices and fused sentences

❖ Make the clauses into separate sentences when the ideas expressed are only loosely related.

COMMA SPLICE   Chemistry has contributed much to our understanding of foods, many foods such as wheat and beans can be produced in the laboratory.

REVISED   Chemistry has contributed much to our understanding of foods. Many foods such as wheat and beans can be produced in the laboratory.

❖ Insert a coordinating conjunction in a comma splice when the ideas in the main clauses are closely related and equally important.

COMMA SPLICE   Some laboratory-grown foods taste good, they are nutritious.

REVISED   Some laboratory-grown foods taste good, *and* they are nutritious.

In a fused sentence insert a comma and a coordinating conjunction.

FUSED   Chemists have made much progress they still have a way to go.

REVISED   Chemists have made much progress, *but* they still have a way to go.

❖ Insert a semicolon between clauses if the relation between the ideas is very close and obvious without a conjunction.

COMMA SPLICE   Good taste is rare in laboratory-grown vegetables, they are usually bland.

REVISED   Good taste is rare in laboratory-grown vegetables; they are usually bland.

❖ Subordinate one clause to the other when one idea is less important than the other. The subordinated element will modify something in the main clause.

COMMA SPLICE   The vitamins are adequate, the flavor and color are deficient.

REVISED   *Even though* the vitamins are adequate, the flavor and color are deficient.

31b Separate main clauses related by *however, thus,* or another conjunctive adverb.

CONJUNCTIVE ADVERBS are modifiers that describe a relation between two main clauses.

Common conjunctive adverbs

accordingly	furthermore	moreover	similarly
also	hence	namely	still
anyway	however	nevertheless	then
besides	incidentally	next	thereafter
certainly	indeed	nonetheless	therefore
consequently	instead	now	thus
finally	likewise	otherwise	undoubtedly
further	meanwhile		

When two clauses are related by a conjunctive adverb, they must be separated by a period or by a semicolon. The adverb is also generally set off by a comma or commas.

COMMA SPLICE	Most Americans refuse to give up unhealthful habits, consequently our medical costs are higher than those of many other countries.
REVISED	Most Americans refuse to give up unhealthful habits. *Consequently,* our medical costs are higher than those of many other countries.
REVISED	Most Americans refuse to give up unhealthful habits; *consequently,* our medical costs are higher than those of many other countries.

Unlike coordinating and subordinating conjunctions, conjunctive adverbs do not join two clauses into a grammatical unit but merely describe the way the clauses relate in meaning. To test whether a word is a conjunctive adverb, try moving it around in its clause. Unlike coordinating and subordinating conjunctions, conjunctive adverbs can move.

Most Americans refuse to give up unhealthful habits; our medical costs, *consequently,* are higher than those of many other countries.

Note that commas set off the conjunctive adverb.

Mixed Sentences

A MIXED SENTENCE contains parts that do not fit together.

32a Match subjects and predicates in meaning.

In a sentence with mixed meaning, the subject is said to do or be something illogical. Such a mixture is sometimes called FAULTY PREDICATION because the predicate conflicts with the subject.

1. Illogical equation with *be*

When a form of *be* connects a subject and a word that describes the subject (a complement), the subject and complement must be logically related.

MIXED   A *compromise* between the city and the country would be the ideal *place* to live.

REVISED   A *community* that offered the best qualities of both city and country would be the ideal *place* to live.

2. *Is when, is where*

Definitions require nouns on both sides of *be*. Definition clauses beginning *when* or *where* are common in speech but should be avoided in writing.

MIXED   An *examination* is *when you are tested* on what you know.

REVISED   An *examination* is a *test* of what you know.

SUBJECT   The part of a sentence that names who or what performs the action or makes the assertion of the verb: *Geese* fly.

PREDICATE   The part of a sentence containing the verb and asserting something about the subject or describing an action by the subject: *Geese* <u>fly</u>.

3. *Reason is because*

The commonly heard construction *The reason is because* . . . is redundant since *because* means "for the reason that."

MIXED   The *reason* the temple requests donations *is because* the school needs expansion.

REVISED   The *reason* the temple requests donations *is that* the school needs expansion.

REVISED   The temple requests donations *because* the school needs expansion.

4. Other mixed meanings

Faulty predications are not confined to sentences with *be.*

MIXED   The *use* of emission controls *was created* to reduce air pollution.

REVISED   Emission *controls were created* to reduce air pollution.

32b Untangle sentences that are mixed in grammar.

Many mixed sentences start with one grammatical plan or construction but end with a different one.

MIXED   *In all her efforts to please others got* her into trouble.

REVISED   *All her efforts to please others got* her into trouble.

MIXED   *Although he was seen with a convicted thief does not make* him a thief.

REVISED   *That he was seen with a convicted thief does not make* him a thief.

32c State parts of sentences, such as subjects, only once.   ESL

In some languages other than English, certain parts of sentences may be repeated. These include the subject in any kind of clause or an object or adverb in an adjective clause. In English, however, these parts are stated only once in a clause.

1. Repetition of subject

You may be tempted to restate a subject as a pronoun before the verb. But the subject needs stating only once in its clause.

FAULTY   The *liquid it* reached a temperature of 180°F.
REVISED   The *liquid* reached a temperature of 180°F.

FAULTY   *Gases* in the liquid *they* escaped.
REVISED   *Gases* in the liquid escaped.

2. Repetition in an adjective clause

Adjective clauses begin with *who, whom, whose, which, that, where,* and *when.* The beginning word replaces another word: the subject (*He is the person who called*), an object of a verb or preposition (*He is the person whom I mentioned*), or a preposition and pronoun (*He knows the office where [in which] the conference will occur*). Do not state the word being replaced in an adjective clause.

FAULTY   The technician *whom* the test depended on *her* was burned. [*Whom* should replace *her.*]
REVISED   The technician *whom* the test depended on was burned.

In adjective clauses beginning with *where* or *when,* no adverb such as *there* or *then* is needed.

FAULTY   Gases escaped at a moment *when* the technician was unprepared *then.*
REVISED   Gases escaped at a moment *when* the technician was unprepared.

NOTE: *Whom, which,* and similar words are sometimes omitted but are still understood by the reader. Thus the word being replaced should not be stated.

FAULTY   Accidents rarely happen to technicians the lab has trained *them.* [*Whom* is understood: . . . *technicians whom the lab has trained.*]
REVISED   Accidents rarely happen to technicians the lab has trained.

IV

Punctuation

33

End Punctuation

End a sentence with one of three punctuation marks: a period (.), a question mark (?), or an exclamation point (!).

33a Use a period after most sentences and in many abbreviations.

1. Statements, mild commands, and indirect questions

STATEMENT
The airline went bankrupt.
It no longer flies.

MILD COMMAND
Think of the possibilities.
Please consider others.

INDIRECT QUESTION
An INDIRECT QUESTION reports what someone asked but not in the exact words of the original question.

The judge asked why I had been driving with my lights off.
No one asked how we got home.

2. Abbreviations

p.	B.C.	B.A.	Mr.
M.D.	A.D.	Ph.D.	Mrs.
Dr.	A.M., a.m.	e.g.	Ms.
St.	P.M., p.m.	i.e.	

Omit periods from most abbreviations of three or more words. These include ACRONYMS, pronounceable words, such as NATO, formed from the initial letters of the words in a name.

IBM	USMC	JFK	VISTA

NOTE: When an abbreviation falls at the end of a sentence, use only one period: *The school offers a B.A.*

33b Use a question mark after a direct question and sometimes to indicate doubt.

1. Direct questions

Who will follow her**?**
What is the difference between these two people**?**

After indirect questions, use a period: *We wondered who would follow her.* (See the facing page.)
Questions in a series are each followed by a question mark.

The officer asked how many times the suspect had been arrested. Three times**?** Four times**?** More than that**?**

2. Doubt

A question mark within parentheses can indicate doubt about a number or date.

The Greek philosopher Socrates was born in 470 (**?**) B.C. and died in 399 B.C. from drinking poison. [Socrates's birthdate is not known for sure.]

Use sentence structure and words, not a question mark, to express sarcasm or irony.

NOT   Her friendly (?) criticism did not escape notice.
BUT   Her criticism, *too rough to be genuinely friendly,* did not escape notice.

33c Use an exclamation point after an emphatic statement, interjection, or command.

No**!** We must not lose this election**!**
"Oh**!**" she gasped.
Come here immediately**!**

INTERJECTION   A word that expresses feeling or commands attention, either alone or within a sentence: *Oh! Hey! Wow!*

Follow mild interjections and commands with commas or periods, as appropriate: *Oh,* *call whenever you can.*

NOTE: Use exclamation points sparingly, even in informal writing. Overused, they'll fail to impress readers and they may make you sound overemphatic.

The Comma

The comma (,) is the most common punctuation mark inside sentences. Its main uses are shown in the box on the facing page.

34a Use a comma before *and, but,* or another coordinating conjunction linking main clauses.

She was perfectly at home in what she knew, *and* what she knew has remained what all of us want to know.
                                        —EUDORA WELTY (on Jane Austen)

He would have turned around again without a word, *but* I seized him.   —FYODOR DOSTOYEVSKY

Near evening I was too jittery to attend to chores, *so* Bailey volunteered to do all before his bath.   —MAYA ANGELOU

EXCEPTION: When main clauses are very short and closely related in meaning, you may omit the comma between them as long as the resulting sentence is clear: *My heart raced and I felt ill.* If you are in doubt about whether to use the comma in such sentences, use it. It will always be correct.

COORDINATING CONJUNCTIONS   *And, but, or, nor,* and sometimes *for, so, yet.*

MAIN CLAUSE   A word group that contains a subject and a verb and does not begin with a subordinating word: *The President was not an overbearing man.*

Main uses of the comma

❖ To separate main clauses linked by a coordinating conjunction (34a):

The building is finished, *but* it has no tenants.

❖ To set off most introductory elements (34b):

Unfortunately, the only tenant pulled out.

❖ To set off nonrestrictive elements (34c):

The empty building symbolizes a weak local economy, *which affects everyone.*

The main cause, *the decline of local industry,* is not news.

❖ To separate items in series (34e):

The city needs *healthier businesses, new schools, and improved housing.*

❖ To separate coordinate adjectives (34f):

A *tall, sleek* skyscraper is not needed.

❖ Other uses of the comma:

To set off other nonessential elements: absolute phrases, parenthetical expressions, phrases expressing contrast, tag questions, *yes* and *no,* words of direct address, mild interjections (34d).

To separate parts of dates, addresses, long numbers (34g).

To separate quotations and explanatory words such as *she said* (34h).

See also 34i for when *not* to use the comma.

34b Use a comma to set off most introductory elements.

An INTRODUCTORY ELEMENT begins a sentence and modifies a word or words in the main clause that follows.

SUBORDINATE CLAUSE

If Ernest Hemingway had written comic books, they would have been just as good as his novels.   —STAN LEE

VERBAL OR VERBAL PHRASE

Exhausted, the runner collapsed at the finish line.

To win the most important race of her career, she had nearly killed herself.

PREPOSITIONAL PHRASE

With the end of the century in sight, futurists are multiplying.

SENTENCE MODIFIER

Fortunately, the news is good.

You may omit the comma after a short subordinate clause or prepositional phrase if its omission does not create confusion: <u>*When snow falls the city collapses*</u>. <u>*By the year 2000*</u> *the world population will top 6 billion*. But the comma is never wrong.

NOTE: Take care to distinguish verbals used as modifiers from verbals used as subjects. The former almost always take a comma; the latter never do.

VERBAL AS MODIFIER

To dance professionally, he trained for years.

VERBAL AS SUBJECT

To dance professionally is his one desire.

34c Use a comma or commas to set off nonrestrictive elements.

Commas around part of a sentence often signal that the element is not essential to the meaning. This NONRESTRICTIVE ELEMENT may modify or rename the word it refers to, but it does not limit the word to a particular individual or group.

SUBORDINATE CLAUSE   A word group that contains a subject and a verb, begins with a subordinating word such as *because* or *who,* and is not a question: <u>*When water freezes,*</u> *crystals form.*

VERBAL   A verb form used as an adjective, adverb, or noun. A verbal plus any object or modifier is a VERBAL PHRASE: <u>*frozen*</u> *water, ready <u>to freeze</u>, rapid <u>freezing</u>.*

PREPOSITIONAL PHRASE   A word group consisting of a preposition, such as *for* or *in,* followed by a noun or pronoun plus any modifiers: *in a jar, with a spoon.* Prepositional phrases usually serve as adjectives or adverbs.

A test for nonrestrictive and restrictive elements

1. Identify the element.

   Hai Nguyen *who emigrated from Vietnam* lives in Denver.
   Those *who emigrated with him* live elsewhere.

2. Remove the element. Does the fundamental meaning of the sentence change?

   Hai Nguyen lives in Denver. No.
   Those live elsewhere. YES.

3. If NO, the element is *nonrestrictive* and *should* be set off with punctuation.

   Hai Nguyen**,** who emigrated from Vietnam**,** lives in Denver.

   If YES, the element is *restrictive* and should *not* be set off with punctuation.

   Those who emigrated with him live elsewhere.

NONRESTRICTIVE ELEMENT

The company**,** *located in Oklahoma***,** has an excellent reputation.

In contrast, a RESTRICTIVE ELEMENT *does* limit the word it refers to: the element cannot be omitted without leaving the meaning too general. Because it is essential, a restrictive element is *not* set off with commas.

RESTRICTIVE ELEMENT

The company rewards employees *who work hard.*

Nonrestrictive elements are *not* essential, but punctuation *is*. Restrictive elements *are* essential, but punctuation is *not*.

NOTE: When a nonrestrictive element falls in the middle of a sentence, be sure to set it off with a pair of commas, one *before* and one *after* the element.

Nonrestrictive and restrictive elements may be modifiers, as in the examples so far, or appositives. A nonrestrictive appositive merely adds information about the word it refers to.

John Kennedy Toole's only novel**,** *A Confederacy of Dunces***,** won the Pulitzer Prize.

APPOSITIVE   A noun or noun substitute that renames another noun immediately before it: *His wife, Emma Thompson, is also an actor.*

In contrast, a restrictive appositive limits or defines the word it refers to.

> Our language has adopted the words *garage, panache, and fanfare* from French.

34d Use a comma or commas to set off other nonessential elements.

Like nonrestrictive modifiers or appositives, many other elements contribute to texture, tone, or overall clarity but are not essential to the meaning. Unlike nonrestrictive elements, these other nonessential elements generally do not refer to any specific word in the sentence.

ABSOLUTE PHRASES

Their work finished, the bricklayers quit for the day.

His clothes, *the fabric tattered and the seams ripped open,* looked like Salvation Army rejects.

We pointed our canoes toward shore, *the rapids ahead being rough.*

PARENTHETICAL EXPRESSIONS

The Cubist painters, *for example,* were obviously inspired by the families of crystals.   —JACOB BRONOWSKI

Any writer, *I suppose,* feels that the world into which he was born is nothing less than a conspiracy against the cultivation of his talent.
                                                                        —JAMES BALDWIN

(Dashes and parentheses may also set off parenthetical expressions. See pp. 166–67.)

PHRASES OF CONTRAST

The essay needs less wit, *more pith.*

His generosity, *not his good looks,* won him friends.

ABSOLUTE PHRASE   A phrase modifying a whole main clause and consisting of a participle and its subject: *Their homework completed, the children watched TV.*

PARENTHETICAL EXPRESSION   Explanatory, supplemental, or transitional word or phrase, such as *of course, however,* or a brief example or fact.

It is not light that is needed, *but fire*; it is not the gentle shower, *but thunder*.
—FREDERICK DOUGLASS

TAG QUESTIONS

Jones should be allowed to vote, *should he not?*
They don't stop to consider others, *do they?*

YES AND NO

Yes, the editorial did have a point.
No, that can never be.

WORDS OF DIRECT ADDRESS

Cody, please bring me the newspaper.
With all due respect, *sir,* I will not.

MILD INTERJECTIONS

Well, you will never know who did it.
Oh, they forgot all about the baby.

34e   Use commas between items in a series.

A SERIES consists of three or more items of equal importance. The items may be words, phrases, or clauses.

The names *Belial, Beelzebub,* and *Lucifer* sound ominous.

He felt cut off from them *by age, by understanding, by sensibility, by technology, and by his need to measure himself against the mirror of other men's appreciation.* —RALPH ELLISON

The company sought a city *that could supply a workforce, that encouraged new building,* and *that restrained corporate taxes.*

Some writers omit the comma before the coordinating conjunction in a series (*Breakfast consisted of coffee, eggs and kippers*). But the final comma is never wrong, and it always helps the reader see the last two items as separate.

TAG QUESTION   A question attached to the end of a statement, consisting of a pronoun, a helping verb, and sometimes *not*: *It isn't correct, is it?*

INTERJECTION   A word that expresses feeling or commands attention: *Oh, must we?*

34f Use commas between two or more adjectives that equally modify the same word.

Adjectives that equally modify the same word—COORDINATE ADJECTIVES—may be separated either by a coordinating conjunction or by a comma.

The *sleek* and *shiny* car was a credit to the neighborhood.
The *dirty*, *dented* car was an eyesore.

Adjectives are not coordinate—and should not be separated by commas—when the one nearer the noun is more closely related to the noun in meaning.

The house overflowed with *ornate electric* fixtures. [*Ornate* modifies *electric fixtures*.]

Among the junk in the attic was *one lovely* vase. [Numbers are not coordinate with other adjectives.]

Tests for coordinate adjectives

1. Identify the adjectives.

   She was a *faithful sincere* friend.
   They are *dedicated medical* students.

2. Can the adjectives be reversed without changing meaning?

   She was a *sincere faithful* friend. YES.
   They are *medical dedicated* students. No.

3. Can the word *and* be inserted between the adjectives without changing meaning?

   She was a *faithful and sincere* friend. YES.
   They are *dedicated and medical* students. No.

4. If YES to *both* questions, the adjectives *are* coordinate and *should* be separated by a comma.

   She was a *faithful*, *sincere* friend.

   If NO to both questions, the adjectives are *not* coordinate and should *not* be separated by a comma.

   They are *dedicated medical* students.

34g Use commas in dates, addresses, place names, and long numbers.

When they appear within sentences, dates, addresses, and place names punctuated with commas are also ended with commas.

DATES

July 4, 1776, was the day the Declaration was signed.

The bombing of Pearl Harbor on Sunday, December 7, 1941, prompted American entry into World War II.

Commas are not used between the parts of a date in inverted order (*15 December 1992*) or in dates consisting of a month or season and a year (*December 1941*).

ADDRESSES AND PLACE NAMES

Use the address 5262 Laurie Lane, Memphis, Tennessee, for all correspondence.

Columbus, Ohio, is the location of Ohio State University.

Commas are not used between state names and zip codes in addresses: *Berkeley, California 94720, is the place of my birth.*

LONG NUMBERS

Use the comma to separate the figures in long numbers into groups of three, counting from the right. With numbers of four digits, the comma is optional.

The new assembly plant cost $7,525,000.
A kilometer is 3,281 feet (*or* 3281 feet).

34h Use a comma or commas to set off explanatory words such as *she said* from a quotation.

The words used to explain a quotation (*she said, he replied,* and so on) should be separated from the quotation by punctuation, usually a comma or commas.

General Sherman said, "War is Hell."

"Knowledge is power," wrote Francis Bacon.

"When you got nothin'," Kris Kristofferson sings, "you got nothin' to lose."

EXCEPTIONS: When explanatory words interrupt a quotation between main clauses, follow the explanatory words with a semicolon or a period. The choice depends on the punctuation of the original.

NOT   "That part of my life was over," she wrote, "his words had sealed it shut."

BUT   "That part of my life was over," she wrote. "His words had sealed it shut." [*She wrote* interrupts the quotation at a period.]

OR   "That part of my life was over," she wrote; "his words had sealed it shut." [*She wrote* interrupts the quotation at a semicolon.]

Do not use a comma when explanatory words follow a quotation ending in an exclamation point or a question mark.

"Claude!" Mrs. Harrison called.
"Why must I come home?" he asked.

Do not use commas with a quotation introduced by *that* or with a short quotation that is merely one element in a longer sentence.

The warning that "cigarette smoking is dangerous to your health" has fallen on many deaf ears.

The children were trained to say "Excuse me" when they bumped into others.

34i Delete commas where they are not required.

Commas can make sentences choppy and even confusing if they are used more often than needed or in violation of rules 34a–34h. The most common spots for misused commas are discussed below.

1. **Between subject and verb, verb and object, or preposition and object**

NOT   The returning *soldiers, received* a warm welcome. [Separated subject and verb.]

BUT   The returning *soldiers received* a warm welcome.

NOT   They had *chosen, to fight* for their country *despite, the risks.* [Separated verb *chosen* and its object; separated preposition *despite* and its object.]

BUT   They had *chosen to fight* for their country *despite the risks.*

2. In compound constructions

Compound constructions consisting of two elements almost never require a comma. The only exception is the sentence consisting of two main clauses linked by a coordinating conjunction: *The computer failed, but employees kept working* (see 34a).

NOT   Banks *could, and should* help older people manage their money. [Compound helping verbs.]

BUT   Banks could and should help older people manage their money.

NOT   Older people need special assistance *because they live on fixed incomes, and because they are not familiar with new accounts.* [Compound subordinate clauses.]

BUT   Older people need special assistance because they live on fixed incomes and because they are not familiar with new accounts.

NOT   One bank *established* special accounts for older depositors, *and counseled* them on investments. [Compound predicate.]

BUT   One bank established special accounts for older depositors and counseled them on investments.

3. Around restrictive elements

NOT   Hawthorne's work, *The Scarlet Letter,* was the first major American novel. [The title is essential to distinguish the novel from the rest of Hawthorne's work.]

BUT   Hawthorne's work *The Scarlet Letter* was the first major American novel.

NOT   The symbols, *that Hawthorne used,* influenced other novelists. [The clause identifies which symbols were influential.]

BUT   The symbols that Hawthorne used influenced other novelists.

4. Around a series

Use commas to separate the items within a series, but not to set the series off from the rest of the sentence.

COMPOUND CONSTRUCTION   Two or more words, phrases, or clauses connected by a coordinating conjunction, usually *and, but, or, nor: man and woman, old or young, leaking oil and spewing steam.*

RESTRICTIVE ELEMENT   Limits (or restricts) the word it refers to and thus can't be omitted without leaving the meaning too general. See also 34c.

NOT	*Agriculture, herding, and hunting,* sustained the Native Americans.
BUT	Agriculture, herding, and hunting sustained the Native Americans.
NOT	Europeans introduced, *horses, advanced technology, and new diseases.*
BUT	Europeans introduced horses, advanced technology, and new diseases.

5. Before an indirect quotation

NOT	The report *concluded, that* dieting could be more dangerous than overeating.
BUT	The report concluded that dieting could be more dangerous than overeating.

The Semicolon

The semicolon (**;**) separates equal and balanced sentence elements—usually main clauses (35a, 35b) and occasionally items in series (35c).

 Use a semicolon between main clauses not joined by *and, but,* or another coordinating conjunction.

When no coordinating conjunction links two main clauses, the clauses should be separated by a semicolon.

INDIRECT QUOTATION   Reports what someone said or wrote, but not in the exact words of the original.

MAIN CLAUSE   A word that contains a subject and a verb and does not begin with a subordinating word: *Parks help cities breathe.*

COORDINATING CONJUNCTIONS   *And, but, or, nor,* and sometimes *for, so, yet.*

I was not led to the university by conventional middle-class ambitions; my grip on the middle class was more tenuous than that on the school system.   —ROBIN FOX

Directing movies was only one of his ambitions; he also wanted to direct theatrical productions of Shakespeare's plays.

NOTE: This rule prevents the errors known as comma splice and fused sentence. (See 31a.)

35b Use a semicolon between main clauses related by *however, thus,* or another conjunctive adverb.

When a conjunctive adverb relates two main clauses, the clauses should be separated by a semicolon.

Blue jeans have become fashionable all over the world; *however,* the American originators still wear more jeans than anyone else.

The position of the semicolon between main clauses never changes, but the conjunctive adverb may move around within the second clause. The adverb is usually set off with a comma or commas.

Blue jeans have become fashionable all over the world; the American originators, *however,* still wear more jeans than anyone else.

Blue jeans have become fashionable all over the world; the American originators still wear more jeans than anyone else, *however.*

NOTE: This rule prevents the errors known as comma splice and fused sentence. (See 31b.)

35c Use semicolons between main clauses or series items containing commas.

Normally, commas separate main clauses linked by coordinating conjunctions (*and, but, or, nor*) and items in a series. But when

---

CONJUNCTIVE ADVERBS   Modifiers that describe the relation of the ideas in two clauses, such as *consequently, hence, however, indeed, instead, nonetheless, otherwise, still, then, therefore, thus.* (See p. 136 for a fuller list.)

the clauses or series items contain commas, a semicolon between them makes the sentence easier to read.

> Lewis and Clark led the men of their party with consummate skill, inspiring and encouraging them, doctoring and caring for them; *and* they kept voluminous journals.   —PAGE SMITH

> The custody case involved Amy Dalton, the child; Ellen and Mark Dalton, the parents; and Ruth and Hal Blum, the grandparents.

35d Delete or replace unneeded semicolons.

Too many semicolons can make writing choppy. And semicolons are often misused in certain constructions that call for other punctuation or no punctuation.

1. Between a main clause and subordinate clause or phrase

The semicolon does not separate unequal parts, such as main clauses and subordinate clauses or phrases.

> **NOT**   According to African authorities; only about 35,000 Pygmies exist today.

> **BUT**   According to African authorities, only about 35,000 Pygmies exist today.

> **NOT**   The world will not be more interesting; in twenty years.

> **BUT**   The world will not be more interesting in twenty years.

2. Before a series or explanation

Colons and dashes, not semicolons, introduce series, explanations, and so forth. (See 36a, 39a.)

> **NOT**   Teachers have heard all sorts of reasons why students do poorly; psychological problems, family illness, too much work, too little time.

> **BUT**   Teachers have heard all sorts of reasons why students do poorly: psychological problems, family illness, too much work, too little time.

The Colon

The colon (:) is mainly a mark of introduction: it signals that the words following will explain or amplify (see below). The colon also has several conventional uses, such as in expressions of time (see 36b).

36a Use a colon to introduce a concluding explanation, series, appositive, or long or formal quotation.

As an introducer, a colon is always preceded by a complete main clause. It may or may not be followed by a main clause. This is one way the colon differs from the semicolon, which generally separates main clauses only. (See 35a, 35b.)

EXPLANATION

Soul food has a deceptively simple definition: the ethnic cooking of African-Americans.

Sometimes a concluding explanation is preceded by *the following* or *as follows* and a colon.

A more precise definition might be *the following*: ingredients, cooking methods, and dishes originating in Africa, brought to the New World by slaves, and modified or supplemented in the Caribbean and the American South.

NOTE: A complete sentence *after* a colon may begin with a capital letter or a small letter (as in the example below). Just be consistent throughout an essay.

Soul food recipes, rarely written down, are passed orally from one generation to another: they form part of African-Americans' oral tradition.

MAIN CLAUSE   A word group that contains a subject and a verb and does not begin with a subordinating word: *Soul food is varied.*

SERIES

At least three soul food dishes are familiar to most Americans: fried chicken, barbecued spareribs, and sweet potatoes.

APPOSITIVE

Soul food has one disadvantage: fat.

Namely, that is, and other expressions that introduce appositives *follow* the colon: *Soul food has one disadvantage: namely, fat.*

LONG OR FORMAL QUOTATION

One soul food chef has a solution: "Soul food doesn't have to be greasy to taste good. . . . Instead of using ham hocks to flavor beans, I use smoked turkey wings. The soulful, smoky taste remains, but without all the fat of pork."

36b Use a colon after the salutation of a business letter, between a title and subtitle, between divisions of time, and in biblical citations.

SALUTATION OF BUSINESS LETTER

Dear Ms. Burak:

TITLE AND SUBTITLE

Charles Dickens: An Introduction to His Novels

TIME		**BIBLICAL CITATION**
12:26	6:00	1 Corinthians 3:6–7

36c Delete or replace unneeded colons.

Use the colon only at the end of a main clause. Do not use it between parts of clauses, such as verb and complement or preposition and object.

NOT   Two entertaining movies directed by Steven Spielberg are: *E.T.* and *Raiders of the Lost Ark.*

BUT   Two entertaining movies directed by Steven Spielberg are *E.T.* and *Raiders of the Lost Ark.*

APPOSITIVE   A noun or noun substitute that renames another noun immediately before it: *my brother, Jack.*

NOT   Shakespeare had the qualities of a Renaissance thinker, such as: humanism and a deep interest in classical Greek and Roman literature.

BUT   Shakespeare had the qualities of a Renaissance thinker, such as humanism and a deep interest in classical Greek and Roman literature.

The Apostrophe

The apostrophe (') appears as part of a word to indicate possession (37a), the omission of one or more letters (37c), or (in a few cases) plural number (37d).

37a Use the apostrophe and sometimes -*s* to form possessive nouns and indefinite pronouns.

A noun or indefinite pronoun shows possession with an apostrophe and, usually, an -*s*: *the <u>dog's</u> hair, <u>everyone's</u> hope.*

NOTE: The apostrophe or apostrophe-plus-*s* is an *addition*. Before this addition, always spell the name of the owner or owners without dropping or adding letters.

1. Singular words: add -*'s*

Bill *Boughton's* skillful card tricks amaze children.
Anyone's eyes would widen.
Most tricks will pique an *adult's* curiosity, too.

The -*'s* ending for singular words pertains also to singular words ending in -*s*.

Henry *James's* novels reward the patient reader.
The *business's* customers filed suit.

INDEFINITE PRONOUN   A pronoun that does not refer to a specific person or thing, such as *anyone, each, everybody, no one,* or *something.*

Uses and misuses of the apostrophe

USES	MISUSES

USES

Possessives of nouns and indefinite pronouns (37a)

SINGULAR	PLURAL
Ms. Park's	the Parks'
everyone's	two weeks'

Contractions (37c)

it's	shouldn't
you're	won't

Plurals of letters, numbers, and words named as words (37d)

C's	*6*'s	*if*'s

MISUSES

Possessives of personal pronouns (37b)

NOT	BUT
it's	its
your's	yours

Third-person singulars of verbs (37b)

NOT	BUT
swim's	swims

Plurals of nouns (37b)

NOT	BUT
book's are	books are
the Freed's	the Freeds

EXCEPTION: An apostrophe alone may be added to a singular word ending in -*s* when another *s* would make the word difficult to say: *Moses' mother, Joan Rivers' jokes.* But the added -*s* is never wrong (*Moses's, Rivers's*).

2. **Plural words ending in -*s*: add -' only**

Workers' incomes have fallen slightly over the past year.
Many students benefit from several *years'* work after high school.
The *Jameses'* talents are extraordinary.

Note the difference in the possessives of singular and plural words ending in -*s*. The singular form usually takes -'*s*: *James's*. The plural takes only the apostrophe: *Jameses'*.

3. **Plural words not ending in -*s*: add -'*s***

Children's educations are at stake.
We need to attract the *media's* attention.

4. **Compound words: add -'*s* only to the last word**

The *council president's* address was a bore.
The *brother-in-law's* business failed.
Taxes are always *somebody else's* fault.

5. **Two or more owners: add -'s depending on possession**

INDIVIDUAL POSSESSION

Youngman's and Mason's comedy techniques are similar. [Each comedian has his own technique.]

JOINT POSSESSION

The child recovered despite her *mother and father's* neglect. [The mother and father were jointly neglectful.]

37b Delete or replace any apostrophe in a plural noun, a singular verb, or a possessive personal pronoun.

1. Plural nouns

The plurals of nouns are generally formed by adding *-s* or *-es*: *boys, families, Joneses*. Don't add an apostrophe to form the plural.

NOT   The unleashed *dog's* belonged to the *Jones'*.

BUT   The unleashed *dogs* belonged to the *Joneses*.

2. Singular verbs

Verbs ending in *-s never* take an apostrophe.

NOT   The subway *break's* down less often now.

BUT   The subway *breaks* down less often now.

3. Possessives of personal pronouns

His, its, ours, yours, theirs, and *whose* are possessive forms of *he, it, we, you, they,* and *who*. They do not take apostrophes.

NOT   The credit is *her's*, not *their's*.

BUT   The credit is *hers*, not *theirs*.

Don't confuse possessive pronouns with contractions. See below.

37c Use the apostrophe to form contractions.

A CONTRACTION replaces one or more letters, numbers, or words with an apostrophe.

it is	it's	cannot	can't
you are	you're	does not	doesn't
they are	they're	were not	weren't
who is	who's	class of 1997	class of '97

NOTE: Don't confuse the possessive pronouns *its, their, your,* and *whose* with the contractions *it's, they're, you're,* and *who's.*

37d Use an apostrophe plus *-s* to form plurals of letters, numbers, and words named as words.

This sentence has too many <u>but</u>'s.
Remember to dot your <u>i</u>'s and cross your <u>t</u>'s.
At the end of each poem, the author had written two <u>3</u>'s.

Notice that the letters, numbers, and words are underlined (italicized) but the apostrophe and added *-s* are not. (See 44d on this use of underlining or italics.)

38

Quotation Marks

Quotation marks—either double (" ") or single (' ')—mainly enclose direct quotations from speech and from writing.
NOTE: Always use quotation marks in pairs, one at the beginning of a quotation and one at the end.

38a Use double quotation marks to enclose direct quotations.

A DIRECT QUOTATION reports what someone said or wrote, in the exact words of the original.

"If a sentence does not illuminate your subject in some new and useful way," says Kurt Vonnegut, "scratch it out."

Do not use quotation marks with an INDIRECT QUOTATION, which reports what someone said or wrote but not in the exact words of the original.

> Kurt Vonnegut advises writers to cross out any sentence that does not say something new and useful about their subject.

38b Use single quotation marks to enclose a quotation within a quotation.

> "In formulating any philosophy," Woody Allen writes, "the first consideration must always be: What can we know? . . . Descartes hinted at the problem when he wrote, 'My mind can never know my body, although it has become quite friendly with my leg.' "

Notice that two different quotation marks appear at the end of the sentence—one single (to finish the interior quotation) and one double (to finish the main quotation).

38c Put quotation marks around the titles of works that are parts of other works.

Use quotation marks to enclose the titles of works that are published or released within larger works (see the box below). Use

---

Titles to be enclosed in quotation marks

Other titles should be underlined (italicized). (See 44a.)

SONG
"Lucy in the Sky with Diamonds"

SHORT STORY
"The Gift of the Magi"

SHORT POEM
"Stopping by Woods on a Snowy Evening"

ARTICLE IN A PERIODICAL
"Does 'Scaring' Work?"

ESSAY
"Joey: A 'Mechanical Boy' "

EPISODE OF A TELEVISION OR RADIO PROGRAM
"The Mexican Connection" (on Sixty Minutes)

SUBDIVISION OF A BOOK
"The Mast Head" (Chapter 35 of Moby Dick)

underlining (italics) for all other titles, such as books, plays, periodicals, movies, and works of art. (See 44a.)

NOTE: Use single quotation marks for a quotation within a quoted title, as in the article and essay titles in the box. And enclose all punctuation in the title within the quotation marks, as in the article title.

Quotation marks may be used to enclose words being defined or used in a special sense.

By "charity" I mean the love of one's neighbor as oneself.

On movie sets movable "wild walls" make a one-walled room seem four-walled on film.

NOTE: Underlining (italics) may also highlight defined words. (See 44d.)

38e Delete quotation marks where they are not required.

TITLE OF YOUR PAPER

NOT   "The Death Wish in One Poem by Robert Frost"

BUT   The Death Wish in One Poem by Robert Frost

OR   The Death Wish in "Stopping by Woods on a Snowy Evening"

COMMON NICKNAME

NOT   Even as President, "Jimmy" Carter preferred to use his nickname.

BUT   Even as President, Jimmy Carter preferred to use his nickname.

SLANG OR TRITE EXPRESSION

Quotation marks will not excuse slang or a trite expression that is inappropriate to your writing. If slang is appropriate, use it without quotation marks.

NOT   We should support the President in his "hour of need" rather than "wimp out on him."

BUT   We should give the President the support he needs rather than turn away like cowards.

38f Place other punctuation marks inside or outside quotation marks according to standard practice.

1. Commas and periods: inside quotation marks

Swift uses irony in his essay "A Modest Proposal**.**"

When he says he hopes his proposal "will not be liable to the least objection**,**" he is being ironic.

" 'A Modest Proposal**,**' " wrote one critic, "is so outrageous that it cannot be believed."

2. Colons and semicolons: outside quotation marks

A few years ago the slogan in elementary education was "learning by playing"**;** now educators are concerned with teaching basic skills.

We all know the meaning of "basic skills"**:** reading, writing, and arithmetic.

3. Dashes, question marks, and exclamation points: inside quotation marks only if part of the quotation

When a dash, question mark, or exclamation point is part of the quotation, place it *inside* quotation marks. Don't use any other punctuation, such as a period or comma.

"But must you**—**" Marcia hesitated, afraid of the answer.
The stranger asked, "Where am I**?**"
"Go away**!**" I yelled.

When a dash, question mark, or exclamation point applies only to the larger sentence, not to the quotation, place it *outside* quotation marks—again, with no other punctuation.

One of the most evocative lines in English poetry**—**"After many a summer dies the swan"**—**was written by Alfred, Lord Tennyson.

Who said, "Now cracks a noble heart"**?**

The woman called me "stupid"**!**

When both the quotation and the larger sentence take a question mark or exclamation point, use only the one *inside* the quotation mark.

Did you say, "Who is she**?**"

Other Marks

The other marks of punctuation are the dash (39a), parentheses (39b), the ellipsis mark (39c), brackets (39d), and the slash (39e).

39a Use the dash or dashes to indicate shifts and to set off some sentence elements.

The dash (—) is mainly a mark of interruption: it signals a shift, insertion, or break.

NOTE: In handwritten and typewritten papers, form a dash with two hyphens (--). Do not add extra space before, after, or between the hyphens.

1. Shifts in tone or thought

He tells us—does he really mean it?—that he will speak the truth from now on.

If she found out—he did not want to think what she would do.

2. Nonrestrictive elements

Dashes may be used instead of commas to set off and emphasize modifiers and other nonrestrictive elements, especially when these elements are internally punctuated. Be sure to use a pair of dashes when the element interrupts the sentence.

The qualities Monet painted—sunlight, rich shadows, deep colors—abounded near the rivers and gardens he used as subjects.

Though they are close together—separated by only a few blocks—the two neighborhoods could be in different countries.

3. Introductory series and concluding series and explanations

Shortness of breath, skin discoloration or the sudden appearance of moles, persistent indigestion, the presence of small lumps—all these may signify cancer. [Introductory series.]

NONRESTRICTIVE ELEMENT   Gives added information but does not limit (or restrict) the word it refers to. (See also 34c.)

The patient undergoes a battery of tests—CAT scan, bronchoscopy, perhaps even biopsy. [Concluding series.]

Many patients are disturbed by the CAT scan—by the need to keep still for long periods in an exceedingly small space. [Concluding explanation.]

A colon could be used instead of a dash in the last two examples. The dash is more informal.

4. Overuse

Too many dashes can make writing jumpy or breathy.

NOT   In all his life—eighty-seven years—my great-grandfather never allowed his picture to be taken—not even once. He claimed the "black box"—the camera—would steal his soul.

BUT   In all his eighty-seven years, my great-grandfather did not allow his picture to be taken even once. He claimed the "black box"—the camera—would steal his soul.

39b Use parentheses to enclose nonessential elements.

Parentheses always come in pairs, one before and one after the punctuated material.

1. Parenthetical expressions

PARENTHETICAL EXPRESSIONS are explanatory, supplemental, or transitional words or phrases, such as *of course, however,* or a brief example or fact. Parentheses de-emphasize parenthetical expressions. (Commas emphasize them more and dashes still more.)

The population of Philadelphia (now about 1.6 million) has declined since 1950.

NOTE: Don't put a comma before a parenthetical expression enclosed in parentheses. Punctuation after the parenthetical expression should be placed outside the closing parenthesis.

NOT   We were haunted by the dungeon, (really the basement.)

BUT   We were haunted by the dungeon (really the basement).

When it falls between other complete sentences, a complete sentence enclosed in parentheses has a capital letter and end punctuation.

In general, coaches will tell you that scouts are just guys who can't coach. (But then, so are brain surgeons.)   —ROY BLOUNT

2. Labels for lists

My father could not, for his own special reasons, even *like* me. He
spent the first twenty-five years of my life acting out that painful
fact. Then he arrived at two points in his own life: **(1)** his last years,
and **(2)** the realization that he had made a tragic mistake.

—RAY WEATHERLY

39c Use the ellipsis mark to indicate omissions from quotations.

The ellipsis mark consists of three spaced periods (**. . .**). It generally indicates an omission from a quotation, as illustrated in the
following excerpts from this quotation about the Philippines:

ORIGINAL QUOTATION

"It was the Cuba of the future. It was going the way of Iran. It was
another Nicaragua, another Cambodia, another Vietnam. But all
these places, awesome in their histories, are so different from each
other that one couldn't help thinking: this kind of talk was a shorthand for a confusion. All that was being said was that something
was happening in the Philippines. Or more plausibly, a lot of different things were happening in the Philippines. And a lot of people
were feeling obliged to speak out about it."

—JAMES FENTON, "The Philippine Election"

OMISSION OF THE MIDDLE OF A SENTENCE

"But all these places . . . are so different from each other that one
couldn't help thinking: this kind of talk was a shorthand for a confusion."

OMISSION OF THE END OF A SENTENCE

"It was another Nicaragua. . . ."

OMISSION OF PARTS OF TWO SENTENCES

"All that was being said was that . . . a lot of different things were
happening in the Philippines."

OMISSION OF ONE OR MORE SENTENCES

"It was the Cuba of the future. It was going the way of Iran. It was
another Nicaragua, another Cambodia, another Vietnam. . . . All
that was being said was that something was happening in the Philippines."

Note these features of the examples:

❖ A quotation need not begin with an ellipsis mark or end with one except when you omit the end of a sentence (second example).

❖ When the ellipsis mark follows a grammatically complete sentence (second and last examples), four equally spaced periods result: the sentence period (closed up to the last word of the sentence) and the three periods of the ellipsis mark.

NOTE: If you omit one or more lines of poetry or paragraphs of prose from a quotation, use a separate line of ellipsis marks across the full width of the quotation to show the omission.

39d Use brackets to indicate changes in quotations.

Brackets have only one use: to indicate that you have altered a quotation to explain, clarify, or correct it.

"That Texaco station [just outside Chicago] is one of the busiest in the nation," said a company spokesperson.

The word *sic* (Latin for "in this manner") in brackets indicates that an error in the quotation appeared in the original and was not made by you.

According to the newspaper report, "The car slammed thru [*sic*] the railing and into oncoming traffic."

But don't use *sic* to make fun of a writer or to note errors in a passage that is clearly nonstandard.

39e Use the slash between options and between lines of poetry.

Use the slash between options:

Some teachers oppose pass/fail courses.

The slash also separates lines of poetry that you run into your text. (Surround the slash with space.)

Many readers have sensed a reluctant turn away from death in Frost's lines "The woods are lovely, dark and deep, / But I have promises to keep."

V

Conventions of Form and Appearance

Manuscript Format

Legible, consistent, and attractive papers and letters are a service to your readers. This chapter describes and illustrates formats for your college papers (40a), for business letters and résumés (40b), and for business memos (40c).

40a Use an appropriate format for your academic papers.

The guidelines below are adapted from the *MLA Handbook for Writers of Research Papers*, the style book for English and some other disciplines. Most of these guidelines are standard, but instructors in various courses may expect you to follow different conventions. Check with your instructor for his or her preferences.

1. Materials

Typewritten papers

For typewritten papers, use $8^1/_2'' \times 11''$ white bond paper of sixteen- or twenty-pound weight. Use the same type of paper throughout a project. Type on only one side of a sheet.

Use a black typewriter ribbon that is fresh enough to make a dark impression, and make sure the keys of the typewriter are clean. To avoid smudging the page when correcting mistakes, use correction fluid or tape. Don't use hyphens or x's to cross out mistakes, and don't type corrections (strikeovers) on top of mistakes.

Papers produced on a word processor

Some printers form characters out of tiny dots, and the legibility of their type varies considerably. If you use such a printer, make sure the dots are close enough together to produce legible characters. (Show your instructor a sample of the type to be sure it is acceptable.) Also be sure the printer ribbon or cartridge produces a dark impression. Use standard-sized ($8^1/_2'' \times 11''$) white bond paper of sixteen- or twenty-pound weight. If you use continuous paper folded like a fan at perforations, remove the strips of holes along the sides, and separate the pages at the folds.

Handwritten papers

For handwritten papers, use regular white paper, $8\frac{1}{2}'' \times 11''$, with horizontal lines spaced between one-quarter and three-eighths of an inch apart. Write on only one side of a sheet, using black or blue ink, not pencil. If possible, use an ink eraser or eradicator to correct mistakes. If you must cross out material, draw a single line through it. Don't write corrections on top of mistakes.

2. Format

The samples below show the format of a paper. For the special formats of source citations and a list of works cited or references, see Chapters 49 (MLA style) and 50 (APA style).

FIRST PAGE OF PAPER

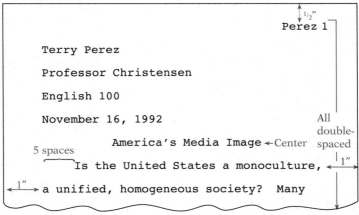

A LATER PAGE OF THE PAPER

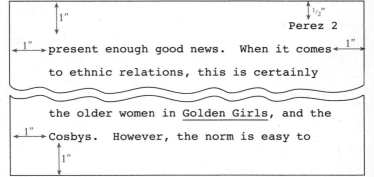

Margins and spacing

Use one-inch margins on all sides of each page. The top margin will contain the page numbers. If you have a word processor or electronic typewriter that produces an even (or justified) right margin, use the feature only if it does not leave wide spaces between words and thus interfere with readability.

Indent the first line of every paragraph five spaces, and double-space throughout.

Paging

Begin numbering your paper in the upper right of the first text page, and number consecutively through the end. Use Arabic numerals (1, 2, 3), and place your last name before the page number in case the pages become separated after you submit your paper.

Title and identification

Provide your name and the date, plus any other information requested by your instructor, in the upper left of the first text page. Double-space between this identification and the title. Center the title, capitalize words in it according to the guidelines in 43c, and double-space between the title and the first line of text.

Punctuation

Type punctuation as follows:

❖ Leave one space after a comma, semicolon, colon, and apostrophe closing a word.
❖ Leave one space after a closing quotation mark, closing parenthesis, and closing bracket when these marks fall within a sentence. When they fall after the sentence period, leave two spaces.
❖ Leave two spaces after a sentence period, question mark, or exclamation point.
❖ Do not add any space before or after a dash, a hyphen, or an apostrophe within a word. Form a dash with two hyphens (--).
❖ Leave one space before and after an ellipsis mark (. . .).

Quotations

POETRY

❖ When you quote a single line from a poem, song, or verse play, run the line into your text and enclose it in quotation marks.

Dylan Thomas remembered childhood as an idyllic time: "About the lilting house and happy as the grass was green."

❖ Poetry quotations of two or three lines may be placed in the text or displayed separately. In the text enclose the quotation in quotation marks and separate the lines with a slash surrounded by space.

An example of Robert Frost's incisiveness is in two lines from "Death of the Hired Man": "Home is the place where, when you have to go there / They have to take you in."

❖ Quotations of more than three lines of poetry should always be separated from the text with space and an indention. *Do not add quotation marks.*

Emily Dickinson rarely needed more than a few lines to express her complex thoughts:

> To wait an Hour–is long–
> If Love be just beyond–
> To wait Eternity–is short–
> If Love reward the end–

❖ Double-space above, below, and throughout a displayed quotation. Indent the quotation ten spaces from the left margin.

PROSE

❖ Run a prose quotation of four or fewer lines into your text, and enclose it in quotation marks.
❖ Separate quotations of five lines or more from the body of your paper.

In his 1967 study of the lives of unemployed black men, Eliot Lebow observes that "unskilled" construction work requires more experience and skill than generally assumed.

> A healthy, sturdy, active man of good intelligence requires from two to four weeks to break in on a construction job. . . . It frequently happens that his foreman or the craftsman he services is not willing to wait that long for him to get into condition or to learn at a glance the difference in size between a rough 2 × 8 and a finished 2 × 10.

❖ Double-space before, after, and throughout a displayed quotation. *Do not add quotation marks.*

DIALOGUE

❖ When quoting conversations, begin a new paragraph for each speaker.

> "What shall I call you? Your name?" Andrews whispered rapidly, as with a high squeak the latch of the door rose.
> "Elizabeth," she said. "Elizabeth."
> —GRAHAM GREENE, *The Man Within*

❖ When you quote a single speaker for more than one paragraph, put quotation marks at the beginning of each paragraph but at the end of only the last paragraph.

40b Use standard formats for business letters and résumés.

1. Business letters

In a letter to the businessperson, you are addressing someone who wants to see quickly why you are writing and how to respond to you. State your purpose at the start. Be straightforward, clear, objective, and courteous.

For a job application, announce right off what job you are applying for and how you heard about it. (See the sample letter on the facing page.) Summarize your qualifications for the job, including relevant facts about your education and employment history. Include your reason for applying, such as a specific career goal. At the end of the letter mention when you are available for an interview.

Use either unlined white paper measuring $8^1/_2'' \times 11''$ or what is called letterhead stationery with your address printed at the top of the sheet. Type the letter single-spaced (with double space between elements) on only one side of a sheet.

A common form for business letters is described below and illustrated on the facing page.

❖ The RETURN-ADDRESS HEADING gives your address (but not your name) and the date. (If you are using stationery with a printed heading, you need only give the date.) Place your heading at least an inch from the top of the page. Align all lines of the heading on the left, and position the whole heading to the right of the center of the paper.

❖ The INSIDE ADDRESS shows the name, title, and complete address of the person you are writing to, just as this information will appear on the envelope. Place the address at least two lines below the return-address heading.

❖ The SALUTATION greets the addressee. Position it at the left margin, two lines below the inside address and two lines above the body of the letter. Follow it with a colon. If you are not addressing someone whose name you know, use a job title (*Dear Personnel Manager*) or use a general salutation (*Dear Sir or Madam, Dear Smythe Shoes*). Use *Ms.* as the title for a woman when she has no other title, when you don't know how she prefers to be addressed, or when you know that she prefers *Ms.*

```
                        3712 Swiss Avenue ⌉  Return
                        Dallas, TX 75204   ├  address
                        March 2, 1993      ⌋  heading

Personnel Manager                     ⌉
Dallas News                           │
Communications Center                 ├  Inside address
Dallas, TX 75222                      ⌋

Dear Personnel Manager:  ⌉├ Salutation

In response to your posting in the English De-  ⌉
partment of Southern Methodist University, I am │
applying for the summer job of part-time editor- │
ial assistant for the Dallas News.               │
                                                 │
I am now enrolled at Southern Methodist Univer-  │
sity as a sophomore, with a dual major in English│
literature and journalism.  As the enclosed      │
résumé shows, I have worked on the university    │ Body
newspaper for nearly two years, and I worked a   │
summer on my hometown newspaper as a copy aide.  │
My goal is a career in journalism.  I believe my │
educational background and my work experience    │
qualify me for the opening you have.             │
                                                 │
I am available for an interview at any time and  │
would be happy to show samples of my newspaper   │
work.  My telephone number is 744—3816.          ⌋

                    Sincerely,  ⌉├ Close

                    Ian M. Irvine        ⌉
                    Ian M. Irvine        ├ Signature
                                         ⌋

Enc.
```

* The BODY of the letter, containing its substance, begins at the left margin. Instead of indenting the first line of each paragraph, insert an extra line of space between paragraphs.
* The letter's CLOSE begins two lines below the last line of the body and aligns with the return-address heading to the right of the center of the page. The close should reflect the level of formality in the salutation: *Respectfully, Cordially, Yours truly,* and *Sin-*

cerely are more formal closes; *Regards* and *Best wishes* are less formal. Capitalize only the first word, and follow the close with a comma.

❖ The SIGNATURE falls below the close and has two parts: your name typed four lines below the close; and your handwritten signature in the space between. Give your name as you sign checks and other documents.

❖ Below the signature at the left margin, you may want to include additional information such as *Enc.* (indicating an enclosure with the letter) or *cc: Margaret Zusky* (indicating that a copy is being sent to the person named).

❖ The envelope should show your name and address in the upper-left corner and the addressee's name, title, and address in the center. Use an envelope that will accommodate the letter once it is folded horizontally in thirds.

2. Résumés

The résumé that you enclose with a letter of application should contain, in table form, your name and address, career objective, and education and employment history, along with information about how to obtain your references. (See the sample on the facing page.) Use headings to mark the various sections of the résumé, spacing around them and within sections so that important information stands out. Try to limit your résumé to one page so that it can be quickly scanned. However, if your experience and education are extensive, a two-page résumé is preferable to a single cramped, un-readable page.

In preparing your résumé, you may wish to consult one of the many books devoted to application letters, résumés, and other elements of a job search. Two helpful guides are Richard N. Bolles, *What Color Is Your Parachute? A Practical Manual for Job-Hunters and Career Changers*, and Tom Jackson, *The Perfect Résumé*.

40c Use a standard form for business memos.

Business memorandums (memos, for short) address people within the same organization. A memo reports briefly and directly on a very specific topic: an answer to a question, a progress report, an evaluation.

Both the form and the structure of a memo are designed to get to the point and dispose of it quickly. State your reason for writing in the first sentence. Devote the first paragraph to a concise presen-

Ian M. Irvine
3712 Swiss Avenue
Dallas, Texas 75204
Telephone: 214-744-3816

Position desired
Part-time editorial assistant.

Education
Southern Methodist University, 1991 to present.
Current standing: sophomore.
Major: English literature and journalism.

Abilene (Texas) Senior High School, 1987-1991.
Graduated with academic, college-preparatory
degree.

Employment history
Daily Campus, student newspaper of Southern
Methodist University, 1991 to present.
Responsibilities include writing feature stories
and sports coverage.

Longhorn Painters, summer 1992.
Responsibilities included exterior and interior
house painting.

Abilene Reporter-News, summer 1991.
Responsibilities as a copy aide included routing
copy, monitoring teleprinter, running errands,
and assisting reporters.

References
Academic: Placement Office
                 Southern Methodist University
                 Dallas, TX 75275

Employment: Ms. Millie Stevens
                 Abilene Reporter-News
                 Abilene, TX 79604

Personal: Ms. Sheryl Gipstein
                 26 Overland Drive
                 Abilene, TX 79604

Bigelow Wax Company

```
TO:  Aileen Rosen, Director of Sales
FROM:  Patricia Phillips, Territory 12
DATE:  March 15, 1993
SUBJECT:  1992 sales of Quick Wax in Territory 12
```

Since it was introduced in January of 1992, Quick Wax has been unsuccessful in Territory 12 and has not affected the sales of our Easy Shine. Discussions with customers and my own analysis of Quick Wax suggest three reasons for its failure to compete with our product.

1. Quick Wax has not received the promotion necessary for a new product. Advertising-- primarily on radio--has been sporadic and has not developed a clear, consistent image for the product. In addition, the Quick Wax sales representative in Territory 12 is new and inexperienced; he is not known to cus- tomers, and his sales pitch (which I once overheard) is weak. As far as I can tell, his efforts are not supported by phone calls or mailings from his home office.

2. When Quick Wax does make it to the store shelves, buyers do not choose it over our product. Though priced competitively with our product, Quick Wax is poorly packaged. The container seems smaller than ours, though in fact it holds the same eight ounces. The lettering on the Quick Wax package (red on blue) is difficult to read, in contrast to the white-on-green lettering on the Easy Shine package.

3. Our special purchase offers and my increased efforts to serve existing customers have had the intended effect of keeping customers satisfied with our product and reducing their inclination to stock something new.

```
Copies: L. Goldberger, Director of Marketing
        L. MacGregor, Customer Service Manager
```

tation of your answer, conclusion, or evaluation. In the rest of the memo explain your reasoning or evidence. Use headings or lists as appropriate to highlight key information. (See the sample on the facing page.)

Most companies have their own conventions for memo formats. The heading usually consists of the company name, the addressee's name, the writer's name, the date, and a subject description or title. (See the sample.) The body of the memo is usually single-spaced, with double-spacing between paragraphs and no paragraph indentions. An indication of who receives copies of the memo can be given two spaces below the last line of the body.

Spelling

You can train yourself to spell better, and this chapter will tell you how. But you can also improve instantly by acquiring three habits:

- ❖ Carefully proofread your writing.
- ❖ Cultivate a healthy suspicion of your spellings.
- ❖ Compulsively check a dictionary whenever you doubt a spelling.

NOTE: The spelling checkers for computerized word processors can help you find and track spelling errors in your papers. But their usefulness is limited, mainly because they can't spot the very common error of confusing words with similar spellings, such as *their/ there/they're* or *to/too/two*. A spelling checker can supplement but can't substitute for your own care and attention.

41a Anticipate typical spelling problems.

Certain situations, such as misleading pronunciation, commonly lead to misspelling.

1. Pronunciation

In English, pronunciation of words is an unreliable guide to how they are spelled. Pronunciation is especially misleading with

HOMONYMS, words pronounced the same but spelled differently. Some commonly confused homonyms and other pairs that sound similar are listed below.

accept (to receive)
except (other than)

affect (to have an influence on)
effect (result)

all ready (prepared)
already (by this time)

allusion (indirect reference)
illusion (erroneous belief or
    perception)

ascent (a movement up)
assent (agreement)

bare (unclothed)
bear (to carry, or an animal)

board (a plane of wood)
bored (uninterested)

brake (stop)
break (smash)

buy (purchase)
by (next to)

cite (to quote an authority)
sight (the ability to see)
site (a place)

desert (to abandon)
dessert (after-dinner course)

discreet (reserved, respectful)
discrete (individual, distinct)

fair (average, or lovely)
fare (a fee for transportation)

forth (forward)
fourth (after *third*)

hear (to perceive by ear)
here (in this place)

heard (past tense of *hear*)
herd (a group of animals)

hole (an opening)
whole (complete)

its (possessive of *it*)
it's (contraction of *it is*)

know (to be certain)
no (the opposite of *yes*)

meat (flesh)
meet (encounter)

passed (past tense of *pass*)
past (after, or a time gone by)

patience (forbearance)
patients (persons under medi-
    cal care)

peace (the absence of war)
piece (a portion of something)

plain (clear)
plane (a carpenter's tool, or an
    airborne vehicle)

presence (the state of being at
    hand)
presents (gifts)

principal (most important, or
    the head of a school)
principle (a basic truth or law)

rain (precipitation)
reign (to rule)
rein (a strap for controlling an
    animal)

right (correct)
rite (a religious ceremony)
write (to make letters)

road (a surface for driving)
rode (past tense of *ride*)

scene (where an action occurs)
seen (past participle of *see*)

stationary (unmoving)
stationery (writing paper)

their (possessive of *they*)
there (opposite of *here*)
they're (contraction of *they
    are*)

to (toward)
too (also)
two (following *one*)

waist (the middle of the body)
waste (discarded material)

weak (not strong)
week (Sunday through Saturday)
which (one of a group)
witch (a sorcerer)

who's (contraction of *who is*)
whose (possessive of *who*)
your (possessive of *you*)
you're (contraction of *you are*)

2. Different forms of the same word

Often, the noun form and the verb form of the same word are spelled differently: for example, *advice* (noun) and *advise* (verb). Sometimes the noun and the adjective forms of the same word differ: *height* and *high*. Similar changes occur in the parts of some irregular verbs (*know, knew, known*) and the plurals of irregular nouns (*man, men*).

41b Follow spelling rules.

1. *Ie* vs. *ei*

To distinguish between *ie* and *ei,* use the familiar jingle:

I before *e,* except after *c,* or when pronounced "ay" as in *neighbor* and *weigh.*

i BEFORE *e*	believe	thief	hygiene
ei AFTER *c*	ceiling	conceive	perceive
ei SOUNDED AS "AY"	sleigh	eight	beige

EXCEPTIONS: For some of the exceptions, remember this sentence:

The weird foreigner neither seizes leisure nor forfeits height.

2. Final *-e*

When adding an ending to a word ending in *-e,* drop the *-e* if the ending begins with a vowel.

advise + able = advisable   surprise + ing = surprising

Keep the *-e* if the ending begins with a consonant.

care + ful = careful   like + ly = likely

EXCEPTIONS: Retain the -*e* after a soft *c* or *g*, to keep the sound of the consonant soft rather than hard: *courageous, changeable*. And drop the -*e* before a consonant when the -*e* is preceded by another vowel: *argue* + *ment* = *argument*, *true* + *ly* = *truly*.

3. Final -*y*

When adding an ending to a word ending in -*y*, change the *y* to *i* if it follows a consonant.

beauty, beauties   worry, worried   supply, supplies

But keep the *y* if it follows a vowel, if it ends a proper name, or if the ending is -*ing*.

day, days   cry, crying   Minsky, Minskys

4. Final consonants

When adding an ending to a word ending in a consonant, double the consonant if it is preceded by a single vowel or if the stress, once the ending is added, falls on the syllable finished by the consonant.

slap, slapping   submit, submitted   begin, beginning

Don't double the final consonant if it is preceded by two vowels or a vowel and another consonant or if the stress, once the ending is added, falls on some syllable other than the one finished by the consonant.

pair, paired   park, parking   refer, reference

5. Prefixes

When adding a prefix, do not drop a letter from or add a letter to the original word.

unnecessary   disappoint   misspell

6. Plurals

Most nouns form plurals by adding -*s* to the singular form. Those ending in -*s*, -*sh*, -*ch*, or -*x* add -*es* for the plural.

boy, boys   kiss, kisses   church, churches

Nouns ending in *-o* preceded by a vowel usually form the plural with *-s*. Those ending in *-o* preceded by a consonant usually form the plural with *-es*.

ratio, ratio<u>s</u>   hero, hero<u>es</u>

Some English nouns adopted from other languages form the plural according to their original language:

piano, piano<u>s</u>   medium, medi<u>a</u>   datum, dat<u>a</u>

With compound nouns, add *-s* to the main word of the compound. Sometimes this main word is not the last word.

city-state<u>s</u>   father<u>s</u>-in-law   passer<u>s</u>by

The Hyphen

Always use a hyphen to divide a word between syllables from one line to the next. Also use it to form some COMPOUND WORDS expressing a combination of ideas, such as *cross-reference*. The following rules cover many but not all compounds. When you doubt the spelling of a compound word, consult a dictionary.

42a Use the hyphen in some compound adjectives.

When two or more words serve together as a single modifier before a noun, a hyphen forms the modifying words clearly into a unit.

She is a *well-known* actor.
No *English-speaking* people were in the room.

When such a compound adjective follows the noun, the hyphen is unnecessary.

The actor is *well known.*
Those people are *English speaking.*

The hyphen is also unnecessary in a compound modifier containing an *-ly* adverb, even before the noun: *clearly defined terms.*

When part of a compound adjective appears only once in two or more parallel compound adjectives, hyphens indicate which words the reader should mentally join with the missing part.

School-age children should have eight- or nine-o'clock bedtimes.

42b Use the hyphen in fractions and compound numbers.

Hyphens join the numerator and denominator of fractions: *three-fourths, one-half.* And the whole numbers *twenty-one* to *ninety-nine* are always hyphenated.

42c Use the hyphen to attach some prefixes and suffixes.

Prefixes are usually attached to word stems without hyphens: *predetermine, unnatural, disengage.* However, when the prefix precedes a capitalized word or when a capital letter is combined with a word, a hyphen usually separates the two: *un-American, non-European, A-frame.* And some prefixes, such as *self-, all-,* and *ex-* (meaning "formerly"), usually require hyphens no matter what follows: *self-control, all-inclusive, ex-student.* The only suffix that regularly requires a hyphen is *-elect,* as in *president-elect.*

43

Capital Letters

The following conventions and a desk dictionary can help you decide whether to capitalize a particular word. In general, capitalize only when a rule or the dictionary says you must.

43a Capitalize the first word of every sentence.

Every writer should own a good dictionary.

When quoting other writers, you should reproduce the capital letters beginning their sentences or indicate that you have altered the source. Whenever possible, integrate the quotation into your own sentence so that its capitalization coincides with yours.

> "Psychotherapists often overlook the benefits of self-deception," the author argues.

> The author argues that "the benefits of self-deception" are not always recognized by psychotherapists.

If you need to alter the capitalization in the source, indicate the change with brackets.

> "[T]he benefits of self-deception" are not always recognized by psychotherapists, the author argues.

> The author argues that "[p]sychotherapists often overlook the benefits of self-deception."

NOTE: Capitalization of questions in a series is optional. Both of the following examples are correct.

> Is the population a hundred? Two hundred? More?
> Is the population a hundred? two hundred? more?

Also optional is capitalization of the first word in a complete sentence after a colon.

43b Capitalize proper nouns, proper adjectives, and words used as essential parts of proper nouns.

1. Proper nouns and proper adjectives

PROPER NOUNS name specific persons, places, and things: *Shakespeare, California, World War I.* PROPER ADJECTIVES are formed from some proper nouns: *Shakespearean, Californian.* Capitalize all proper nouns and proper adjectives but not the articles (*a, an, the*) that precede them.

SPECIFIC PERSONS AND THINGS

Stephen King   Boulder Dam
Napoleon Bonaparte   the Empire State Building

SPECIFIC PLACES AND GEOGRAPHICAL REGIONS

New York City   the Mediterranean Sea
China   the Northeast, the South
But: northeast of the city, going south

DAYS OF THE WEEK, MONTHS, HOLIDAYS

Monday   Yom Kippur
May   Christmas

HISTORICAL EVENTS, DOCUMENTS, PERIODS, MOVEMENTS

the Vietnam War   the Renaissance
the Constitution   the Romantic Movement

GOVERNMENT OFFICES OR DEPARTMENTS AND INSTITUTIONS

House of Representatives   Polk Municipal Court
Department of Defense   Northeast High School

POLITICAL, SOCIAL, ATHLETIC, AND OTHER ORGANIZATIONS AND
ASSOCIATIONS AND THEIR MEMBERS

Democratic Party, Democrats   League of Women Voters
Sierra Club   Boston Celtics
B'nai B'rith   Chicago Symphony Orchestra

RACES, NATIONALITIES, AND THEIR LANGUAGES

Native American   Germans
African-American, Negro   Swahili
Caucasian   Italian
But: blacks, whites

RELIGIONS, THEIR FOLLOWERS, AND TERMS FOR THE SACRED

Christianity, Christians   God
Catholicism, Catholics   Allah
Judaism, Orthodox Jew   the Bible (*but* biblical)
Islam, Moslems *or* Muslims   the Koran

2. Common nouns used as essential parts of proper nouns

Capitalize the common nouns *street, avenue, park, river, ocean, lake, company, college, county,* and *memorial* when they are part of proper nouns naming specific places or institutions.

Main Street   Lake Superior
Central Park   Ford Motor Company

Mississippi River
Pacific Ocean

Madison College
George Washington Memorial

43c Capitalize most words in titles and subtitles of works.

In all titles and subtitles of works, capitalize the first and last words and all other words *except* articles (*a, an, the*), *to* in infinitives, and connecting words (prepositions and coordinating and subordinating conjunctions) of fewer than five letters. Capitalize even these short words when they are the first or last word in a title or when they fall after a colon or semicolon.

"Courtship Through the Ages"
A Diamond Is Forever
"Knowing Whom to Ask"
Learning from Las Vegas

Management: A New Theory
"Once More to the Lake"
An End to Live For
File Under Architecture

43d Capitalize titles preceding persons' names.

Before a person's name, capitalize his or her title. After the name, do not capitalize the title.

Professor Otto Osborne
Doctor Jane Covington
Senator Robert Dole

Otto Osborne, a professor
Jane Covington, a doctor
Robert Dole, the senator

NOTE: Many writers capitalize a title denoting very high rank even when it follows a name or is used alone: *Lyndon Johnson, past President of the United States.*

44

Underlining (Italics)

<u>Underlining</u> and *italic type* indicate the same thing: the word or words are being distinguished or emphasized. In your papers use a ruler or the underscore on the keyboard to underline. If your type-

writer or word processor can produce italic type, consult your instructor about whether to use it. Many instructors prefer underlining.

44a Underline the titles of works that appear independently.

Underline the titles of works, such as books and periodicals, that are published, released, or produced separately from other works. (See the box below.) Use quotation marks for all other titles, such as short stories, articles in periodicals, and episodes of television series. (See 38c.)

EXCEPTIONS: Legal documents, the Bible, and their parts are generally not underlined.

NOT We studied the <u>Book of Revelation</u> in the <u>Bible</u>.
BUT We studied the Book of Revelation in the Bible.

Titles to be underlined (italicized)

Other titles should be placed in quotation marks (see 38c).

BOOKS

<u>Catch-22</u>
<u>War and Peace</u>

PLAYS

<u>Hamlet</u>
<u>The Phantom of the Opera</u>

PAMPHLETS

<u>The Truth About Alcoholism</u>

LONG MUSICAL WORKS

Tchaikovsky's <u>Swan Lake</u>
The Beatles' <u>Revolver</u>
But: Symphony in C

TELEVISION AND RADIO PROGRAMS

<u>60 Minutes</u>
<u>The Shadow</u>

LONG POEMS

<u>Beowulf</u>
<u>Paradise Lost</u>

PERIODICALS

<u>Time</u>
<u>Philadelphia Inquirer</u>

PUBLISHED SPEECHES

Lincoln's <u>Gettysburg Address</u>

MOVIES

<u>Gone with the Wind</u>
<u>Invasion of the Body Snatchers</u>

WORKS OF VISUAL ART

Michelangelo's <u>David</u>
the <u>Mona Lisa</u>

44b Underline the names of ships, aircraft, spacecraft, and trains.

Challenger   Orient Express   Queen Elizabeth II
Apollo XI   Montrealer   Spirit of St. Louis

44c Underline foreign words that are not part of the English language.

A foreign expression should be underlined when it has not been absorbed into our language. A dictionary will say whether a word is still considered foreign to English.

The scientific name for the brown trout is Salmo trutta. [The Latin scientific names for plants and animals are always underlined.]

The Latin De gustibus non est disputandum translates roughly as "There's no accounting for taste."

44d Underline words, letters, numbers, and phrases named as words.

Some people pronounce th, as in thought, with a faint s or f sound.

Try pronouncing unique New York ten times fast.

The word syzygy refers to a straight line formed by three celestial bodies, as in the alignment of the earth, sun, and moon. [Quotation marks may also be used for words being defined.]

44e Occasionally, underlining may be used for emphasis.

Underlining can stress an important word or phrase, especially in reporting how someone said something. But use such emphasis very rarely, or your writing may sound immature or hysterical.

Abbreviations

The following guidelines on abbreviations pertain to nontechnical writing. Technical writing, such as in the sciences and engineering, generally uses many more abbreviations.

45a Use standard abbreviations for titles immediately before and after proper names.

BEFORE THE NAME	AFTER THE NAME
Dr. James Hsu	James Hsu, M.D.
Mr., Mrs., Ms., Hon.,	D.D.S., D.V.M., Ph.D.,
St., Rev., Msgr., Gen.	Ed.D., O.S.B., S.J., Sr., Jr.

Do not use abbreviations such as *Rev., Hon., Prof., Rep., Sen., Dr.,* and *St.* (for *Saint*) unless they appear before a proper name.

45b Familiar abbreviations and acronyms are acceptable in most writing.

An ACRONYM is an abbreviation that spells a pronounceable word, such as WHO, NATO, and AIDS. These and other abbreviations using initials are acceptable in most writing as long as they are familiar to readers. Abbreviations of three or more words are usually written without periods.

INSTITUTIONS	LSU, UCLA, TCU
ORGANIZATIONS	CIA, FBI, YMCA, AFL-CIO
CORPORATIONS	IBM, CBS, ITT
PEOPLE	JFK, LBJ, FDR
COUNTRIES	U.S.A. (or USA)

NOTE: If a name or term (such as *operating room*) appears often in a piece of writing, then its abbreviation (*O.R.*) can cut down on extra words. Spell out the full term at its first appearance, indicate its abbreviation in parentheses, and then use the abbreviation.

Use *B.C., A.D., A.M., P.M., no.,* and *$* only with specific dates and numbers.

44 B.C.	11:26 A.M. (*or* a.m.)	no. 36 (*or* No. 36)
A.D. 1492	8:05 P.M. (*or* p.m.)	$7.41

The abbreviation B.C. ("before Christ") always follows a date, whereas A.D. (*anno Domini,* Latin for "year of the Lord") precedes a date.

NOTE: B.C.E. ("before the common era") and C.E. ("common era") are increasingly replacing B.C. and A.D., respectively. Both follow the date.

45d Generally, reserve Latin abbreviations for source citations and comments in parentheses.

i.e.	*id est:*	that is
cf.	*confer:*	compare
e.g.	*exempli gratia:*	for example
et al.	*et alii:*	and others
etc.	*et cetera:*	and so forth
N.B.	*nota bene:*	note well

He said he would be gone a fortnight (i.e., two weeks)
Bloom et al., editors, *Anthology of Light Verse*
Trees, too, are susceptible to disease (e.g., Dutch elm disease).

(Note that these abbreviations are generally not italicized or under-lined.)

Some writers avoid these abbreviations in formal writing, even within parentheses.

 Reserve *Inc., Bros., Co.,* or *&* (for *and*) for official names of business firms.

FAULTY	*The Santini bros.* operate a large moving firm in New York City & environs.
REVISED	*The Santini brothers* operate a large moving firm in New York City *and* environs.
REVISED	*Santini Bros.* is a large moving firm in New York City *and* environs.

Spell out units of measurement and names of places, calendar designations, people, and courses.

Units of measurement, geographical names, and other words are often abbreviated in technical writing. In other academic writing and general writing, however, such words should be spelled out.

UNITS OF MEASUREMENT
The dog is thirty *inches* (not *in.*) high.

GEOGRAPHICAL NAMES
The publisher is in *Massachusetts* (not *Mass.* or *MA*).

NAMES OF DAYS, MONTHS, AND HOLIDAYS
The truce was signed on *Tuesday* (not *Tues.*), *April* (not *Apr.*) 16.

NAMES OF PEOPLE
Robert (not *Robt.*) Frost writes accessible poems.

COURSES OF INSTRUCTION
I'm majoring in *political science* (not *poli. sci.*).

Numbers

In scientific and technical writing, all numbers are usually written as figures. In business writing, all numbers over ten are usually written as figures. In other academic and general writing—the subject of this chapter—numbers are more often spelled out.

 Use figures for numbers that require more than two words to spell out.

The leap year has *366* days.
The population of Minot, North Dakota, is about *32,800*.

Spell out numbers of one or two words.

> The ball game drew *forty-two thousand* people. [A hyphenated number may be considered one word.]

EXCEPTIONS: Use a combination of figures and words for round numbers over a million: *26 million, 2.45 billion.* And use either all figures or all words when several numbers appear together in a passage, even if convention would require a mixture.

46b Use figures instead of words according to standard practice.

We conventionally use figures for certain information, even when the numbers could be spelled out in one or two words.

DAYS AND YEARS

June 18, 1985   A.D. 12   456 B.C.   1999

PAGES, CHAPTERS, VOLUMES, ACTS, SCENES, LINES

Chapter 9, page 123
Hamlet, Act 5, Scene 3

DECIMALS, PERCENTAGES, AND FRACTIONS

22.5 $3^1/_2$
48% (*or* 48 percent)

ADDRESSES

355 Clinton Avenue
Washington, D.C. 20036

SCORES AND STATISTICS

21 to 7   a ratio of 8 to 1

EXACT AMOUNTS OF MONEY

$3.5 million $4.50

THE TIME OF DAY

9:00   3:45

EXCEPTIONS: Round dollar or cent amounts of only a few words may be expressed in words: *seventeen dollars; sixty cents.* When the word *o'clock* is used for the time of day, also express the number in words: *two o'clock* (not *2 o'clock*).

46c Spell out numbers that begin sentences.

For clarity, spell out any number that begins a sentence. If the number requires more than two words, reword the sentence so that the number falls later and can be expressed as a figure.

FAULTY   *103* visitors asked for refunds.

AWKWARD   *One hundred three* visitors asked for refunds.

REVISED   Of the visitors, *103* asked for refunds.

VI

Research and Documentation

47

Research Strategy

Research writing is a process involving diverse and overlapping activities. A thoughtful plan (47a) and an appropriate topic (47b) will give you a head start and help direct your progress.

47a   Planning a research project

As soon as you receive an assignment for a research project, you can begin developing a strategy for completing it. The first step should be making a schedule that apportions the available time to the necessary work. A possible schedule appears below. (The section numbers in parentheses refer to relevant discussions in this book.)

Complete
by:

_____   1. Finding a topic (47b)
_____   2. Finding information and refining the topic (48a–48b)

_____   3. Scanning and evaluating sources (48c)
_____   4. Taking notes using summary, paraphrase, and direct quotation (48d–48e)

_____   5. Creating a focus and structure (3a–3b)
_____   6. Drafting the paper (4a–4b, 48f)

_____   7. Revising and editing the paper (5a–5d)
_____   8. Citing sources in your text (49a, 50a)
_____   9. Preparing the list of sources (49b, 50b)
_____   10. Preparing and proofreading the final manuscript (5c, 40a)
_____   11. Final paper due

You can estimate that each segment marked off by a horizontal line will occupy *roughly* one-quarter of the total time—for example, a week in a four-week assignment or two weeks in an eight-week assignment. The most unpredictable segments are the first two, so it's wise to get started early enough to accommodate the unexpected.

47b Finding a topic

Before reading this section, you may want to review the suggestions given in 1a (p. 2) for finding and limiting an essay topic. Selecting and limiting a topic for a research paper present special opportunities and problems. If you have questions about your topic, consult your instructor.

A topic for a research paper has four primary requirements, each with corresponding pitfalls.

1. Ample published sources of information are available on the topic.

   Avoid (*a*) very recent topics, such as the latest medical breakthrough, and (*b*) topics that are too removed geographically, such as a minor event in Australian history.

2. The topic encourages research in the kinds and number of sources required by the assignment.

   Avoid (*a*) topics that depend entirely on personal opinion and experience, such as the virtues of your hobby, and (*b*) topics that require research in only one source, such as a straight factual biography.

3. The topic will lead you to an objective assessment of sources and to defensible conclusions.

   Avoid topics that rest entirely on belief or prejudice, such as when human life begins or why women (or men) are superior. Your readers are unlikely to be swayed from their own beliefs.

4. The topic suits the length of paper assigned and the time given for research and writing.

   Avoid broad topics that have too many sources to survey adequately, such as a major event in history.

48

Using Sources

Research writing is mainly about finding sources and using them to form, support, and extend your own ideas. This chapter discusses keeping track of sources (48a); the kinds of sources available (48b); evaluating sources (48c); taking notes using summary, paraphrase, and quotation (48d); avoiding plagiarism (48e); and introducing borrowed material in your own text (48f).

NOTE: If sources you need are not in your library, your librarian may be able to obtain them from another library. But plan ahead: these interlibrary loans can take a week or even several weeks.

48a Keeping a working bibliography

Keep track of source information as you find it with a WORKING BIBLIOGRAPHY, a file of sources that you believe will help you. Using a 3″ × 5″ index card for each source allows you to rearrange, edit, and add to the list without fuss. Later you can alphabetize the cards for your final list of sources. Pages 217–18 and 224–25 show diagrams of the basic information you'll need for a book and an article in a periodical. In addition, record the library's catalog number for each source so that you can retrieve it easily.

48b Finding sources

Sources are of two basic kinds:

❖ PRIMARY SOURCES are firsthand accounts: historical documents (letters, speeches, and so on), eyewitness reports, works of literature, reports on experiments or surveys, or your own interviews, experiments, observations, or correspondence. Whenever possible, you should seek and rely on primary sources, drawing your own conclusions from them.

❖ SECONDARY SOURCES report and analyze information drawn from other sources, often primary ones: a historian's account of a battle, a critic's reading of a poem, a physicist's evaluation of several studies, an encyclopedia or other standard reference book. Secondary sources may contain helpful summaries and interpretations that direct, support, and extend your thinking. However, most research-writing assignments expect your own ideas to go beyond those you find in such sources.

Your library houses primary and secondary sources in reference works, periodicals, and books and on computerized databases. In addition, you can generate your own primary sources.

A tip for researchers

If you are unsure of how to locate or use your library's resources, ask a reference librarian. This person is familiar with all the library's resources and with general and specialized research techniques, and it is his or her job to help you and others with research. Even experienced researchers often consult reference librarians.

1. Reference works

REFERENCE WORKS include encyclopedias, dictionaries, digests, bibliographies, indexes, atlases, almanacs, and handbooks. Your research *must* go beyond these sources, but they can help you decide whether your topic really interests you and whether it meets the requirements for a research paper (p. 199). Preliminary research in reference works will also direct you to more detailed sources on your topic. A comprehensive catalog and explanation is Eugene P. Sheehy, *Guide to Reference Books*, 10th ed. (1986).

2. Periodicals

PERIODICALS—journals, magazines, and newspapers—are invaluable sources of information in research. The difference between journals and magazines lies primarily in their content, readership, and frequency of issue.

❖ Magazines—such as *Psychology Today*, *Newsweek*, and *Esquire*—are nonspecialist publications intended for diverse readers. Most magazines appear weekly or monthly, and their pages are numbered anew with each issue.

❖ Journals often appear quarterly and contain specialized information intended for readers in a particular field. Examples include *American Anthropologist*, *Journal of Black Studies*, and *Journal of Chemical Education*.

Various indexes to periodicals provide information on the articles in journals, magazines, and newspapers. Many of these indexes are available on computerized databases (see the next page). Examples include *Readers' Guide to Periodical Literature*, *InfoTrac*, *New York Times Index*, and many indexes to the journals of particular disciplines, such as the *Art Index*, the *General Sciences Index*, and the *Social Sciences Index*.

Every library lists its complete periodical holdings either in its main catalog (see below) or in a separate catalog. The recent issues of a periodical are usually held in the library's periodical room. Back issues are usually stored elsewhere, either in bound volumes or on film that requires a special machine to read. A librarian will show you how to operate the machine.

3. Books

The library's main catalog lists books alphabetically by author's name, title of book, and subject. The catalog may be in a card file, in a printed volume, on film, or, increasingly, on a computerized database that you reach by a keyboard and a monitor. Ask a librarian if you are uncertain about the location, form, or use of the catalog.

To search the catalog, you will need specific key words relating to your subject. *Library of Congress Subject Headings* lists headings and subheadings under which the Library of Congress and other catalogers index books.

4. Computerized databases

In addition to its book catalog, your library may have other electronic storehouses of information. For example, most of the indexes listed on the previous page are published on compact disks just like music disks, called CD-ROMs. And many libraries subscribe to commercial information services, such as DIALOG, that provide bibliographic information, reports, and other materials from publishers and corporations. Usually, a librarian must help you use these services, and they cost a fee.

Like a book search, a database search requires identifying the key words relevant to your topic under which information has been indexed. Key words should not be so narrow that they exclude possibly relevant information, nor so broad that they call up many irrelevant sources.

5. Your own sources

Academic writing will often require you to conduct primary research for information of your own. For instance, you may need to analyze a poem, conduct an experiment, survey a group of people, or interview an expert. Such primary research may be the sole basis of your paper or may supplement and extend the information you find in other sources.

48c Evaluating sources

As you look through sources, you should evaluate their usefulness. Scan introductions, tables of contents, and headings. Look for information about authors' backgrounds that will help you understand their expertise and bias. Try to answer the following questions about each source:

❖ Is the work relevant?

Does the source devote some attention to your topic?

Where in the source are you likely to find relevant information or ideas?

Is the source appropriately specialized for your needs? Check the source's treatment of a topic you know something about, to ensure that it is neither too superficial nor too technical.

How important is the source likely to be for your writing?

❖ Is the work reliable?

How up to date is the source? Check the publication date.

Is the author an expert in the field? Look for an author biography, or look up the author in a biographical reference.

What is the author's bias? Check biographical information or the author's own preface or introduction. Consider what others have written about the author or the source.

Whatever his or her bias, does the author reason soundly, provide adequate evidence, and consider opposing views?

Don't expect to find harmony among sources, for reasonable people often disagree in their opinions. Thus you must deal honestly with the gaps and conflicts in sources. Old sources, superficial ones, slanted ones—these should be offset in your research and your writing by sources that are newer, more thorough, or more objective.

48d Taking notes using summary, paraphrase, and direct quotation

Your final paper should show that you have digested and interpreted the information in your sources—work that can be performed most efficiently in note taking. Taking notes is not a mechanical process of copying from books and periodicals. Rather, as you read and take notes you assess and organize the information in your sources.

If you use index cards for your notes, they will be easy to arrange and edit. Write only one idea on each card, give the note a topic heading so that you can see at a glance what it's about, and record the source author's name and the source page number. (Without this information, you won't be able to use the note.)

NOTE: Photocopying from sources postpones decisions about whether to summarize, paraphrase, or quote them. Photocopying can save time, but don't let it prevent you from thinking critically and creatively about your sources.

1. Summary

When you SUMMARIZE, you condense an extended idea or argument into a sentence or more in your own words. Summary is most useful when you want to record the gist of an author's idea without the background or supporting evidence. Here, for example, is a passage summarized in a sentence.

ORIGINAL

Generalizing about male and female styles of management is a tricky business, because stereotypes have traditionally been used to keep women down. Not too long ago it was a widely accepted truth that women were unstable, indecisive, temperamental and manipulative and weren't good team members because they'd never played football. In fighting off these prejudices many women simply tried to adopt masculine traits in the office.
—ANN HUGHEY AND ERIC GELMAN, "Managing the Woman's Way," *Newsweek,* page 47

SUMMARY

Rather than be labeled with the sexist stereotypes that prevented their promotions, many women adopted masculine qualities.

2. Paraphrase

When you PARAPHRASE, you follow much more closely the author's original presentation, but you still restate it in your own words. Paraphrase is most useful when you want to reconstruct an author's line of reasoning but don't feel the original words merit direct quotation. Here is a paraphrase of the passage above by Hughey and Gelman.

PARAPHRASE

Because of the risk of stereotyping, which has served as a tool to block women from management, it is difficult to characterize a feminine management style. Women have been cited for their emotionality, instability, and lack of team spirit, among other qualities.

Many women have defended themselves at work by adopting the qualities of men.

3. Direct quotation

In a paper analyzing primary sources such as literary works, you will use direct quotation extensively to illustrate and support your analysis. But you should quote from secondary sources only in the following circumstances:

1. The author's original satisfies one of these requirements:

   The language is unusually vivid, bold, or inventive.

   The quotation cannot be paraphrased without distortion or loss of meaning.

   The words themselves are at issue in your interpretation.

   The quotation represents and emphasizes the view of an important expert.

   The quotation is a graph, diagram, or table.

2. The quotation is as short as possible.

   It includes only material relevant to your point.

   It is edited to eliminate unneeded examples and other material. (See below.)

When taking a quotation from a source, copy the material *carefully*. Take down the author's exact wording, spelling, capitalization, and punctuation. Proofread every direct quotation *at least twice*, and be sure you have supplied big quotation marks so that later you won't confuse the direct quotation with a paraphrase or summary. If you want to make changes for clarity, use brackets (see 39d). If you want to omit irrelevant words or sentences, use ellipsis marks, usually three spaced periods (see 39c).

48e Avoiding plagiarism

PLAGIARISM (from a Latin word for "kidnapper") is the presentation of someone else's ideas or words as your own. Whether deliberate or accidental, plagiarism is a serious and often punishable offense.

❖ *Deliberate* plagiarism:

   Copying a phrase, a sentence, or a longer passage from a source and passing it off as your own by omitting quotation marks and a source citation.

Summarizing or paraphrasing someone else's ideas without acknowledging your debt in a source citation.

Buying a term paper and handing it in as your own.

❖ *Accidental* plagiarism:

Forgetting to place quotation marks around another writer's words.

Omitting a source citation for another's idea because you are unaware of the need to acknowledge the idea.

Carelessly copying a source when you mean to paraphrase.

1. What you need not acknowledge

Your independent material

Your own observations, thoughts, compilations of facts, or experimental results, expressed in your words and format, do not require acknowledgment. Though you generally should describe the basis for your conclusions so that readers can evaluate your thinking, you need not cite sources for them.

Common knowledge

Common knowledge consists of the standard information of a field of study as well as folk literature and commonsense observations.

❖ Standard information includes the major facts of history, such as the dates of Charlemagne's rule as emperor of Rome (800–814). It does not include interpretations of facts, such as a historian's opinion that Charlemagne was sometimes needlessly cruel in extending his power.

❖ Folk literature, such as the fairy tale "Snow White," is popularly known and cannot be traced to a particular writer. Literature traceable to a writer is not folk literature, even if it is very familiar.

❖ A commonsense observation is something most people know, such as that inflation is most troublesome for people with low and fixed incomes. An economist's argument about the effects of inflation on Chinese immigrants is not a commonsense observation.

If you do not know a subject well enough to determine whether a piece of information is common knowledge, make a record of the source as you would for any other quotation, paraphrase, or summary. As you read more about the subject, the information may come up repeatedly without acknowledgment, in which case it is

Checklist for avoiding plagiarism

1. What type of source are you using: your own independent material, common knowledge, or someone else's independent material? You must acknowledge someone else's material.
2. If you are quoting someone else's material, is the quotation exact? Have you inserted quotation marks around quotations run into the text? Have you shown omissions with ellipses and additions with brackets?
3. If you are paraphrasing or summarizing someone else's material, have you used your own words and sentence structures? Does your paraphrase or summary employ quotation marks when you resort to the author's exact language? Have you represented the author's meaning without distortion?
4. Is each use of someone else's material acknowledged in your text? Are all your source citations complete and accurate? (See 49a or 50a.)
5. Does your list of works cited include all the sources you have drawn from in writing your paper? (See 49b or 50b.)

probably common knowledge. But if you are still in doubt when you finish your research, always acknowledge the source.

2. What you must acknowledge

You must always acknowledge other people's independent material—that is, any facts or ideas that are not common knowledge or your own. The source may be anything, including a book, an article, a movie, an interview, a microfilmed document, or a computer program. You must acknowledge not only ideas or facts themselves but also the language and format in which the ideas or facts appear, if you use them. That is, the wording, sentence structures, arrangement of ideas, and special graphics (such as a diagram) created by another writer belong to that writer just as his or her ideas do.

The following example baldly plagiarizes both the structure and the words of the original quotation from Jessica Mitford's *Kind and Usual Punishment*, page 9.

ORIGINAL	The character and mentality of the keepers may be of more importance in understanding prisons than the character and mentality of the kept.
PLAGIARISM	But the character of prison officials (the keepers) is more important in understanding prisons than the character of prisoners (the kept).

The next example is more subtle plagiarism, because it changes Mitford's sentence structure. But it still uses her words.

PLAGIARISM   In understanding prisons, we should know more about the character and mentality of the keepers than of the kept.

The plagiarism in these examples can be remedied by placing Mitford's exact words in quotation marks, changing her sentence structure when not quoting, and citing the source properly (here, in MLA style).

REVISION   According to one critic of the penal system, "The
(QUOTATION)   character and mentality of the keepers may be of more importance in understanding prisons than the character and mentality of the kept" (Mitford 9).

REVISION   One critic of the penal system maintains that we
(PARAPHRASE)   may be able to learn more about prisons from the psychology of the prison officials than from that of the prisoners (Mitford 9).

48f Introducing borrowed material

When using summaries, paraphrases, and quotations, integrate them smoothly into your own sentences. In the passage below, the writer has not meshed the structures of her own and her source's sentences.

AWKWARD   One editor disagrees with this view and "a good reporter does not fail to separate opinions from facts" (Lyman 52).

REVISED   One editor disagrees with this view, maintaining that "a good reporter does not fail to separate opinions from facts" (Lyman 52).

Even when not conflicting with your own sentence structure, borrowed material will be ineffective if you merely dump it in readers' laps without explaining how you intend it to be understood.

DUMPED   Many news editors and reporters maintain that it is impossible to keep personal opinions from influencing the selection and presentation of facts. "True, news reporters, like everyone else, form impressions of what they see and hear. However, a good reporter does not fail to separate opinions from facts" (Lyman 52).

REVISED   Many news editors and reporters maintain that it is impossible to keep personal opinions from influencing the selection and presentation of facts. <u>Yet not all authorities agree with this view. One editor grants that</u> "news reporters, like everyone else, form impressions of what they see and hear." But, <u>he insists</u>, "a good reporter does not fail to separate opinions from facts" (Lyman 52).

You can do even more to integrate a quotation into your text and inform readers why you are using it. If your readers will recognize it, you can provide the author's name in the text:

AUTHOR   . . . <u>Harold Lyman</u> grants that "news reporters, like
NAMED   everyone else, form impressions of what they see and hear." But, Lyman insists, "a good reporter does not fail to separate opinions from facts" (52).

If the source title contributes information about the author or the context of the quotation, you can provide it in the text:

TITLE   . . . Harold Lyman, <u>in his book *The Conscience of the*
GIVEN   *Journalist,*</u> grants that "news reporters, like everyone else, form impressions of what they see and hear." But, Lyman insists, "a good reporter does not fail to separate opinions from facts" (52).

Finally, if the quoted author's background and experience clarify or strengthen the quotation, you can provide these credentials in the text:

CREDENTIALS   . . . Harold Lyman, <u>a newspaper editor for more than
GIVEN   forty years,</u> grants that "news reporters, like everyone else, form impressions of what they see and hear." But, Lyman insists, "a good reporter does not fail to separate opinions from facts" (52).

You need not name the author, source, or credentials in your text when you are simply establishing facts or weaving together facts and opinions from varied sources. In the following passage, the information is more important than the source, so the name of the source is confined to a parenthetical acknowledgment:

To end the abuses of the British, many colonists were urging three actions: forming a united front, seceding from Britain, and taking control of their own international trade and diplomacy (Wills 325–36).

See pages 174–75 for when to run quotations into your own text and when to display them separately from your text.

Documenting Sources: MLA Style

Every time you borrow the words, facts, or ideas of others, you must DOCUMENT the source—that is, supply a reference (or document) telling readers that you borrowed the material and where you borrowed it from.

Editors and teachers in most academic disciplines require special documentation formats (or styles) in their scholarly journals and in students' papers. This chapter concentrates on a style of in-text citation widely used in the arts and humanities: that of the Modern Language Association, published in the *MLA Handbook for Writers of Research Papers*, 3rd ed. (1988). The next chapter presents a style widely used in the social sciences, that of the American Psychological Association (APA). Beyond this book several guides outline other documentation styles:

> American Anthropological Association. "Style Guide and Information for Authors." *American Anthropologist* (1977): 774–79.
>
> American Chemical Society. *Handbook for Authors of Papers in American Chemical Society Publications.* 1978.
>
> American Institute of Physics. *Style Manual for Guidance in the Preparation of Papers.* 3rd ed. 1978.
>
> American Mathematical Society. *A Manual for Authors of Mathematical Papers.* 8th ed. 1980.
>
> American Medical Association. *Style Book: Editorial Manual.* 6th ed. 1976.
>
> American Sociological Association. "Editorial Guidelines." Inside front cover of each issue of *American Sociological Review.*
>
> *The Chicago Manual of Style.* 13th ed. 1982.
>
> Council of Biology Editors. *CBE Style Manual: A Guide for Authors, Editors, and Publishers in the Biological Sciences.* 5th ed. 1983.
>
> Turabian, Kate L. *A Manual for Writers of Term Papers, Theses, and Dissertations.* 5th ed. Rev. and exp. Bonnie Birtwistle Honigsblum. 1987.

Ask your instructor which style he or she prefers.

49a Writing MLA parenthetical citations

The documentation system of the *MLA Handbook* employs brief parenthetical citations within the text that direct readers to the list

Index to MLA parenthetical citations

of works cited at the end of the text. The following pages describe this documentation system: what must be included in a citation (below), where to place citations (p. 215), and when to use footnotes or endnotes in addition to parenthetical citations (p. 216).

1. Citation formats

The in-text citations of sources have two requirements:

❖ They must include just enough information for the reader to locate the appropriate source in your list of works cited.
❖ They must include just enough information for the reader to locate the place in the source where the borrowed material appears.

Usually, you can meet both these requirements by providing the author's last name and the page(s) in the source on which the material appears. The reader can find the source in your list of works cited and find the borrowed material in the source itself.

1. AUTHOR NOT NAMED IN THE TEXT

```
One researcher concludes that "women impose a
distinctive construction on moral problems,
seeing moral dilemmas in terms of conflicting
responsibilities" (Gilligan 105).
```

When you have not already named the author in your sentence, provide the author's last name and the page number(s), with no punctuation between them, in parentheses.

2. AUTHOR NAMED IN THE TEXT

```
One researcher, Carol Gilligan, concludes that
"women impose a distinctive construction on
moral problems, seeing moral dilemmas in terms
of conflicting responsibilities" (105).
```

If the author's name is already given in your text, you need not repeat it in the parenthetical citation. The citation gives just the page number(s).

3. A WORK WITH TWO OR THREE AUTHORS

```
As Frieden and Sagalyn observe, "The poor and
the minorities were the leading victims of
highway and renewal programs" (29).
```

```
According to one study, "The poor and the
minorities were the leading victims of high-
way and renewal programs" (Frieden and Sagalyn
29).
```

If the source has two or three authors, give all their names in the text or in the citation.

4. A WORK WITH MORE THAN THREE AUTHORS

```
It took the combined forces of the Americans,
Europeans, and Japanese to break the rebel siege
of Peking in 1900 (Lopez et al. 362).
```

```
It took the combined forces of the Americans,
Europeans, and Japanese to break the rebel siege
of Peking in 1900 (Lopez, Blum, Cameron, and
Barnes 362).
```

If the source has more than three authors, you may list all their last names or use only the first author's name followed by "et al." (the abbreviation for the Latin "and others"). The choice depends on what you do in your list of works cited (see p. 219).

5. AN ENTIRE WORK (NO PAGE NUMBERS)

```
Boyd deals with the need to acknowledge and come
to terms with our fear of nuclear technology.
```

When you cite an entire work rather than a part of it, the reference will not include any page number. If the author's name appears in the text, no parenthetical reference is needed. But remember that the source must appear in the list of works cited.

6. A MULTIVOLUME WORK

```
After issuing the Emancipation Proclamation,
Lincoln said, "What I did, I did after very full
deliberations, and under a very heavy and solemn
sense of responsibility" (5: 438).
```

If you consulted only one volume of a multivolume work, your list of works cited will indicate as much (see p. 222), and you can treat the volume as any book. But if you consulted two or more volumes, your citation must indicate which one you are referring to. In the example the number 5 indicates the volume from which the quotation was taken; the number 438 indicates the page number in that volume.

7. A WORK BY AN AUTHOR OF TWO OR MORE WORKS

```
At about age seven, most children begin to use
appropriate gestures to reinforce their stories
(Gardner, Arts 144-45).
```

If your list of works cited includes two or more works by the same author, give the appropriate title or a shortened version of it in the parenthetical citation. For this reference the full title is *The Arts and Human Development*.

8. An unsigned work

```
One article notes that a death-row inmate may

demand his own execution to achieve a fleeting

notoriety ("Right").
```

Anonymous works are alphabetized by title in the list of works cited. In the text they are referred to by full or shortened title. This citation refers to an unsigned article titled "The Right to Die." (A page number is unnecessary because the article is no longer than a page.)

9. A government document or a work with a corporate author

```
A 1983 report by the Hawaii Department of

Education predicts a gradual increase in

enrollments (6).
```

If the author of the work is listed as a government body or a corporation, cite the work by that organization's name. If the name is long, work it into the text to avoid an intrusive parenthetical citation.

10. An indirect source

```
George Davino maintains that "even small

children have vivid ideas about nuclear energy"

(qtd. in Boyd 22).
```

When you quote or paraphrase one source's quotation of someone else, your citation must indicate as much. In the citation above, "qtd. in" ("quoted in") says that Davino was quoted by Boyd. The list of works cited then includes only Boyd (the work consulted), not Davino.

11. A literary work

```
Toward the end of James's novel, Maggie suddenly

feels "the intimate, the immediate, the fa-

miliar, as she hadn't had them for so long"

(535; pt. 6, ch. 41).
```

Novels, plays, and poems are often available in many editions, so your instructor may ask you to provide information that will help readers find the passage you cite no matter what edition they consult.

For novels, as in the example above, the page number comes first, followed by a semicolon and then information on the appropriate part or chapter of the work.

```
Later in King Lear Shakespeare has the disguised

Edgar say, "The prince of darkness is a gentle-

man" (3.4.147).
```

For poems and verse plays, as above, you can omit the page number and instead cite the appropriate part or act (and scene, if any) plus the line number(s). Use Arabic numerals for acts and scenes ("3.4") unless your instructor specifies Roman numerals ("III.iv"). For prose plays, provide the page number followed by the act and scene, if any (see the reference to *Death of a Salesman* on the next page).

12. MORE THAN ONE WORK

```
Two recent articles point out that a computer

badly used can be less efficient than no

computer at all (Richards 162; Gough and Hall

201).
```

If you use a parenthetical citation to refer to more than a single work, separate the references by a semicolon. Since long citations in the text can distract the reader, you may choose to cite several or more works in an endnote or footnote rather than in the text. See the next page.

2. Placement of parenthetical citations

Generally, place a parenthetical citation at the end of the sentence in which you summarize, paraphrase, or quote a work. The citation should follow a closing quotation mark but precede the sentence punctuation. (See the examples in the previous section.) When a citation pertains to only part of a sentence, place the citation after the borrrowed material and at the least intrusive point—usually at the end of a clause.

```
Though Spelling argues that American automobile

manufacturers "have done the best that could be

expected" in meeting consumer needs (26), not

everyone agrees with him.
```

When a citation appears after a quotation that ends in an ellipsis mark (. . .), place the citation between the closing quotation mark and the sentence period.

```
One observer maintains that "American

manufacturers must bear some blame for the

current recession . . ." (Rosenbaum 12).
```

When a citation appears at the end of a quotation set off from the text, place it two spaces *after* the punctuation ending the quotation. No additional punctuation is necessary.

```
In Arthur Miller's Death of a Salesman, the most

poignant defense of Willie Loman comes from his

wife, Linda:

              He's not the finest character that

              ever lived.  But he's a human being,

              and a terrible thing is happening to

              him. . . .  Attention, attention must

              finally be paid to such a person.  (56;

              act 1)
```

(This citation of a play includes the act number as well as the page number. See model 11 on p. 214.)

3. Footnotes or endnotes in special circumstances

Footnotes or endnotes may replace parenthetical citations when you cite several sources at once, when you comment on a source, or when you provide information that does not fit easily in the text. Signal a footnote or endnote in your text with a numeral raised above the appropriate line. Then write a note with the same numeral.

```
TEXT  At least five subsequent studies have con-

      firmed these results.[1]
```

Note   ¹ Abbott and Winger 266-68; Casner 27;

Hoyenga 78-79; Marino 36; Tripp, Tripp, and

Walk 179-83.

In a note the raised numeral is indented five spaces and followed by a space. If the note appears as a footnote, place it at the bottom of the page on which the citation appears, set it off from the text with quadruple spacing, and single-space the note itself. If the note appears as an endnote, place it in numerical order with the other endnotes on a page between the text and the list of works cited; double-space all the endnotes.

49b Preparing the MLA list of works cited

At the end of your paper, a list titled "Works Cited" includes all the sources you quoted, paraphrased, or summarized in your paper. (If your instructor asks you to include sources you examined but did not cite, title the list "Works Consulted.")

For the list of works cited, arrange your sources in alphabetical order by the last name of the author. If an author is not given in the source, alphabetize the source by the first main word of the title (excluding *A*, *An*, or *The*). Type the entire list double-spaced (both within and between entries). Indent the second and subsequent lines of each entry five spaces from the left. (See the sample on p. 240.)

NOTE: You may have to combine some of the following formats for particular sources. For example, to list a work by four authors appearing in a monthly periodical, you will have to draw on model 3 ("A book with more than three authors") and model 23 ("A signed article in a monthly or bimonthly magazine").

1. Books

The basic format for a book includes the following elements:

(a)   (b)
Gilligan, Carol. In a Different Voice: Psycho-

logical Theory and Women's Development.

(c)
Cambridge: Harvard UP, 1982.
①   ②   ③

Index to MLA works-cited models

a. The author's full name: the last name first, followed by a comma, and then the first name and any middle name or initial. End the name with a period and two spaces.
b. The full title of the book, including any subtitle. Underline the complete title, capitalize all important words (see 43c), separate the main title and the subtitle with a colon and one space, and end the title with a period and two spaces.
c. The publication information:
   (1) The city of publication, followed by a colon and one space.
   (2) The name of the publisher, followed by a comma. Shorten most publishers' names—in many cases to a single word. For instance, use "Little" for Little, Brown. For university presses, use the abbreviation "UP," as in the example above.
   (3) The date of publication, ending with a period.

1. A BOOK WITH ONE AUTHOR

Gilligan, Carol. <u>In a Different Voice: Psycho-
    logical Theory and Women's Development</u>.
    Cambridge: Harvard UP, 1982.

2. A BOOK WITH TWO OR THREE AUTHORS

Frieden, Bernard J., and Lynne B. Sagalyn.
    <u>Downtown, Inc.: How America Rebuilds Cities</u>.
    Cambridge: MIT, 1989.

Give the authors' names in the order provided on the title page. Reverse the first and last names of the first author *only,* and separate the authors' names with a comma.

3. A BOOK WITH MORE THAN THREE AUTHORS

Lopez, Robert S., et al. <u>Civilizations: Western
    and World</u>. Boston: Little, 1975.

You may, but need not, give all authors' names if the work has more than three authors. If you do not give all names, provide the name of the first author only, and follow the name with a comma and the abbreviation "et al." (for the Latin *et alii,* meaning "and others").

4. TWO OR MORE WORKS BY THE SAME AUTHOR(S)

Gardner, Howard. <u>The Arts and Human Development</u>.
    New York: Wiley, 1973.

```
---.   The Quest for Mind: Piaget, Lévi-Strauss,

       and the Structuralist Movement.   New York:

       Knopf, 1973.
```

Give the author's name only in the first entry. For the second and any subsequent works by the same author, substitute three hyphens for the author's name. Within the set of entries for the author, list the sources alphabetically by the first main word of the title. Note that the three hyphens stand for *exactly* the same name or names. If the second source above were by Gardner and somebody else, both names would have to be given in full.

5. A BOOK WITH AN EDITOR

```
Ruitenbeek, Hendrick, ed.   Freud as We Knew Him.

       Detroit: Wayne State UP, 1973.
```

The abbreviation "ed.," separated from the name by a comma, identifies Ruitenbeek as the editor of the work.

6. A BOOK WITH AN AUTHOR AND AN EDITOR

```
Melville, Herman.   The Confidence Man: His

       Masquerade.   Ed. Hershel Parker.   New York:

       Norton, 1971.
```

When citing the work of the author, give his or her name first, and give the editor's name after the title, preceded by "Ed." ("Edited by"). When citing the work of the editor, use the form above for a book with an editor, and give the author's name after the title preceded by "By": "Parker, Hershel, ed. The Confidence Man: His Masquerade. By Herman Melville."

7. A TRANSLATION

```
Alighieri, Dante.   The Inferno.   Trans. John

       Ciardi.   New York: NAL, 1971.
```

When citing the work of the author, give his or her name first, and give the translator's name after the title, preceded by "Trans." ("Translated by"). When citing the work of the translator, give his or her name first, followed by a comma and "trans.," and after the title give the author's name preceded by "By": "Ciardi, John, trans. The Inferno. By Dante Alighieri."

8. A BOOK WITH A CORPORATE AUTHOR

```
Lorenz, Inc.  Research in Social Studies
     Teaching.  Baltimore: Arrow, 1992.
```

List the name of the corporation, institution, or other body as author.

9. AN ANONYMOUS BOOK

```
Webster's Ninth New Collegiate Dictionary.
     Springfield: Merriam, 1987.
```

List the book under its title. Do not use "anonymous" or "anon."

10. A LATER EDITION

```
Bollinger, Dwight L.  Aspects of Language.  2nd
     ed.  New York: Harcourt, 1975.
```

For any edition after the first, place the edition number between the title and the publication information. Use the appropriate designation for editions that are named or dated rather than numbered—for instance, "Rev. ed." for "Revised edition."

11. A REPUBLISHED BOOK

```
James, Henry.  The Golden Bowl.  1904.  London:
     Penguin, 1966.
```

Place the original date of publication after the title, and then provide the full publication information for the source you are using.

12. A BOOK WITH A TITLE IN ITS TITLE

```
Eco, Umberto.  Postscript to The Name of the
     Rose.  Trans. William Weaver.  New York:
     Harcourt, 1983.
```

When a book's title contains another book title (as here: The Name of the Rose), do not underline the shorter title. When a book's title contains the title of a work normally placed in quotation marks, keep the quotation marks and underline both titles: Critical Response to Henry James's "Beast in the Jungle." (Note that the underlining extends under the closing quotation mark.)

13. A WORK IN MORE THAN ONE VOLUME

```
Lincoln, Abraham.   The Collected Works of Abra-
      ham Lincoln.   Ed. Roy P. Basler.   8 vols.
      New Brunswick: Rutgers UP, 1953.
Lincoln, Abraham.   The Collected Works of Abra-
      ham Lincoln.   Ed. Roy P. Basler.   Vol. 5.
      New Brunswick: Rutgers UP, 1953.   8 vols.
```

If you use two or more volumes of a multivolume work, give the work's total number of volumes before the publication information ("8 vols." in the first example). Your text citation will indicate which volume you are citing (see p. 213). If you use only one volume, give that volume number before the publication information ("Vol. 5" in the second example). You may add the total number of volumes to the end of the entry ("8 vols." in the second example).

14. A WORK IN A SERIES

```
Bergman, Ingmar.   The Seventh Seal.   Modern Film
      Scripts Series.   New York: Simon, 1968.
```

Place the name of the series (no quotation marks or underlining) after the title.

15. PUBLISHED PROCEEDINGS OF A CONFERENCE

```
Watching Our Language: A Conference Sponsored by
      the Program in Architecture and Design
      Criticism.   6-8 May 1991.   New York:
      Parsons School of Design, 1991.
```

Whether in or after the title of the conference, supply information about who sponsored the conference, when it was held, and who published the proceedings. If you are citing a particular presentation at the conference, treat it as a selection from an anthology or collection (model 16).

16. A SELECTION FROM AN ANTHOLOGY OR COLLECTION

```
Auden, W. H.   "A Healthy Spot."   The Collected
```

<u>Poetry of W. H. Auden</u>. New York: Random,

1945. 134.

Give the author and the title of the selection you are citing, placing the title in quotation marks and ending it with a period. Then give the title of the anthology. If the anthology has an editor, add the name as in model 6. At the end of the entry give the inclusive page numbers for the entire selection, but do not include the abbreviation "pp."

17. TWO OR MORE SELECTIONS FROM THE SAME ANTHOLOGY

Brooks, Rosetta. "Streetwise." Martin 38-39.

Martin, Richard, ed. <u>The New Urban Landscape</u>.

New York: Rizzoli, 1990.

Plotkin, Mark J. "Tropical Forests and the

Urban Landscape." Martin 50-51.

When citing more than one selection from the same source, avoid unnecessary repetition by giving the source in full (as in the Martin entry) and then simply cross-referencing it in entries for the works you used. Thus, instead of full information for the Brooks and Plotkin articles, give Martin's name and the appropriate pages in his book. Note that each entry appears in its proper alphabetical place among other works cited.

18. AN ARTICLE FROM A COLLECTION OF REPRINTED ARTICLES

Gibian, George. "Traditional Symbolism in <u>Crime</u>

<u>and Punishment</u>." <u>PMLA</u> 70 (1955): 979-96.

Rpt. in <u>Crime and Punishment</u>. By Feodor

Dostoevsky. Ed. George Gibian. Norton

Critical Editions. New York: Norton, 1964.

575-92.

Some collections contain articles reprinted from other sources. For an article from such a collection, provide the author and title of the article, placing the title in quotation marks and ending it with a period. Then, unless your instructor specifies otherwise, provide the complete information for the earlier publication of the piece, followed by "Rpt. in" ("Reprinted in") and the information for the source in which you found the piece. If you are not required to provide the earlier publication information, use model 16.

19. AN INTRODUCTION, PREFACE, FOREWORD, OR AFTERWORD

```
Donaldson, Norman.  Introduction.  The

     Claverings.  By Anthony Trollope.  New

     York: Dover, 1977.  vii-xv.
```

An introduction, foreword, or afterword is often written by someone other than the book's author. When citing such a work, give its name without quotation marks or underlining. Follow the title of the book with its author's name preceded by "By." Give the inclusive page numbers of the part you cite. (In the example above, the small Roman numerals indicate that the cited work is in the front matter of the book, before page 1.)

When the author of a preface or introduction is the same as the author of the book, give only the last name after the title:

```
Gould, Stephen Jay.  Prologue.  The Flamingo's

     Smile: Reflections in Natural History.  By

     Gould.  New York: Norton, 1985.  13-20.
```

20. AN ENCYCLOPEDIA OR ALMANAC

```
"Mammoth."  The New Columbia Encyclopedia.  1975.

Mark, Herman F.  "Polymers."  Encyclopaedia

     Britannica: Macropaedia.  1974.
```

Give the name of an author only when the article is signed; otherwise, give the title first. If the articles are alphabetized in the reference work, you needn't list any page numbers. For familiar sources like those in the examples, full publication information is not needed. Just provide the year of publication.

2. Periodicals: Journals, magazines, and newspapers

The basic format for an article from a periodical includes the following information:

```
       a                    b
Lever, Janet.  "Sex Differences in the Games
```

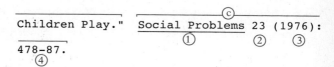

Children Play." <u>Social Problems</u> 23 (1976):
478-87.

a. The author's full name: last name first, followed by a comma, and then the first name and any middle name or initial. End the name with a period and two spaces.
b. The full title of the article, including any subtitle. Place the title in quotation marks, capitalize all important words in the title (see 43c), and end the title with a period (inside the final quotation mark) and two spaces.
c. The publication information:
 (1) The underlined title of the periodical (minus any *A*, *An*, or *The* at the beginning).
 (2) The volume or issue number (in Arabic numerals).
 (3) The date of publication, followed by a colon and a space.
 (4) The inclusive page numbers of the article (without the abbreviation "pp."). For the second number in inclusive page numbers over 100, provide only as many digits as needed for clarity (usually two): 100–01, 1026–36, 1190–206, 398–401.

21. A SIGNED ARTICLE IN A JOURNAL WITH CONTINUOUS PAGINATION THROUGHOUT THE ANNUAL VOLUME

Lever, Janet. "Sex Differences in the Games

 Children Play." <u>Social Problems</u> 23 (1976):

 478-87.

Some journals page all issues of an annual volume consecutively, so that issue 3 may begin on page 261. For this kind of journal, give the volume number after the title ("23" in the example above) and place the year of publication in parentheses.

22. A SIGNED ARTICLE IN A JOURNAL THAT PAGES ISSUES SEPARATELY OR THAT NUMBERS ONLY ISSUES, NOT VOLUMES

Boyd, Sarah. "Nuclear Terror." <u>Adaptation to</u>

 <u>Change</u> 7.4 (1981): 20-23.

Some journals page each issue separately (starting each issue at page 1). For these journals, give the volume number, a period, and the issue number (as in "7.4" in the Boyd entry). When citing an article in a journal that numbers only issues, not annual volumes, treat the issue number as if it were a volume number, as in model 21.

23. A SIGNED ARTICLE IN A MONTHLY OR BIMONTHLY MAGAZINE

```
Stein, Harry.   "Living with Lies."  Esquire Dec.

     1981: 23.
```

Follow the periodical title with the month (abbreviated) and the year of publication. Don't place the date in parentheses, and don't provide a volume or issue number.

24. A SIGNED ARTICLE IN A WEEKLY OR BIWEEKLY MAGAZINE

```
Stevens, Mark.   "Low and Behold."  New Republic

     24 Dec. 1990: 27-33.
```

Follow the periodical title with the day, the month (abbreviated), and the year of publication. Don't place the date in parentheses, and don't provide a volume or issue number.

25. A SIGNED ARTICLE IN A DAILY NEWSPAPER

```
Gargan, Edward A.   "Buffalo Concern Gives Pop

     Sound to Player Pianos."  New York Times 16

     Feb. 1984: B1.
```

Give the name of the newspaper as it appears on the first page (but without *A*, *An*, or *The*). Then follow model 24, with one difference if the newspaper is divided into sections that are paged separately. In that case, provide the section designation before the page number when the newspaper does the same (as in "B1" above), or provide the section designation before the colon when the newspaper does not combine the two in its numbering (as in "sec. 1: 1 +" below).

26. AN UNSIGNED ARTICLE

```
"The Right to Die."  Time 11 Oct. 1976: 101.

"Protests Greet Pope in Holland."  Boston Sunday

     Globe 12 May 1985, sec. 1: 1+.
```

Begin the entry for an unsigned article with the title of the article. The number "1 +" indicates that the article does not run on consecutive pages but starts on page 1 and continues later in the issue.

27. AN EDITORIAL OR LETTER TO THE EDITOR

```
"Bodily Intrusions."  Editorial.  New York Times

     29 Aug. 1990: A20.
```

Don't use quotation marks or underlining for the word "Editorial."
For a signed editorial, give the author's name first.

> Dowding, Michael. Letter. <u>Economist</u> 5-11 Jan.
>
> 1985: 4.

Don't use quotation marks or underlining for the word "Letter."

28. A REVIEW

> Dunne, John Gregory. "The Secret of Danny
>
> Santiago." Rev. of <u>Famous All over Town</u>,
>
> by Danny Santiago. <u>New York Review of</u>
>
> <u>Books</u> 16 Aug. 1984: 17-27.

"Rev." is an abbreviation for "Review." The name of the author of
the work being reviewed follows the work's title, a comma, and "by."

29. AN ABSTRACT OF A DISSERTATION

> Steciw, Steven K. "Alterations to the Pessac
>
> Project of Le Corbusier." <u>DAI</u> 46 (1986):
>
> 565C. Cambridge U, England.

For an abstract appearing in *Dissertation Abstracts* (*DA*) or *Dissertation Abstracts International* (*DAI*), give the author's name and the
title as for any article. Then give publication information for the
source and the name of the institution granting the author's degree.

3. Other sources

30. A GOVERNMENT DOCUMENT

> Hawaii. Dept. of Education. <u>Kauai District</u>
>
> <u>Schools, Profile 1983-84</u>. Honolulu: Hawaii
>
> Dept. of Education, 1983.
>
> United States. Cong. House. Committee on Ways
>
> and Means. <u>Medicare Payment for Outpatient</u>
>
> <u>Occupational Therapy Services</u>. 102nd
>
> Cong., 1st sess. Washington: GPO, 1991.

Unless an author is listed for a government document, give the appropriate agency as author. Begin with the name of the government, then the name of the agency (which may be abbreviated), then the title and publication information. For a Congressional document (second example), give the house and committee involved before the title, and give the number and session of Congress after the title. In the second example, "GPO" stands for the U.S. Government Printing Office.

31. A PAMPHLET

Resource Notebook. Washington: Project on

        Institutional Renewal Through the

        Improvement of Teaching, 1976.

Most pamphlets can be treated as books. In the example above, the pamphlet has no listed author, so the title comes first. If the pamphlet has an author, list his or her name first.

32. AN UNPUBLISHED DISSERTATION OR THESIS

Wilson, Stuart M. "John Stuart Mill as a Liter-

        ary Critic." Diss. U of Michigan, 1970.

The title is quoted rather than underlined. "Diss." stands for "Dissertation." "U of Michigan" is the institution that granted the author's degree.

33. A MUSICAL COMPOSITION OR WORK OF ART

Mozart, Wolfgang Amadeus. Piano Concerto no. 20

        in D Minor, K. 466.

Don't underline musical compositions identified only by form, number, and key. Do underline titled operas, ballets, and compositions (Carmen, Sleeping Beauty).

Sargent, John Singer. Venetian Doorway.

        Metropolitan Museum of Art, New York.

Underline the title of a work of art. Include the name and location of the institution housing the work.

34. A FILM OR VIDEOTAPE

Allen, Woody, dir. Manhattan. With Allen,

Diane Keaton, Michael Murphy, Meryl Streep,

and Anne Byrne.   United Artists, 1979.

Start with the name of the individual whose work you are citing. (If you are citing the work as a whole, start with the title, as in the next model.) Give additional information (writer, lead actors, and so on) as seems appropriate. For a film, end with the film's distributor and date.

<u>Serenade</u>.   Videotape.   Chor. George Balanchine.

With San Francisco Ballet.   Dir. Hilary

Bean.   San Francisco Ballet, 1987.   24 min.

For a videotape, filmstrip, or slide program, include the name of the medium after the title, without underlining or quotation marks. Add the running time to the end.

35. A TELEVISION OR RADIO PROGRAM

<u>King of America</u>.   Writ. B. J. Merholz.   Music

Elizabeth Swados.   With Larry Atlas,

Andreas Katsulas, Barry Miller, and Michael

Walden.   American Playhouse.   PBS.   WNET,

New York.   19 Jan. 1982.

Start with the title of the program or the name of the individual whose work you are citing, and provide other participants' names as seems appropriate. Also give the series title (if any), the broadcasting network (if any), and the local station, city, and date.

36. A PERFORMANCE

<u>The English Only Restaurant</u>.   By Silvio Martinez

Palau.   Dir. Susana Tubert.   Puerto Rico

Traveling Theater, New York.   27 July 1990.

Ozawa, Seiji, cond.   Boston Symphony Orch. Con-

cert.   Symphony Hall, Boston.   25 Apr. 1991.

As with films and television programs, place the title first unless you are citing the work of an individual (second example). Provide additional information about participants after the title, as well as the theater, city, and date. Note that the orchestra concert in the second example is neither quoted nor underlined.

37. A RECORDING

Mitchell, Joni. <u>For the Roses</u>. Asylum,

      SD-5057, 1972.

Brahms, Johannes. Concerto no. 2 in B-flat, op.

      83. Perf. Artur Rubinstein. Cond. Eugene

      Ormandy. Philadelphia Orch. RCA, RK-1243,

      1972.

Begin with the name of the individual whose work you are citing. Then provide the title of the recording (first example) or the title of the work recorded (second example), the names of any artists not already listed, the manufacturer of the recording, the catalog number, and the date.

38. A LETTER

Buttolph, Mrs. Laura E. Letter to Rev. and Mrs.

      C. C. Jones. 20 June 1857. In <u>The</u>

      <u>Children of Pride: A True Story of Georgia</u>

      <u>and the Civil War</u>. Ed. Robert Manson

      Myers. New Haven: Yale UP, 1972. 334-35.

A published letter is listed under the writer's name. Specify that the source is a letter and to whom it was addressed, and give the date on which it was written.

Packer, Ann E. Letter to the author. 15 June

      1988.

For a letter you receive, give the name of the writer, note the fact that the letter was sent to you, and provide the date of the letter.

39. A LECTURE OR ADDRESS

Carlone, Dennis J. "Urban Design in the 1990s."

      Sixth Symposium on Urban Issues. City of

      Cambridge. Cambridge, 16 Oct. 1988.

Give the speaker's name, the title if known (in quotation marks), the title of the meeting, the name of the sponsoring organization, the location of the lecture, and the date.

40. AN INTERVIEW

```
Graaf, Vera.  Personal interview.  19 Dec. 1990.

Martin, William.  Interview.  "Give Me That Big

     Time Religion."  Frontline.  PBS.  WGBH,

     Boston.  13 Feb. 1984.
```

Begin with the name of the person interviewed. Then specify "Personal interview" (if you conducted the interview in person), "Telephone interview" (if you conducted the interview over the phone), or "Interview" (if you did not conduct the interview)—without quotation marks or underlining. Finally, provide a date (first example) or provide other bibliographic information and then a date (second example).

41. A MAP OR OTHER ILLUSTRATION

```
Women in the Armed Forces.  Map.  Women in the

     World: An International Atlas.  By Joni

     Seager and Ann Olson.  New York: Touch-

     stone, 1986.  44-45.
```

List the illustration by its title (underlined). Provide a descriptive label ("Map," "Chart," "Table"), without underlining or quotation marks, and the publication information. If the creator of the illustration is credited in the source, put his or her name first in the entry, as with any author.

42. AN INFORMATION OR COMPUTER SERVICE

```
Jolson, Maria K.  Music Education for

     Preschoolers.  ERIC, 1981.  ED 264 488.

Palfry, Andrew.  "Choice of Mates in Identical

     Twins."  Modern Psychology Jan. 1979:

     16-27.  DIALOG file 261, item 5206341.
```

A source you get from an information or computer service should be treated like a book or a periodical article, as appropriate, with

62 Documenting sources: MLA style

the author's name and then the title. If the source has not been
published before, simply name the service (ERIC in the Jolson entry
above), and give the year of release and the service's identifying
number. If the source has been published before, give full publication information and then the name of the service and its identifying
numbers, as in the Palfry entry.

43. COMPUTER SOFTWARE

<u>Project Scheduler 6000</u>. Computer software.

      Scitor, 1991. MS-DOS, 256 KB, disk.

Include the title of the software, the name of the writer (if known),
the name of the distributor, and the date. As in this example, you
may also provide information about the computer or operating system for which the software is designed, the amount of computer
memory it requires, and its format.

49c Examining a sample research paper in MLA style

The sample paper on the next page follows the guidelines of the
MLA Handbook for manuscript format, as outlined in 40a, and for
parenthetical citations and the list of works cited, as outlined in this
chapter. Marginal annotations highlight features of the paper.

Andrea Joseph

English 101

Ms. Diodati

April 19, 1992

Drinking the Pounds Away

"Give us a week, we'll take off the weight" is a familiar jingle advertising the Slim·Fast liquid diet. In our weight-conscious society, liquid-diet programs such as Slim·Fast and Optifast promise quick weight loss with little effort on the dieter's part. But many of these programs fail to emphasize that successful weight loss demands more than drinking a tasty low-calorie shake; it demands a fundamental change in behavior.

When liquid diets were first introduced in the 1970s, they were so deficient nutritionally that they were actually dangerous. But according to Victor Frattali, a nutritionist at the U.S. Food and Drug Administration, manufacturers have now raised calorie levels and use "high-quality protein" (qtd. in Sachs 48). In addition, liquid diets are now divided into two categories: those sold over the counter in drugstores and markets

Writer's name and page number.

Writer's name, course, instructor's name, date.

Title centered.

Double-space throughout.

Thesis sentence.

Background information.

Citation form: indirect source (Frattali quoted by Sachs). Citation falls between quotation mark and sentence period.

Joseph 2

and those supervised by health-care professionals (Simko et al. 231).

Medically supervised programs, such
as Optifast and Medifast, became popular
when the talk-show host Oprah Winfrey
broadcast that she lost sixty-seven pounds
on the Optifast diet (Kirschner et al.
902). The twenty-six-week Optifast regimen
consists of three stages: a fasting period
when patients consume only liquid-protein
shakes providing 420 to 800 calories a
day; a "refeeding" stage when food is
reintroduced into the diet; and a maintenance stage when patients practice eating
sensibly (Beek 56).

Medical supervision and psychological
counseling are crucial parts of the
Optifast program. Before admittance,
patients must pass a physical examination
to ensure that they do not have any conditions that might make the diet dangerous
for them. One such condition, according to
Dr. Thomas A. Wadden, a leading expert on
obesity, is too little body fat, which
could lead the body to consume muscle mass
(including heart muscle) instead of fat
(qtd. in Stocker-Ferguson 55). During the

Citation
form: source
with more
than three
authors.

Discussion of
supervised
programs.

Summary of
source.

Citation
form: author
not named
in the text.

Discussion
of risks of
liquid diets.

Introduction
to a para-
phrase, giv-
ing source's
name and
credentials.

Joseph 3

diet, patients undergo frequent weight
checks and blood and urine tests (Stocker-
Ferguson 57). <u>The Mayo Clinic Diet Manual</u>
notes that unmonitored patients can suffer
dehydration and loss of vital minerals
(Pemberton et al. 190).

Oprah Winfrey's weight loss "provoked
a new frenzy of public interest" in liquid
diets (Kirschner et al. 902), but most
people were medically ineligible for
programs like Optifast. Over-the-counter
liquid diets such as Slim·Fast and Dyna-
trim quickly appeared to meet consumer
demand, and now celebrities speaking for
these products almost guarantee weight
loss. The drinks are indeed easy to
obtain and inexpensive (less than a dollar
a serving), and their packaging makes
losing weight seem effortless. According
to the Slim·Fast instructions, the dieter
can shed one or two pounds per week with a
simple regimen: "Enjoy a Slim·Fast shake
for breakfast, a mid-morning snack,
another shake for lunch, a mid-afternoon
snack . . . , then a satisfying, well-
balanced dinner." Unlike with medically
supervised programs, dieters are not

Paragraph integrates information from two sources to describe risks.

Transition to unsupervised programs.

The writer uses Slim·Fast packaging as a primary source. Her analysis and conclusions are her own unless otherwise acknowledged.

Citation form: no parenthetical citation needed here because the author's name (Slim·Fast) is in the text and the product packaging has no pages.

Joseph 4

required to attend meetings or consult
health-care professionals. Medical supervision is not required because the addition of snacks and regular meals raises the
calorie intake to at least 1200 compared
to Optifast's maximum 800 (Lowe 48).

Citation form: paraphrased source not named in the text.

Although consumers overwhelmingly
support the over-the-counter liquid diets,
some health-care professionals are concerned about how the products are marketed.
Kirschner et al., writing in New Jersey
Medicine, believe that the marketing has
"sensationalized weight loss and deempha-
sized the role of carefully supervised
programs" (902). A can of Slim·Fast shake
mix does post a warning in small type:

Transition to professionals' concerns.

Citation form: author named in the text.

> Slim·Fast shakes should not be
> used as a sole source of nutri-
> tion; eat at least one well-
> balanced meal daily. . . . Any-
> one who is pregnant, nursing,
> has a health problem, is under
> the age of 18, or wants to lose
> more than 15 percent of their
> starting body weight should con-
> sult a physician before starting
> this or any weight loss program.

Quotation over four lines is indented ten spaces and double-spaced.

Joseph 5

But the advertisements for Slim·Fast make **Writer's own analysis.**
the required meal sound like an optional
treat, and they do not advise users to
have a physical exam. Without supervision, dieters might easily under-
eat, losing weight faster than is safe
for anyone, not just the categories of
people listed in the warning (Beek 53).

The insert in a can of Slim·Fast mentions regular exercise and other forms of
behavior modification, but the can label
does not, nor, again, do the advertise-
ments. And the insert actually encourages **Writer's own analysis.**
the use of the product as a crutch: "Behav-
ior modification is a way of learning to
change habits and Slim·Fast can help
you. . . . Drink a satisfying Slim·Fast **Ellipsis mark indicating omission from the quotation.**
shake every day for breakfast or lunch."
This advice shifts the responsibility for
weight loss from the dieter to the product.

Most doctors and nutritionists agree
that the will and effort of the dieter--
especially in changing lifelong eating
habits--are essential for long-term weight
loss (Simko et al. 232). As <u>Newsweek</u>'s
Melinda Beek observes, people who have
followed a liquid diet without behavior

Joseph 6

modification "haven't done anything to improve their eating habits--unless they plan to drink the powder for the rest of their lives" (55).

Indeed, long-term results with Slim· Fast and other liquid diets are poor. One study of dieters on the closely monitored Optifast program found that only 32 per- cent of the patients reached their goal weights, and only 10 percent of these maintained their new weight after eighteen months (Segal 13). (Oprah Winfrey's well- publicized battles with her weight provide anecdotal evidence of the diet's weak- ness.) Dieters using over-the-counter products have even less success at losing pounds and keeping them off (Kirschner et al. 903; Segal 14).

What is the alternative? Two nutritionists offer some simple modi- fications in behavior that can help dieters learn to manage eating:

> Eat only at specified times and
> places; learn to eat more slowly;
> omit other activities, such as
> reading or watching television,

Paragraph integrates evidence from several sources.

Summary of supporting data.

Citation form: two sources.

Question emphasizing transition to behavior modification.

Joseph 7

while eating; use smaller plates
and place portions directly on
the plate rather than serve family style; and use a reward system.   (Robinson and Lawler 481)

Citation form: after displayed quotation, citation follows sentence period and two spaces.

Weight Watchers and some other group
programs combine sensible eating of real
foods (as opposed to shakes and other
substitutes) with counseling in nutrition
and behavior modification. During group
sessions conducted by nutritionists or
therapists, dieters try to identify and
correct unhealthful eating habits. One
Weight Watchers participant, Ann Lorden,
explains that the counseling "helps you
realize what triggers your desire to eat,
other than hunger, so that you can keep
yourself from having food you really don't
want or need."

Primary source: personal interview.

Liquid diets lure consumers with
promises of quick and easy weight loss,
but the formulas are not magic potions
that absorb excess weight. A liquid diet
just lets a person avoid food. Only behavior modification helps a dieter learn
to eat.

Conclusion: sharp contrast between liquid diets and behavior modification.

Joseph **8**

Works Cited

Beek, Melinda. "The Losing Formula."

Newsweek 17 Apr. 1990: 53-58.

Kirschner, M. A., et al. "Responsible

Weight Loss in New Jersey." New Jer-

sey Medicine 87 (1990): 901-04.

Second and
subsequent
lines of each
source are in-
dented five
spaces.

Lorden, Ann. Personal interview. 22

March 1992.

Lowe, Carl. "Diet in a Glass." Health

Oct. 1989: 48-50.

Pemberton, Cecelia M., et al. Mayo Clinic

Diet Manual: A Handbook of Dietary

Practices. 6th ed. Philadelphia:

Decker, 1988.

Robinson, Corrine H., and Marilyn R. Law-

ler. Normal and Therapeutic Nutri-

tion. New York: Macmillan, 1982.

Sachs, Andrea. "Drinking Yourself Skinny."

Time 22 Dec. 1988: 48-49.

Segal, Marian. "Modified Fast: A Sometime

Solution to a Weighty Problem." FDA

Consumer Apr. 1990: 11-15.

Simko, Margaret D., et al. Practical Nutri-

tion: A Quick Reference for Health Care

Practitioners. Rockville: Aspen, 1989.

Slim·Fast Foods. Label and insert with a

```
                              Joseph 8

    can of Slim·Fast powdered mix.  New

    York: Slim·Fast, 1991.

Stocker-Ferguson, Sharon.  "Inside Amer-

    ica's Hottest Diet Programs."  Pre-

    vention Jan. 1990: 53-57.
```

Documenting Sources: APA Style

The documentation style of the American Psychological Association is used in psychology and some other social sciences and is very similar to the styles in sociology, economics, and other disciplines. The following adapts the APA style from the *Publication Manual of the American Psychological Association,* 3rd ed. (1983).

NOTE: The APA style resembles the MLA style (Chapter 49), but there are important differences. For instance, APA parenthetical citations include the date of publication, whereas MLA citations do not. Don't confuse the two styles.

50a Writing APA parenthetical citations

In the APA style, parenthetical citations in the text refer to a list of sources at the end of the text. The basic parenthetical citation contains the author's last name, the date of publication, and often the page number from which material is borrowed.

1. AUTHOR NOT NAMED IN THE TEXT

```
One critic of Milgram's experiments insisted

that the subjects should have been fully
```

Index to APA parenthetical citations

```
informed of the possible effects on them

(Baumrind, 1968, p. 34).
```

When you do not name the author in your text, place in parentheses the author's name, the date of the source, and the page number(s) preceded by "p." or "pp." Separate the elements with commas. Position the reference so that it is clear what material is being documented *and* so that the reference fits as smoothly as possible into your sentence structure.

2. AUTHOR NAMED IN THE TEXT

```
Baumrind (1968, p. 34) insisted that the

subjects in Milgram's study should have been

fully informed of the possible effects on them.
```

When you use the author's name in the text, do not repeat it in the reference. Position the reference next to the author's name. If you cite the same source again in the paragraph, you need not repeat the reference as long as the page number (if any) is the same and it is clear that you are using the same source.

3. A WORK WITH TWO AUTHORS

```
Pepinsky and DeStefano (1977) demonstrate that a

teacher's language often reveals hidden biases.

One study (Pepinsky & DeStefano, 1977) demon-

strated hidden biases in teachers' language.
```

When given in the text, two authors' names are connected by "and." In a parenthetical citation, they are connected by an ampersand, "&."

4. A WORK WITH THREE TO SIX AUTHORS

```
Pepinsky, Dunn, Rentl, and Corson (1973) further

demonstrated the biases evident in gestures.
```

In the first citation of a work with three to six authors, name all the authors, as in the example above. In the second and subsequent references to the work, give only the first author's name, followed by "et al." (Latin for "and others"):

```
In the work of Pepinsky et al. (1973), the

loaded gestures included head shakes and eye

contact.
```

5. A WORK WITH MORE THAN SIX AUTHORS

```
One study (Rutter et al., 1976) attempts to

explain these geographical differences in

adolescent experience.
```

For more than six authors, even in the first citation of the work, give only the first author's name, followed by "et al."

6. A WORK WITH A CORPORATE AUTHOR

```
An earlier prediction was even more somber

(Lorenz, Inc., 1970).
```

For a work with a corporate or group author, treat the name of the corporation or group as if it were an individual's name.

7. AN ANONYMOUS WORK

```
One article ("Right to Die," 1976) noted that a

death-row inmate may crave notoriety.
```

For an anonymous or unsigned work, use the first two or three words of the title in place of an author's name, excluding an initial *The, A,* or *An.* Underline book and journal titles. Place quotation marks around article titles. (In the list of references, however, do not use quotation marks for article titles. See pp. 248–49.) Capitalize the significant words in all titles cited in the text. (But in the reference list, treat only journal titles this way. See pp. 248–49.)

8. ONE OF TWO OR MORE WORKS BY THE SAME AUTHOR(S)

```
At about age seven, most children begin to use
appropriate gestures to reinforce their stories
(Gardner, 1973a, pp. 144-145).
```

If your reference list includes two or more works published by the same author(s) *in the same year*, the works should be lettered in the reference list (see p. 247). Then your parenthetical citation should include the appropriate letter, as here.

9. TWO OR MORE WORKS BY DIFFERENT AUTHORS

```
Two studies (Herskowitz, 1974; Marconi & Hamblen,
1980) found that periodic safety instruction
can dramatically reduce employees' accidents.
```

List the sources in alphabetical order by the first author's name. Insert a semicolon between sources.

10. AN INDIRECT SOURCE

```
Supporting data appear in a study by Wong (cited
in Marconi & Hamblen, 1980).
```

The phrase "cited in" indicates that the reference to Wong's study was found in Marconi and Hamblen. You are obliged to acknowledge that you did not consult the original source (Wong) yourself. In the list of references, give only Marconi and Hamblen.

50b   Preparing the APA reference list

In APA style, the in-text parenthetical citations refer to the list of sources at the end of the text. This list, titled "References," includes full publication information on every source cited in the paper. The sources are arranged alphabetically by the author's last name or, if there is no author, by the first main word of the title. (See the sample reference list on p. 259.) In the models that follow for various sources, observe these features:

Index to APA references

- ❖ Double-space all entries. Type the first line of each entry at the left margin, and indent all subsequent lines three spaces.
- ❖ List all authors last-name first, separating names and parts of names with commas. Use initials for first and middle names. Use an ampersand (&) rather than "and" before the last author's name.
- ❖ In titles of books and articles, capitalize only the first word of the title, the first word of the subtitle, and proper names; all other words begin with small letters. In titles of journals, capitalize all significant words. Underline the titles of books and journals. Do not underline or use quotation marks around the titles of articles.
- ❖ Give full names of publishers, excluding "Co.," "Inc.," and the like.
- ❖ Use the abbreviation "p." or "pp." before page numbers in books, magazines, and newspapers, but *not* for scholarly journals. For inclusive page numbers, include all figures: "667–668."

❖ Separate the parts of the reference (author, date, title, and publication information) with a period and two spaces.

NOTE: You may have to combine models to provide the necessary information on a source—for instance, combining "A book with one author" (1) and "A book with an editor" (3) for a book with only one editor.

1. A BOOK WITH ONE AUTHOR

Rodriguez, R. (1982). <u>A hunger of memory: The education of Richard Rodriguez</u>. Boston: David R. Godine.

The initial "R" appears instead of the author's first name, even though the author's full first name appears on the source. In the title, only the first words of title and subtitle and the proper name are capitalized.

2. A BOOK WITH TWO OR MORE AUTHORS

Nesselroade, J. R., & Baltes, P. B. (1979). <u>Longitudinal research in the study of behavioral development</u>. New York: Academic Press.

An ampersand (&) separates the authors' names.

3. A BOOK WITH AN EDITOR

Dohrenwend, B. S., & Dohrenwend, B. P. (Eds.). (1974). <u>Stressful life events: Their nature and effects</u>. New York: John Wiley.

List the editors' names as if they were authors, but follow the last name with "(Eds.)."—or "(Ed.)." with only one editor. Note the periods inside and outside the final parenthesis.

4. A BOOK WITH A TRANSLATOR

Trajan, P. D. (1927). <u>Psychology of animals</u>. (H. Simone, Trans.). Washington, DC: Halperin & Bros.

The name of the translator appears in parentheses after the title,

followed by a comma, "Trans.," a closing parenthesis, and a final
period.

5. A BOOK WITH A CORPORATE AUTHOR

Lorenz, Inc. (1992). <u>Research in social</u>

   <u>studies teaching</u>. Baltimore: Arrow Books.

For a work with a corporate or group author, begin the entry with
the corporate or group name. In the reference list, alphabetize the
work as if the first main word (excluding *The, A,* and *An*) were an
author's last name.

6. AN ANONYMOUS BOOK

<u>Webster's seventh new collegiate dictionary</u>.

   (1963). Springfield: G. & C. Merriam.

When no author is named, list the work under its title, and alphabetize it by the first main word (excluding *The, A, An*).

7. TWO OR MORE WORKS BY THE SAME AUTHOR(S)

Gardner, H. (1973a). <u>The arts and human</u>

   <u>development</u>. New York: John Wiley.

Gardner, H. (1973b). <u>The quest for mind:</u>

   <u>Piaget, Lévi-Strauss, and the structuralist</u>

   <u>movement</u>. New York: Alfred A. Knopf.

When citing two or more works by exactly the same author(s), arrange the sources in order of their publication dates, earliest first.
When citing two or more works by exactly the same author(s), published in the same year—as in the examples above—arrange them
alphabetically by the first main word of the title and distinguish the
sources by adding a letter to the date. Both the date *and* the letter
are used in citing the source in the text (see p. 244).

8. A LATER EDITION

Bollinger, D. L. (1975). <u>Aspects of language</u>

   (2nd ed.). New York: Harcourt Brace Jovano-

   vich.

The edition number in parentheses follows the title and is followed by a period.

9. **A WORK IN MORE THAN ONE VOLUME**

```
Lincoln, A.  (1953).  The collected works of

    Abraham Lincoln (R. P. Basler, Ed.).  (Vol.

    5).  New Brunswick: Rutgers University Press.

Lincoln, A.  (1953).  The collected works of

    Abraham Lincoln (R. P. Basler, Ed.).  (Vols.

    1-8).  New Brunswick: Rutgers University

    Press.
```

The first entry cites a single volume (5) in the eight-volume set. The second cites all eight volumes. In the absence of an editor's name, the description of volumes would follow the title directly: "The collected works of Abraham Lincoln (Vol. 5)."

10. **AN ARTICLE OR CHAPTER IN AN EDITED BOOK**

```
Paykel, E. S.  (1974).  Life stress and

    psychiatric disorder: Applications of the

    clinical approach.  In B. S. Dohrenwend &

    B. P. Dohrenwend (Eds.), Stressful life

    events: Their nature and effects (pp. 239-

    264).  New York: John Wiley.
```

Give the publication date of the collection (1974) as the publication date of the article or chapter. After the word "In" use model 3 (p. 246) for an edited book, but add the page numbers of the cited selection after the book title.

11. **AN ARTICLE IN A JOURNAL WITH CONTINUOUS PAGINATION THROUGHOUT THE ANNUAL VOLUME**

```
Emery, R. E.  (1982).  Marital turmoil: Inter-

    personal conflict and the children of

    discord and divorce.  Psychological Bulletin,

    92, 310-330.
```

Some journals page all issues of an annual volume consecutively, so that issue 3 may begin on page 261. For these journals, include only the volume number, underlined and separated from the title by a comma. No "pp." precedes the page numbers.

12. AN ARTICLE IN A JOURNAL THAT PAGES ISSUES SEPARATELY

Boyd, S. (1981). Nuclear terror. Adaptation

  to Change, 7(4), 20-23.

For journals that page issues separately (each beginning with page 1), give the issue number in parentheses immediately after the volume number. The issue number is *not* underlined.

13. AN ARTICLE IN A MAGAZINE

Van Gelder, L. (1986, December). Countdown to

  motherhood: When should you have a baby?

  Ms., pp. 37-39, 74.

In the absence of a volume number, give the month of publication after the year and a comma. Give all page numbers even when the article appears on discontinuous pages. Use "pp." before the page numbers.

14. AN ARTICLE IN A NEWSPAPER

Herbers, J. (1988, March 6). A different

  Dixie: Few but sturdy threads tie new South

  to old. The New York Times, sec. 4, p. 1.

Give month *and* date along with year of publication. Use The in the newspaper name if the paper itself does.

15. AN UNSIGNED ARTICLE

The right to die. (1976, October 11). Time, p.

  101.

List and alphabetize the article under its title, as you would an anonymous book (model 6, p. 247).

16. A REVIEW

Dinnage, R. (1987, November 29). Against the

master and his men. [Review of A mind of her

own: The life of Karen Horney]. The New York

Times Book Review, pp. 10-11.

If the review is not titled, use the bracketed information as the title, keeping the brackets.

17. A REPORT

Gerald, K. (1958). Micro-moral problems in

obstetric care (Report No. NP-71). St.

Louis: Catholic Hospital Association.

Treat the report like a book, but provide any report number in parentheses after the title, with no punctuation between them.

18. AN INFORMATION SERVICE

Jolson, Maria K. (1981). Music education for

preschoolers. New York: Teachers College,

Columbia University. (ERIC Document Repro-

duction Service No. ED 264 488)

Place the name of the service and the document number in parentheses after the original publisher and a period. No period follows the number.

19. A GOVERNMENT DOCUMENT

United States Commission on Civil Rights.

(1983). Greater Baltimore commitment.

Washington DC: Author.

If no individual is listed as author, list the document under the name of the sponsoring agency. When the agency is both the author and the publisher, use "Author" in place of the publisher's name.

20. AN INTERVIEW

William C. Brisick. (1988, July 1). [Interview

with Ishmael Reed]. Publishers Weekly,

pp. 41-42.

List a published interview under the interviewer's name. Provide the publication information appropriate for the kind of source the interview appears in (here, a magazine). Immediately after the title (if any), specify in brackets that the piece is an interview and, if necessary, provide other identifying information.

Note that interviews you conduct yourself are not included in the list of references. Instead, use an in-text parenthetical citation: if the subject is already named, "(personal communication, July 7, 1991)"; if not, "(L. Kogod, personal communication, July 7, 1991)."

21. A VIDEOTAPE OR OTHER NONPRINT SOURCE

Heeley, D. (Director), & Kramer, J. (Producer).

(1988). <u>Bacall on Bogart</u> [Videotape]. New

York: WNET Films.

The names of major contributors are followed by parenthetical designation of their function. The medium is specified in brackets after the title, with no intervening punctuation. Other nonprint sources include films, slides, art works, and musical performances.

22. COMPUTER SOFTWARE

<u>Project scheduler 6000</u>. (1991). [Computer

program]. Orlando: Scitor.

If no individual is given as author, list the software under its title. Identify the entry as a "Computer program" in brackets, add a period, and provide the name of the producer. If there is a catalog or other reference number, give it at the end of the entry, as in model 18.

50c Examining a sample research paper in APA style

The following excerpts from a sociology paper illustrate elements of a research paper using APA documentation style.

❖ The title page, abstract, opening of the paper, and reference list should all begin on new pages.
❖ The paper is double-spaced throughout.
❖ Pages are numbered consecutively, starting with the title page. Each page (including the title page) is identified by a shortened version of the title as well as a page number.

❖ Different levels of headings are distinct: the title and main headings are centered and are not underlined; subheadings begin at the left margin and are underlined.

[New page.]

Dating Violence

1

Heading: shortened title and page number

An Assessment of

Dating Violence on Campus

Karen M. Tarczyk

Sociology 213

Mr. Durkan

May 6, 1990

Title page: copy centered vertically and horizontally, double-spaced.

[New page.]

Dating Violence

2

Abstract

Little research has examined the patterns of abuse and violence occurring within couples during courtship. With a questionnaire administered to a sample of college students, the extent and nature of such abuse and violence were investigated. The results, some interpretations, and implications for further research are discussed.

Abstract: summary of subject, research method, conclusions. Heading centered. Double-space.

[New page.]

Dating Violence

Double-space throughout.

3

An Assessment of

Dating Violence on Campus

Title repeated on first text page.

In recent years, a great deal of attention has been devoted to family violence.
Numerous studies have been done on spouse
and child abuse. However, violent behavior
occurs in dating relationships as well.
The problem of dating violence has been relatively ignored by sociological research.
It should be examined further since the
premarital relationship is one context in
which individuals learn and adopt behaviors that surface later in marriage.

Introduction: presentation of the problem researched by the writer.

The sociologist James Makepeace
(1979) contends that courtship violence is
a "potential mediating link" between
violence in one's family of orientation
and violence in one's later family of
procreation (p. 103). His provocative study
examining dating behaviors at Bemidji
State University in Minnesota caused a
controversy. Makepeace reported that one-
fifth of the respondents had had at least
one encounter with dating violence. He concluded by extending these percentages to

Citation form: author named in the text followed by date; combined quotation and paraphrase followed by page number.

Dating Violence

4

students nationwide, suggesting the existence of a major hidden social problem.

Supporting Makepeace's research,
another study found that 22.3% of respondents at Oregon State University had
been either the victim or the perpetrator
of premarital violence (Cates, Rutter,
Karl, Linton, & Smith, 1982). In addition, in over one-half of the cases,
the abuse was reciprocal. Cates et al.
concluded that premarital violence was a
problem of "abusive relationships" as well
as "abusive individuals" (p. 90).

[The introduction continues.]

All these studies indicate a problem
that is being neglected. The present
study's objective was to gather information on the extent and nature of
premarital violence and to discuss some
possible interpretations.

Method

Sample

I conducted a survey of 200 students
(134 females, 66 males) at a large state
university in the northeast United States.

Citation form: authors not named in the text; all authors named for first citation.

Citation form: after first citation of multiple authors, "et al." is used.

Objective of the study being reported.

Main heading.

Subheading.

"Method" section: how writer conducted her own research (primary source).

Dating Violence

5

The sample consisted of students enrolled
in an introductory sociology course.
[The explanation of method continues.]

The Questionnaire

A questionnaire exploring the
personal dynamics of relationships was
distributed during regularly scheduled
class. Questions were answered anon-
ymously in a 30-minute time period.
The survey consisted of three sections.
[The explanation of method continues.]

Section 3 required participants to
provide information about their current
dating relationships. Levels of stress
and frustration, communication between
partners, and patterns of decision making
were examined. These variables were
expected to influence the amount of
violence in a relationship. The next part
of the survey was adopted from Murray
Strauss's Conflict Tactics Scales (1982).
These scales contain 19 items designed to
measure conflict and the means of conflict
resolution, including reasoning, verbal
aggression, and actual violence. The

final page of the questionnaire contained
general questions on the couple's use of
alcohol, sexual activity, and overall
satisfaction with the relationship.

Results

The incidence of verbal aggression
and threatened and actual dating violence
was examined. A high number of students,
50% (62 of 123 subjects), reported that
they had been the victim of verbal abuse,
either being insulted or sworn at. In
addition, 14% (17 of 123) of respondents
admitted being threatened with some type
of violence. Low percentages were
reported for the various types of actual
physical violence. (See Table 1.)

[The explanation of results continues.]

"Results" section: summary and presentation of data.

Discussion

Violence within premarital relationships has been relatively ignored. The results of the present study indicate that
abuse and force do occur in dating relationships. Although the percentages are small,
so was the sample. Extending them to the
entire campus population would mean significant numbers. For example, if the 6% inci-

"Discussion" section: interpretation of data and presentation of conclusions.

Table 1

Incidence of Courtship Violence

Type of violence	Number of students reporting	Percentage of sample
Insulted or swore	62	50.4
Threatened to hit or throw something	17	13.8
Threw something	8	6.6
Pushed, grabbed, or shoved	18	14.9
Slapped	8	6.6
Kicked, bit, or hit with fist	7	6.0
Hit or tried to hit with something	2	1.6
Threatened with a knife or gun	1	0.8
Used a knife or gun	1	0.8

dence of being kicked, bitten, or hit with
a fist is typical, then 300 students of a
5,000-member student body might have experienced this type of violence.
[The discussion continues.]

If the courtship period is char-
acterized by abuse and violence, what
accounts for it? The other sections of
the survey examined some variables that
appear to influence the relationship.
Level of stress and frustration, both
within the relationship and in the
respondent's life, was one such variable.
The communication level between partners,
both the frequency of discussion and the
frequency of agreement, was another.
[The discussion continues.]

The method of analyzing the data in
this study, utilizing frequency distribu-
tions, provided a clear overview. However,
more tests of significance and correlation
and a closer look at the social and individual variables affecting the relationship
are warranted. The courtship period may
set the stage for patterns of married life.
It merits more attention.

Dating Violence New page for reference list.

8

References

Heading centered.

Cates, R. L., Rutter, C. H., Karl, J.,
    Linton, M., & Smith, K. (1982). Pre-
    marital abuse: A social psychological
    perspective. Journal of Family Issues,
    3(1), 79-90.

Glaser, R., and Rutter, C. H. (Eds.).
    (1984). Familial violence [Special
    issue]. Family Relations, 33(3).

Laner, M. (1983). Recent increases in
    dating violence. Social Problems, 22,
    152-166.

Makepeace, J. M. (1979). Courtship
    violence among college students.
    Family Relations, 30, 97-103.

Socko performance on campus. (1981, June
    7). Time, pp. 66-67.

Strauss, M. L. (1982). Conflict tactics
    scales. New York: Sociological Tests.

Sources are alphabetized by authors' last names.

Double-space throughout.

Second and subsequent lines of each source are indented three spaces.

Glossary of Usage

This glossary provides notes on words or phrases that often cause problems for writers. The recommendations for standard written English are based on current dictionaries and usage guides. Items labeled NONSTANDARD should be avoided in speech and especially in writing. Those labeled COLLOQUIAL and SLANG occur in speech and in some informal writing but are best avoided in the more formal writing usually expected in college and business. (Words and phrases labeled *colloquial* include those labeled by many dictionaries with the equivalent term *informal.*)

a, an   Use *a* before words beginning with consonant sounds, including those spelled with an initial pronounced *h* and those spelled with vowels that are sounded as consonants: *a historian, a one-o'clock class, a university.* Use *an* before words that begin with vowel sounds, including those spelled with an initial silent *h: an orgy, an L, an honor.*

The article before an abbreviation depends on how the abbreviation is to be read: *She was once an HEW undersecretary* (*HEW* is to be read as three separate letters, and *h* is pronounced "aitch"). *Many Americans opposed a SALT treaty* (*SALT* is to be read as one word, *salt*).

See also 28f on the uses of *a, an,* and *the.*

accept, except   *Accept* is a verb meaning "receive." *Except* is usually a preposition or conjunction meaning "but for" or "other than"; when it is used as a verb, it means "leave out." *I can accept all your suggestions except the last one. I'm sorry you excepted my last suggestion from your list.*

advice, advise   *Advice* is a noun, and *advise* is a verb: *Take my advice; do as I advise you.*

affect, effect   Usually *affect* is a verb, meaning "to influence," and *effect* is a noun, meaning "result": *The drug did not affect his driving; in fact, it seemed to have no effect at all.* But *effect* occasionally is used as a verb meaning "to bring about": *Her efforts effected a change.* And *affect* is used in psychology as a noun meaning "feeling or emotion": *One can infer much about affect from behavior.*

agree to, agree with   *Agree to* means "consent to," and *agree with* means "be in accord with": *How can they agree to a treaty when they don't agree with each other about the terms?*

all ready, already   *All ready* means "completely prepared," and *already* means "by now" or "before now": *We were all ready to go to the movie, but it had already started.*

all right   *All right* is always two words. *Alright* is a common misspelling.

all together, altogether   *All together* means "in unison," or "gathered in one place." *Altogether* means "entirely." *It's not altogether true that our family never spends vacations all together.*

allusion, illusion   An *allusion* is an indirect reference, and an *illusion* is a deceptive appearance: *Paul's constant allusions to Shakespeare created the illusion that he was an intellectual.*

almost, most   *Almost* is an adverb meaning "nearly"; *most* is an adjective meaning "the greater number (or part) of." In formal writing, *most* should not be used as a substitute for *almost: We see each other almost* (not *most*) *every day.*

a lot   *A lot* is always two words, used informally to mean "many." *Alot* is a common misspelling.

among, between   In general, *among* is used for relationships involving more than two people or for comparing one thing to a group to which it belongs. *The four of them agreed among themselves that the choice was between New York and Los Angeles.*

amount, number   *Amount* refers to a quantity of something (a singular noun) that cannot be counted. *Number* refers to countable items (a plural noun). *The amount of tax depends on the number of deductions.*

and/or   *And/or* is awkward and often confusing. A sentence such as *The decision is made by the mayor and/or the council* implies that one or the other or both make the decision. If you mean both, use *and;* if you mean either, use *or.* Use *and/or* only when you mean three options.

ante-, anti-   The prefix *ante-* means "before" (*antedate, antebellum*); *anti-* means "against" (*antiwar, antinuclear*). Before a capital letter or *i, anti-* takes a hyphen: *anti-Freudian, anti-isolationist.*

anxious, eager   *Anxious* means "nervous" or "worried" and is usually followed by *about. Eager* means "looking forward" and is usually followed by *to. I've been anxious about getting blisters. I'm eager* (not *anxious*) *to get new running shoes.*

anybody, any body; anyone, any one   *Anybody* and *anyone* are indefinite pronouns; *any body* is a noun modified by an adjective; *any one* is a pronoun or adjective modified by *any. How can anybody communicate with any body of government? Can anyone help Amy? She has more work than any one person can handle.*

any more, anymore   *Any more* is used in negative constructions to mean "no more." *Anymore,* an adverb meaning "now," is also used in negative constructions. *He doesn't want any more. She doesn't live here anymore.*

anyplace   Colloquial for *anywhere.*

anyways, anywheres   Nonstandard for *anyway* and *anywhere.*

apt, liable, likely   *Apt* and *likely* are interchangeable. Strictly speaking, though, *apt* means "having a tendency to": *Horace is apt to forget his lunch in the morning. Likely* means "probably going to": *Horace is leaving so early today that he's likely to catch the first bus.*

   Liable normally means "in danger of" and should be confined to situations with undesirable consequences: *Horace is liable to trip over that hose.* Strictly, *liable* means "responsible" or "exposed to": *The owner will be liable for Horace's injuries.*

as   Substituting for *because, since,* or *while, as* may be vague or ambiguous: *As we were stopping to rest, we decided to eat lunch.* (Does *as* mean "while" or "because"?) Usually a more precise word is preferable.

   As never should be used as a substitute for *whether* or *who. I'm not sure whether* (not *as*) *we can make it. That's the man who* (not *as*) *gave me directions.*

as, like   In formal speech and writing, *as* may be either a preposition or a conjunction; *like* functions as a preposition only. Thus, if the construction being introduced is a full clause rather than a word or phrase, the preferred choice is *as* or *as if*: *The plan succeeded as* (not *like*) *we hoped. It seemed as if* (not *like*) *it might fail. Other plans like it have failed.*

as, than   In comparisons, *as* and *than* may be followed by either subjective- or objective-case pronouns: *You are as tall as he* (subjective). *They treated you better than him* (objective). The case depends on whether the pronoun is the subject or object of a verb: *I love you more than he* (*loves you*). *I love you more than* (*I love*) *him.* See also 25d.

assure, ensure, insure   *Assure* means "to promise": *He assured us that we would miss the traffic. Ensure* and *insure* often are used interchangeably to mean "make certain," but some reserve *insure* for matters of legal and financial protection and use *ensure* for more general meanings: *We left early to ensure that we would miss the traffic. It's expensive to insure yourself against floods.*

at   The use of *at* after *where* is wordy and should be avoided: *Where are you meeting him?* is preferable to *Where are you meeting him at?*

at this point in time   Wordy for *now, at this point,* or *at this time.*

awful, awfully   Strictly speaking, *awful* means "awe-inspiring." As intensifiers meaning "very" or "extremely" (*He tried awfully hard*), *awful* and *awfully* should be avoided in formal speech or writing.

a while, awhile   *Awhile* is an adverb; *a while* is an article and a noun. *I will be gone awhile* (not *a while*). *I will be gone for a while* (not *awhile*).

bad, badly   In formal speech and writing, *bad* should be used only as an adjective; the adverb is *badly. He felt bad because his tooth ached badly.* In *He felt bad,* the verb *felt* is a linking verb and the adjective *bad* is a subject complement. See also 28b.

being as, being that   Colloquial for *because,* the preferable word in formal speech or writing: *Because* (not *Being as*) *the world is round, Columbus never did fall off the edge.*

beside, besides   *Beside* is a preposition meaning "next to." *Besides* is a preposition meaning "except" or "in addition to" as well as an adverb meaning "in addition." *Besides, several other people besides you want to sit beside Dr. Christensen.*

better, had better   *Had better* (meaning "ought to") is a verb modified by an adverb. The verb is necessary and should not be omitted: *You had better* (not *better) go.*

between, among   See *among, between.*

bring, take   Use *bring* only for movement from a farther place to a nearer one and *take* for any other movement. *First, take these books to the library for renewal, then take them to Mr. Daniels. Bring them back to me when he's finished.*

but, hardly, scarcely   These words are negative in their own right; using *not* with any of them produces a double negative (see 28d). *We have but* (not *haven't got but*) *an hour before our plane leaves. I could hardly* (not *couldn't hardly*) *make out her face.*

but, however, yet   Each of these words is adequate to express contrast. Don't combine them. *He said he had finished, yet* (not *but yet*) *he continued.*

can, may   Strictly, *can* indicates capacity or ability, and *may* indicates permission: *If I may talk with you a moment, I believe I can solve your problem.*

censor, censure   To *censor* is to edit or remove from public view on moral or some other grounds; to *censure* is to give a formal scolding. *The lieutenant was censured by Major Taylor for censoring the letters his soldiers wrote home from boot camp.*

center around   *Center on* is more logical than, and preferable to, *center around.*

climatic, climactic   *Climatic* comes from *climate* and refers to weather: *Last winter's temperatures may indicate a climatic change. Climactic* comes from *climax* and refers to a dramatic high point: *During the climactic duel between Hamlet and Laertes, Gertrude drinks poisoned wine.*

complement, compliment   To *complement* something is to add to, complete, or reinforce it: *Her yellow blouse complemented her black hair.* To *compliment* something is to make a flattering remark about it: *He complimented her on her hair. Complimentary* can also mean "free": *complimentary tickets.*

conscience, conscious   *Conscience* is a noun meaning "a sense of right and wrong"; *conscious* is an adjective meaning "aware" or "awake." *Though I was barely conscious, my conscience nagged me.*

contact   Often used imprecisely as a verb instead of a more exact word such as *consult, talk with, telephone,* or *write to.*

continual, continuous   *Continual* means "constantly recurring": *Most movies on television are continually interrupted by commercials. Continuous* means "unceasing": *Cable television often presents movies continuously without commercials.*

could of   See *have, of.*

credible, creditable, credulous   *Credible* means "believable": *It's a strange story, but it seems credible to me. Creditable* means "deserving of credit" or "worthy": *Steve gave a creditable performance. Credulous* means "gullible": *The credulous Claire believed Tim's lies.* See also *incredible, incredulous.*

criteria   The plural of *criterion* (meaning "standard for judgment"): *Of all our criteria for picking a roommate, the most important criterion is a sense of humor.*

data   The plural of *datum* (meaning "fact"). Though *data* is often used as a singular noun, most careful writers still treat it as plural: *The data fail* (not *fails*) *to support the hypothesis.*

device, devise   *Device* is the noun, and *devise* is the verb: *Can you devise some device for getting his attention?*

differ from, differ with   To *differ from* is to be unlike: *The twins differ from each other only in their hairstyles.* To *differ with* is to disagree with: *I have to differ with you on that point.*

different from, different than   *Different from* is preferred: *His purpose is different from mine.* But *different than* is widely accepted when a construction using *from* would be wordy: *I'm a different person now than I used to be* is preferable to *I'm a different person now from the person I used to be.*

discreet, discrete   *Discreet* (noun form *discretion*) means "tactful": *What's a discreet way of telling Maud to be quiet? Discrete* (noun form *discreteness*) means "separate and distinct": *Within a computer's memory are millions of discrete bits of information.*

disinterested, uninterested   *Disinterested* means "impartial": *We chose Pete, as a disinterested third party, to decide who was right. Uninterested* means "bored" or "lacking interest": *Unfortunately, Pete was completely uninterested in the question.*

don't   *Don't* is the contraction for *do not,* not for *does not: I don't care, you don't care,* but *he doesn't* (not *don't*) *care.*

due to   *Due* is an adjective or noun; thus *due to* is always acceptable as a subject complement: *His gray hairs were due to age.* Many object to *due to* as a preposition meaning "because of" (*Due to the holiday, class was canceled*). A rule of thumb is that *due to* is always correct after a form of the verb *be* but questionable otherwise.

due to the fact that   Wordy for *because.*

eager, anxious   See *anxious, eager.*

effect   See *affect, effect.*

elicit, illicit   *Elicit* is a verb meaning "bring out" or "call forth." *Illicit* is an adjective meaning "unlawful." *The crime elicited an outcry against illicit drugs.*

ensure   See *assure, ensure, insure.*

enthused   Used colloquially as an adjective meaning "showing enthusiasm." The preferred adjective is *enthusiastic: The coach was enthusiastic* (not *enthused*) *about the team's victory.*

et al., etc.   *Et al.,* the Latin abbreviation for "and other people," is often used in source references for works with more than three authors: *Jones et al. Etc.,* the Latin abbreviation for "and other things," should be avoided in formal writing and should not be used to refer to people. When used, it should not substitute for precision, as in *The government provides health care, etc.*

everybody, every body; everyone, every one   *Everybody* and *everyone* are indefinite pronouns: *Everybody* (*everyone*) *knows Tom steals. Every one* is a pronoun modified by *every,* and *every body* a noun modified by *every.* Both refer to each thing or person of a specific group and are typically followed by *of: The game commissioner has stocked every body of fresh water in the state with fish, and now every one of our rivers is a potential trout stream.*

everyday, every day   *Everyday* is an adjective meaning "used daily" or "common"; *every day* is a noun modified by *every: Everyday problems tend to arise every day.*

everywheres   Nonstandard for *everywhere.*

except   See *accept, except.*

except for the fact that   Wordy for *except that.*

explicit, implicit   *Explicit* means "stated outright": *I left explicit instructions. Implicit* means "implied, unstated": *We had an implicit understanding.*

farther, further   *Farther* refers to additional distance (*How much farther is it to the beach?*), and *further* refers to additional time, amount, or other abstract matters (*I don't want to discuss this any further*).

fewer, less   *Fewer* refers to individual countable items (a plural noun), *less* to general amounts (a singular noun): *Skim milk has fewer calories than whole milk. We have less milk left than I thought.*

flaunt, flout   *Flaunt* means "show off": *If you have style, flaunt it. Flout* means "scorn" or "defy": *Hester Prynne flouted convention and paid the price.*

flunk   A colloquial substitute for *fail.*

fun   As an adjective, *fun* is colloquial and should be avoided in most writing: *It was a pleasurable* (not *fun*) *evening.*

further   See *farther, further.*

get   This common verb is used in many slang and colloquial expressions: *get lost, that really gets me, getting on. Get* is easy to overuse; watch out for it in expressions such as *it's getting better* (substitute *improving*) and *we got done* (substitute *finished*).

good, well   *Good* is an adjective, and *well* is nearly always an adverb: *Larry's a good dancer. He and Linda dance well together. Well* is properly used as an adjective only to refer to health: *You don't look well. Aren't you feeling well?* (*You look good*, in contrast, means "Your appearance is pleasing.")

good and   Colloquial for "very": *I was very* (not *good and*) *tired.*

had better   See *better, had better.*

had ought   The *had* is unnecessary and should be omitted: *He ought* (not *had ought*) *to listen to his mother.*

hanged, hung   Though both are past-tense forms of *hang, hanged* is used to refer to executions and *hung* is used for all other meanings: *Tom Dooley was hanged* (not *hung*) *from a white oak tree. I hung* (not *hanged*) *the picture you gave me.*

hardly   See *but, hardly, scarcely.*

have, of   Use *have*, not *of*, after helping verbs such as *could, should, would, may*, and *might*: *You should have* (not *should of*) *told me.*

he, she; he/she   Convention has allowed the use of *he* to mean "he or she": *After the infant learns to creep, he progresses to crawling.* However, many people today object to this use of *he* because readers tend to think of *he* as male, whether or not that is the writer's intention. The construction *he/she*, one substitute for *he*, is awkward and objectionable to most readers. The better choice is to use *he or she*, to make the pronoun plural, or to rephrase. For instance: *After the* *infant learns to creep, he or she progresses to crawling. After infants learn to creep, they progress to crawling. After learning to creep, the infant progresses to crawling.* See also 12a-6 and 26c.

herself, himself   See *myself, herself, himself, yourself.*

hisself   Nonstandard for *himself.*

hopefully   *Hopefully* means "with hope": *Freddy waited hopefully for a glimpse of Eliza.* The use of *hopefully* to mean "it is to be hoped," "I hope," or "let's hope" is now very common; but since many readers continue to object strongly to the usage, you should avoid it. *I hope* (not *Hopefully*) *Eliza will be here soon.*

idea, ideal   An *idea* is a thought or conception. An *ideal* (noun) is a model of perfection or a goal. *Ideal* should not be used in place of *idea: The idea* (not *ideal*) *of the play is that our ideals often sustain us.*

if, whether   For clarity, begin a subordinate clause with *whether* rather than *if* when the clause expresses an alternative: *If I laugh hard, people can't tell whether I'm crying.*

illicit   See *elicit, illicit.*

illusion   See *allusion, illusion.*

implicit   See *explicit, implicit.*

imply, infer   Writers or speakers *imply,* meaning "suggest": *Jim's letter implies he's having a good time.* Readers or listeners *infer,* meaning "conclude": *From Jim's letter I infer he's having a good time.*

incredible, incredulous   *Incredible* means "unbelievable"; *incredulous* means "unbelieving": *When Nancy heard Dennis's incredible story, she was frankly incredulous.* See also *credible, creditable, credulous.*

individual, person, party   *Individual* should refer to a single human being in contrast to a group or should stress uniqueness: *The U.S. Constitution places strong emphasis on the rights of the individual.* For other meanings *person* is preferable: *What person* (not *individual*) *wouldn't want the security promised in that advertisement? Party* means "group" (*Can you seat a party of four for dinner?*) and should not be used to refer to an individual except in legal documents.

infer   See *imply, infer.*

in regards to   Nonstandard for *in regard to* (or *as regards* or *regarding*).

inside of, outside of   The *of* is unnecessary when *inside* and *outside* are used as prepositions: *Stay inside* (not *inside of*) *the house.*

The decision is <u>*outside*</u> *(not* <u>*outside of*</u> *) my authority. Inside of* may refer colloquially to time, though in formal English *within* is preferred: *The law was passed* <u>*within*</u> *(not* <u>*inside of*</u> *) a year.*

insure   See *assure, ensure, insure.*

irregardless   Nonstandard for *regardless.*

is because   See *reason is because.*

is when, is where   These are mixed constructions (faulty predication; see 32a) in sentences that define: *Adolescence* <u>*is a stage*</u> *(not* <u>*is when a person is*</u> *) between childhood and adulthood. Socialism* <u>*is a system in which*</u> *(not* <u>*is where*</u> *) government owns the means of production.*

its, it's   *Its* is a possessive pronoun: *That plant is losing* <u>*its*</u> *leaves.* *It's* is a contraction for *it is:* <u>*It's*</u> *likely to die if you don't water it.* Many people confuse *it's* and *its* because possessives are most often formed with *-'s;* but the possessive *its,* like *his* and *hers,* never takes an apostrophe.

-ize, -wise   The suffix *-ize* changes a noun or adjective into a verb: *revolutionize, immunize.* The suffix *-wise* changes a noun or adjective into an adverb: *clockwise, otherwise, likewise.* Avoid the two suffixes except in established words: *I'm highly* <u>*sensitive*</u> *(not* <u>*sensitized*</u> *) to that kind of criticism.* <u>*Financially*</u> *(not* <u>*Moneywise*</u> *), it's a good time to buy real estate.*

kind of, sort of, type of   In formal speech and writing, avoid using *kind of* or *sort of* to mean "somewhat": *He was* <u>*rather*</u> *(not* <u>*kind of*</u> *) tall.*

   Kind, sort, and *type* are singular and take singular modifiers and verbs: <u>*This kind*</u> *of dog* <u>*is*</u> *easily trained.* Agreement errors often occur when these singular nouns are combined with the plural demonstrative adjectives *these* and *those:* <u>*These kinds*</u> *(not* <u>*kind*</u> *) of dogs* <u>*are*</u> *easily trained. Kind, sort,* and *type* should be followed by *of* but not by *a: I don't know what* <u>*type of*</u> *(not* <u>*type*</u> *or* <u>*type of a*</u> *) dog that is.*

   Use *kind of, sort of,* or *type of* only when the word *kind, sort,* or *type* is important: *That was a* <u>*strange*</u> *(not* <u>*strange sort of*</u> *) statement.*

lay, lie   *Lay* is a transitive verb (principal parts *lay, laid, laid*) that means "put" or "place" and takes a direct object. *If we* <u>*lay*</u> *this tablecloth in the sun next to the shirt Sandy* <u>*laid*</u> *out there this morning, it should dry quickly. Lie* is an intransitive verb (principal parts *lie, lay, lain*) that means "recline" or "be situated": *I* <u>*lay*</u> *awake last night, just as I had* <u>*lain*</u> *awake the night before. The town* <u>*lies*</u> *east of the river.* See also 19b.

leave, let   *Leave* and *let* are interchangeable only when followed by *alone; leave me alone* is the same as *let me alone*. Otherwise, *leave* means "depart" and *let* means "allow": *Jill would not <u>let</u> Sue <u>leave</u>.*

less   See *fewer, less.*

liable   See *apt, liable, likely.*

lie, lay   See *lay, lie.*

like, as   See *as, like.*

like, such as   When you are giving an example of something, use *such as* to indicate that the example is a representative of the thing mentioned, and use *like* to compare the example to the thing mentioned: *Steve has recordings of many great saxophonists, <u>such as</u> Ben Webster and Lee Konitz. Steve wants to be a great jazz saxophonist <u>like</u> Ben Webster and Lee Konitz.*

likely   See *apt, liable, likely.*

literally   This adverb means "actually" or "just as the words say," and it should not be used to qualify or intensify expressions whose words are not to be taken at face value. The sentence *He was <u>literally</u> climbing the walls* describes a person behaving like an insect, not a person who is restless or anxious. For the latter meaning, *literally* should be omitted.

lose, loose   *Lose* is a verb meaning "mislay": *Did you <u>lose</u> a brown glove? Loose* is an adjective meaning "unrestrained" or "not tight": *Ann's canary got <u>loose</u>. Loose* also can function as a verb meaning "let loose": *They <u>loose</u> the dogs as soon as they spot the bear.*

lots, lots of   Colloquial substitutes for *very many, a great many,* or *much.* Avoid *lots* and *lots of* in college or business writing.

may, can   See *can, may.*

may be, maybe   *May be* is a verb, and *maybe* is an adverb meaning "perhaps": *Tuesday <u>may be</u> a legal holiday. <u>Maybe</u> we won't have classes.*

may of   See *have, of.*

media   *Media* is the plural of *medium* and takes a plural verb: *All the news <u>media are</u> increasingly visual.*

might of   See *have, of.*

moral, morale   As a noun, *moral* means "ethical conclusion" or "lesson": *The moral of the story escapes me. Morale* means "spirit" or "state of mind": *Victory improved the team's morale.*

most, almost   See *almost, most.*

must of   See *have, of.*

myself, herself, himself, yourself   The *-self* pronouns are reflexive or intensive, which means they refer to or intensify an antecedent: *Paul and I did it ourselves; Jill herself said so.* The *-self* pronouns are often used colloquially in place of personal pronouns, but that use should be avoided in formal speech and writing: *No one except me* (not *myself*) *saw the accident. Our delegates will be Susan and you* (not *yourself*).

nowheres   Nonstandard for *nowhere.*

number   See *amount, number.*

of, have   See *have, of.*

off of   *Of* is unnecessary. Use *off* or *from* rather than *off of: He jumped off* (or *from*, not *off of*) *the roof.*

OK, O.K., okay   All three spellings are acceptable, but avoid this colloquial term in formal speech and writing.

on account of   Wordy for *because of.*

on the other hand   This transitional expression of contrast should be preceded by its mate, *on the one hand: On the one hand*, we hoped *for snow. On the other hand, we feared that it would harm the animals.* However, the two combined can be unwieldy, and a simple *but, however, yet*, or *in contrast* often suffices: *We hoped for snow. Yet we feared that it would harm the animals.*

outside of   See *inside of, outside of.*

owing to the fact that   Wordy for *because.*

party   See *individual, person, party.*

people, persons   In formal usage, *people* refers to a general group: *We the people of the United States. . . . Persons* refers to a collection of individuals: *Will the person or persons who saw the accident please notify. . . .* Except when emphasizing individuals, prefer *people* to *persons.*

per   Except in technical writing, an English equivalent is usually preferable to the Latin *per: $10 an* (not *per*) *hour; sent by* (not *per*) *parcel post; requested in* (not *per* or *as per*) *your letter.*

percent (per cent), percentage Both these terms refer to fractions of one hundred. *Percent* always follows a numeral (*40 percent of the voters*), and the word should be used instead of the symbol (%) in general writing. *Percentage* usually follows an adjective (*a high percentage*).

person See *individual, person, party*.

persons See *people, persons*.

phenomena The plural of *phenomenon* (meaning "perceivable fact" or "unusual occurrence"): *The Center for Short-Lived Phenomena judged that the phenomenon we had witnessed was not a flying saucer.*

plenty A colloquial substitute for *very: He was going very* (not *plenty*) *fast when he hit that tree.*

plus *Plus* is standard as a preposition meaning "in addition to": *His income plus mine is sufficient.* But *plus* is colloquial as a conjunctive adverb: *Our organization is larger than theirs; moreover* (not *plus*), *we have more money.*

precede, proceed The verb *precede* means "come before": *My name precedes yours in the alphabet.* The verb *proceed* means "move on": *We were told to proceed to the waiting room.*

prejudice, prejudiced *Prejudice* is a noun; *prejudiced* is an adjective. Do not drop the *-d* from *prejudiced: I was fortunate that my parents were not prejudiced* (not *prejudice*).

pretty Overworked as an adverb meaning "rather" or "somewhat": *He was somewhat* (not *pretty*) *irked at the suggestion.*

previous to, prior to Wordy for *before*.

principal, principle *Principal* is a noun meaning "chief official" or, in finance, "capital sum." As an adjective, *principal* means "foremost" or "major." *Principle* is a noun only, meaning "rule" or "axiom." *Her principal reasons for confessing were her principles of right and wrong.*

proceed, precede See *precede, proceed*.

question of whether, question as to whether Wordy substitutes for *whether*.

raise, rise *Raise* is a transitive verb that takes a direct object, and *rise* is an intransitive verb that does not take an object: *The Kirks have to rise at dawn because they raise cows.*

real, really   In formal speech and writing, *real* should not be used as an adverb; *really* is the adverb and *real* an adjective. *Popular re-action to the announcement was <u>really</u>* (not <u>*real*</u>) *enthusiastic.*

reason is because   A mixed construction (faulty predication; see 32a). Although the expression is colloquially common, formal speech and writing require a *that* clause after *reason is: The <u>reason</u> he is absent <u>is that</u>* (not <u>*is because*</u>) *he is sick.* Or: *He is absent <u>because</u> he is sick.*

respectful, respective   *Respectful* means "full of (or showing) re-spect": *Be <u>respectful</u> of other people. Respective* means "separate": *The French and the Germans occupied their <u>respective</u> trenches.*

rise, raise   See *raise, rise.*

scarcely   See *but, hardly, scarcely.*

sensual, sensuous   *Sensual* suggests sexuality; *sensuous* means "pleasing to the senses." *Stirred by the <u>sensuous</u> scent of meadow grass and flowers, Cheryl and Paul found their thoughts growing in-creasingly <u>sensual</u>.*

set, sit   *Set* is a transitive verb (principal parts *set, set, set*) that describes something a person does to an object: *He <u>set</u> the pitcher down. Sit* is an intransitive verb (principal parts *sit, sat, sat*) that describes something done by a person who is tired of standing: *She <u>sits</u> on the sofa.* See also 19b.

shall, will   *Will* is the future-tense helping verb for all persons: *I <u>will</u> go, you <u>will</u> go, they <u>will</u> go.* The main use of *shall* is for first-person questions requesting an opinion or consent: *<u>Shall</u> I order a pizza? <u>Shall</u> we dance? Shall* can also be used for the first person when a formal effect is desired (*I <u>shall</u> expect you around three*), and it is occasionally used with the second or third person to express the speaker's determination (*You <u>shall</u> do as I say*).

should of   See *have, of.*

since   *Since* is often used to mean "because": *<u>Since</u> you ask, I'll tell you.* Its primary meaning, however, relates to time: *I've been waiting <u>since</u> noon.* To avoid confusion, some writers prefer to use *since* only in contexts involving time. If you do use *since* in both senses, watch out for ambiguous constructions, such as *<u>Since</u> you left, my life is empty,* where *since* could mean either "because" or "ever since."

sit, set   See *set, sit.*

so   Avoid using *so* alone or as a vague intensifier: *He was <u>so</u> late. So* needs to be followed by *that* and a clause that states a result: *He was <u>so</u> late <u>that</u> I left without him.*

somebody, some body; someone, some one *Somebody and someone* are indefinite pronouns; *some body* is a noun modified by an adjective; and *some one* is a pronoun or an adjective modified by *some*. *Somebody ought to invent a shampoo that will give hair some body. Someone told Janine she should choose some one plan and stick with it.*

someplace Informal for *somewhere*.

sometime, sometimes, some time *Sometime* means "at an indefinite time in the future": *Why don't you come up and see me sometime? Sometimes* means "now and then": *I still see my old friend Joe sometimes. Some time* means "span of time": *I need some time to make the payments.*

somewheres Nonstandard for *somewhere*.

sort of, sort of a See *kind of, sort of, type of.*

such Avoid using *such* as a vague intensifier: *It was such a cold winter. Such* should be followed by *that* and a clause that states a result: *It was such a cold winter that Napoleon's troops had to turn back.*

such as See *like, such as.*

supposed to, used to In both these expressions, the *-d* is essential: *I used to* (not *use to*) *think so. He's supposed to* (not *suppose to*) *meet us.*

sure Colloquial when used as an adverb meaning *surely*: *James Madison sure was right about the need for the Bill of Rights.* If you merely want to be emphatic, use *certainly*: *Madison certainly was right.* If your goal is to convince a possibly reluctant reader, use *surely*: *Madison surely was right.*

sure and, sure to; try and, try to *Sure to* and *try to* are the preferred forms: *Be sure to* (not *sure and*) *buy milk. Try to* (not *Try and*) *find some decent tomatoes.*

take, bring See *bring, take.*

than, as See *as, than.*

than, then *Than* is a conjunction used in comparisons, *then* an adverb indicating time: *Holmes knew then that Moriarty was wilier than he had thought.*

that, which *That* always introduces restrictive clauses: *We should use the lettuce that Susan bought* (*that Susan bought* identifies the specific lettuce being referred to). *Which* can introduce both restrictive and nonrestrictive clauses, but many writers reserve *which* only for nonrestrictive clauses: *The leftover lettuce, which is in the refrigerator, would make a good salad* (*which is in the refrigerator* simply provides more information about the lettuce). See also 34c.

their, there, they're *Their* is the possessive form of *they: Give them their money. There* indicates place (*I saw her standing there*) or functions as an expletive (*There is a hole behind you*). *They're* is a contraction for *they are: They're going fast.*

theirselves Nonstandard for *themselves.*

then, than See *than, then.*

these kind, these sort, these type, those kind See *kind of, sort of, type of.*

thru A colloquial spelling of *through* that should be avoided in all academic and business writing.

time period Since a *period* is an interval of time, this expression is redundant: *They did not see each other for a long time* (not *time period*). *Six accidents occurred in a three-week period* (not *time period*).

to, too, two *To* is a preposition; *too* is an adverb meaning "also" or "excessively"; and *two* is a number. *I too have been to Europe two times.*

too Avoid using *too* as an intensifier meaning "very": *Monkeys are too mean.* If you do use *too*, explain the consequences of the excessive quality: *Monkeys are too mean to make good pets.*

toward, towards Both are acceptable, though *toward* is preferred. Use one or the other consistently.

try and, try to See *sure and, sure to; try and, try to.*

type of See *kind of, sort of, type of.* Don't use *type* without *of: It was a family type of* (not *type*) *restaurant.* Or, better: *It was a family restaurant.*

uninterested See *disinterested, uninterested.*

unique As an absolute adjective, *unique* cannot sensibly be modified with words such as *very* or *most: That was a unique* (not *a very unique* or *the most unique*) *movie.*

usage, use *Usage* refers to conventions, most often those of a language: *Is "hadn't ought" proper usage? Usage* is often misused in place of the noun *use: Wise use* (not *usage*) *of insulation can save fuel.*

use, utilize   *Utilize* means "make use of ": *We should utilize John's talent for mimicry in our play.* In most contexts, *use* is equally or more acceptable and less stuffy.

used to   See *supposed to, used to.*

wait for, wait on   In formal speech and writing, *wait for* means "await" (*I'm waiting for Paul*), and *wait on* means "serve" (*The owner of the store herself waited on us*).

ways   Colloquial as a substitute for *way: We have only a little way* (not *ways*) *to go.*

well   See *good, well.*

whether, if   See *if, whether.*

which   See *that, which.*

which, who   *Which* never refers to people. Use *who* or sometimes *that* for a person or persons and *which* or *that* for a thing or things: *The baby, who was left behind, opened the door, which we had closed.*

who's, whose   *Who's* is the contraction of *who is: Who's at the door? Whose* is the possessive form of *who: Whose book is that?*

will, shall   See *shall, will.*

-wise   See *-ize, -wise.*

would have   Avoid this construction in place of *had* in clauses that begin *if* and state a condition contrary to fact: *If the tree had* (not *would have*) *withstood the fire, it would have been the oldest in town.*

would of   See *have, of.*

you   In all but very formal writing, *you* is generally appropriate as long as it means "you, the reader." In all writing, avoid indefinite uses of *you,* such as *In one ancient tribe your first loyalty was to your parents.* See also 27c.

your, you're   *Your* is the possessive form of *you: Your dinner is ready. You're* is the contraction of *you are: You're bound to be late.*

yourself   See *myself, herself, himself, yourself.*

Index

Page numbers in **boldface** refer to main definitions in the text.

CORRECTION SYMBOLS

e numbers and letters refer to chapters and sections of the handbook.

Faulty abbreviation, **45**		⌃	Comma, **34**
Misuse of adjective or adverb, **28**		;	Semicolon, **35**
Error in agreement, **23, 26**		:	Colon, **36**
Apostrophe needed or misused, **37**		⸮	Apostrophe, **37**
Inappropriate word, **12a**		" "	Quotation marks, **38**
Awkward construction		— ( ) ... [ ] /	Dash, parentheses, ellipsis mark, brackets, slash, **39**
Error in case form, **25**		**par, ¶**	Start new paragraph, **7**
Use capital letter, **43**		**¶ coh**	Paragraph not coherent, **7b**
Missing source citation or error in form of citation, **49, 50**		**¶ dev**	Paragraph not developed, **7c**
		¶ un	Paragraph not unified, **7a**
Coherence lacking, **3b-3, 7b**		**pass**	Ineffective passive voice, **22a**
Be more concise, **14**		**pn agr**	Error in pronoun-antecedent agreement, **26**
Coordination needed or faulty, **8**		**ref**	Error in pronoun reference, **27**
Comma splice, **31**		**rep**	Unnecessary repetition, **14b**
Ineffective diction (word choice), **12**		**rev**	Revise or proofread, **5**
Add details, **11c**		**shift**	Inconsistency, **20c, 21b, 22b, 27d**
Incorrect word division, **42**		**sp**	Misspelled word, **41**
Dangling modifier, **29b**		**spec**	Be more specific, **7c, 12b-2**
Emphasis lacking or faulty, **10**		**sub**	Subordination needed or faulty, **10**
Inexact word, **12b**		**t**	Error in verb tense, **20**
Sentence fragment, **30**		**t seq**	Error in tense sequence, **20d**
Fused sentence, **31**		**trans**	Transition needed, **7b-6**
See Glossary of Usage, p. 261		**und**	Underline (italicize), **44**
Error in grammar, **15–18**		**var**	Vary sentence structure, **11**
Error in use of hyphen, **42**		**vb**	Error in verb form, **19**
Incomplete construction, **13**		**vb agr**	Error in subject-verb agreement, **23**
Italicize (underline), **44**			
Awkward construction		**w**	Wordy, **14**
Use lowercase letter, **43**		**ww**	Wrong word, **12b-1**
Mixed construction, **32**		**/ /**	Faulty parallelism, **9**
Misplaced modifier, **29a**		**#**	Separate with a space
Meaning unclear		⁀	Close up the space
Error in manuscript form, **40**		ℯ	Delete
Unnecessary capital letter, **43**		t⟋e⟍b	Transpose letters or words
Comma not needed, **34i**		**x**	Obvious error
No new paragraph needed, **7**		∧	Something missing, **13**
Error in use of numbers, **46**		**??**	Manuscript illegible or meaning unclear
Error in punctuation, **33–39**			
Period, question mark, exclamation point, **33**			